IN
TITANIC'S
SHADOW

IN TITANIC'S SHADOW

THE WORLD'S WORST MERCHANT SHIP DISASTERS

DAVID L. WILLIAMS

The use of images reproduced in this book does not imply the endorsement by the contributors of the views expressed herein.

First published 2012

The History Press
The Mill, Brimscombe Port
Stroud, Gloucestershire, GL5 2QG
www.thehistorypress.co.uk

British Library Cataloguing in Publication Data.
A catalogue record for this book is available from the British Library.

ISBN 978 0 7524 7122 8

Typesetting and origination by The History Press
Printed in Great Britain

CONTENTS

ACKNOWLEDGEMENTS

I would like to express my gratitude and appreciation for the help received from the following individuals, organisations and associations, without whom this book could not have been realised. I trust that I have not in error missed anyone who assisted me and would offer my sincere apologies, should that be the case.

Lindsay Bridge, Nereo Castelli, Eugen Chirva, Mario Cicogna, Amos Conti, Frank Heine, Richard de Kerbrech, Rei Kimura, Knut Klippenberg, Arnold Kludas, Enoki Koichi, Siri Holm Lawson, Boris Lemachko, Michael Lynch, Rolf Meinecke, Dr Piotr Mierzejewski, Mervyn Pearson, Björn Pedersen, Luca Ruffato, James Shaw, Yan Shuheng, Erling Skjold, Peter Tschursch, Kihachiro Ueda and Ray Woodmore.

Bundesarchiv (Martina Caspers)
Deep Image Co. (Leigh Bishop)
Deutsches Schiffahrtsmuseum (Klaus Fuest)
French Line Archives (Pauline Maillard and Nancy Chauvet)
Glasgow University Archives (William Bill and Gemma Tougher)
Guildhall Library, Aldermanbury, London (Valerie Hart)
Hapag-Lloyd (Peter Maass)
Imperial War Museum
JAMSTEC (Noriko Kunugiyama)
John Swire & Sons (Rob Jennings)
Lancastria Survivors Association
Maritime Photo Library (Adrian Vicary)
Mitsui-OSK (Yasushi Kikuchi)
Nippon Yusen Kaisha (Captain Masaharu Akamine)
Ostsee Archiv (Heinz Schön)
PoW Research, Japan (Toru Fukubayashi and Yuji Miwa)
Press Association (Jane Speed and Laura Wagg)
Royal Navy Submarine Museum (Debbie Corner)
The National Archives, Kew
United States Navy
University of Bristol (Professor Robert Beckers and Jamie Carstairs)
University of Liverpool, Cunard Archives (Dr Maureen Watry)
World Ship Society Photo Library (Jim McFaul & Tony Smith)

INTRODUCTION

Four days after leaving Southampton on her maiden voyage on 10 April 1912, the White Star Line's new flagship, RMS *Titanic*, struck an iceberg near the Grand Banks, off Newfoundland, and foundered with the loss of 1,507 lives. The disaster sent shock waves around the world and brought about many important yet long overdue improvements to the rules governing maritime safety. Since that time, there has been an enduring fascination with the tragedy, not least because it was claimed the ship was 'virtually unsinkable' and, having been perhaps influenced by such thinking, because there was an inadequate number of lifeboats to rescue all the people she was carrying. The sinking of the *Titanic* rapidly became a metaphor for extreme calamity, especially of a maritime nature, and, ironically, her name has been used as a means of conveying the gravity of far more serious events. Hence, we have 'Asia's *Titanic*', 'The *Titanic* of Germany', and so on.

The *Titanic* story has been told and retold countless times in books and films, so that to each new generation it has become a familiar fable; warning of the consequences of human arrogance and of taking lightly the ever-present dangers of the seas. From this emerged the misconception that the sinking of the *Titanic* was the worst shipping disaster ever, a belief still widely held today, overshadowing many other equally or more serious maritime losses. Indeed, a comparable tragedy that occurred barely two years later, when the Canadian Pacific liner *Empress of Ireland* was run down and sunk in the St Lawrence Seaway, is nowhere near as well known, certainly outside shipping circles, even though 1,098 lives were lost. Although the approaching First World War in part deflected attention away from this second great catastrophe, the impact of the *Titanic*'s loss on the public consciousness had somehow made it easier to accept this equally grave event.

During the First World War, the relentless migration to 'total war', with seemingly diminishing regard for casualties and in which, for the first time, civilians became legitimate targets, heralded the potential for even greater slaughter on the oceans. While the *Titanic* disaster remained, briefly, the most serious deep-sea maritime accident, the destruction by torpedo of ships like the *Lusitania* and *Gallia*, with extremely high casualties, was a clear indication of things to come. It was in this conflict that the *Titanic*'s horrendous death toll would be surpassed, while in the Second World War that followed only twenty years later, the margin by which it was to be exceeded would grow alarmingly.

While it is not the intention of this book to diminish the gravity of the *Titanic* disaster, it is nevertheless fitting at the time when the 100th anniversary of that loss is being commemorated, once more giving it a singularly disproportionate focus, that the losses of those ships that subsequently suffered higher casualties should receive greater recognition. The disparity of attention between these events can be best demonstrated by an experience I had while researching for this very book. A search in a well-known, specialist maritime reference library for any literature on any of the ships described in this volume drew an almost complete blank, whereas there was an entire rack of books devoted to the *Titanic* alone.

By raising the profile of these other losses, it sets the *Titanic* disaster in a broader context. This approach, while perhaps relegating *Titanic* and giving it a less extraordinary status, highlights how in peacetime, despite international conventions, the regard for passenger safety has been increasingly compromised for the sake of commercial competition and operational economics, and, in wartime, how human life has been callously cheapened.

As already alluded to, the ships described in these pages, more than forty in total, all suffered significantly worse human casualties when they were sunk than had the *Titanic*. In some cases, the number of victims was three or four times greater. In total, they account for a death toll of 140,000; a staggering loss of life at sea and an average of 3,250 people killed with each sinking. Thus, while it is not the intention to suggest that the *Titanic* case should not receive the attention it does, these far less well-known tragedies do give the so-called 'worst disaster at sea' a sobering perspective.

Despite the fact that the *Titanic* disaster now ranks far behind many other merchant ship casualties in terms of lost life, these other ships remain, in comparison, largely inconspicuous and unknown, hidden from the media spotlight. There are many reasons for this. If we consider first, by way of contrast, the greater public awareness of the *Titanic* tragedy and, for the purposes of the exercise, disregard its appalling consequences, it can be seen that it had an almost theatrical dimension with all the drama and human interest of a well-plotted novel. It could almost have been conceived as a screenplay or bestseller, with its vivid characters and a gripping storyline advancing relentlessly to its awful climax. Oblivious to the impending danger, each facet of the ship's vulnerability is sinisterly revealed; also, there is the contrast between the prospects for survival of rich and poor as they confronted eternity; a contrast with underlying themes of morality and social injustice.

On the other hand, this is not so for the majority of the ships and incidents described herein. Sunk mainly in wartime while carrying troops, prisoners or evacuees, they lacked the glamorous image that was an integral part of the *Titanic's* story. Grey ships on grey oceans, sparsely reported due to the restrictions of news embargoes imposed at the time – in many cases little more than the barest of facts was ever recorded about these major shipping disasters. Moreover, if we take into consideration the fact that around 85 per cent of these losses involved 'enemy' ships, although not in all cases enemy personnel, it becomes clear there was far less concern about the severity of the loss of life. It was a case of: we were fighting a war; in wartime people get killed; and these victims were invariably enemy people and not our concern.

Similarly, the details of those disasters that befell Allied ships were also suppressed, though for different reasons. Maintaining public morale was regarded as critical during wartime; the authorities, therefore, rightly or wrongly, controlled when and to what extent 'bad' news, especially of the magnitude of these cases, should be leaked to the media. In some instances, it never was fully released and, protected by 100-year security exclusions, more than another thirty years must still pass before the full, official facts will be publicly known.

These ships also lacked the media appeal of the new flagship of one of the most famous shipping companies of all time – an elegant, floating city working the prestigious 'Atlantic ferry' service – and they were rarely the subjects of press photographers' cameras. Being a mix of small passenger vessels and pure cargo ships, they were generally the unsung workhorses of the merchant service, and few photographs exist to record their physical form, other than the odd launching image or trials view. For some ships, it has been impossible to find any photographs at all so that, in those cases, visual anonymity has proved unavoidable.

The ships described in these pages find themselves listed on that roster of the worst ever disasters at sea principally because they were seriously overloaded – it is, in fact, their common denominator. And, for the most part, they were not engaged at the time of their demise on duties for which they had been designed or built. Indeed, many of them were never intended to carry passengers of any description. It may be thought, therefore, that it is stretching things to draw comparisons between the *Titanic* and the ships in this book, which, for the most part, were sunk during wartime by enemy action. After all, the *Titanic* was going about her normal, intended business with a complement that was well within the maximum number permitted by her passenger certificate.

When considering major accidents at sea, as well as the matter of overloading, it is important to bear in mind how close Cunard's great *Queen Mary* came to being one of the ships listed in this book – indeed, how close did she come to being the deadliest shipping disaster of all time? It would have completely overshadowed the loss of the *Titanic*. During the time her construction was suspended and her future was in doubt – to quote *Damned by Destiny* (see Bibliography), while she was 'balanced on the Horns of Destiny' – she had come close to being a failed ship project; no more than a 'might-have-been' in the annals of the sea. But in October 1942, barely six years after her delayed career had begun, in a second more sinister trial with fate, she was involved in a wartime collision that could have brought about her end and, of far greater consequence, cost the lives of the huge complement of servicemen she was carrying. The actual number on board on that occasion is believed to have been around 11,250, but around that time she was routinely transporting some 15,000 or more troops besides her crew on each voyage. In fact, on her previous transatlantic crossing her complement had been a record 15,988, of whom just 863 were crew.

Had she gone down, her only means of rescue – her escort, the cruiser HMS *Curacoa* – had already foundered, cut in two by the impact of the collision. Moreover, operating independently of convoys, there were few ships in the vicinity that could have rendered assistance. Fortuitously (for the *Queen Mary*), she had hit the *Curacoa* bow first and her collision bulkhead held, but it could have been so very different.

Naval architects hold the view that, had the *Titanic* hit the iceberg head on, she too would probably have survived, albeit seriously damaged. Other ships certainly endured after such encounters, such as the Guion liner *Arizona* on 7 November 1879. It was to be the *Titanic's* destiny, though, that an attempt was made to steer her around the iceberg and in so doing she grazed along it, receiving a glancing blow that opened up her side, exposing what may be considered as the Achilles heel of her design: susceptibly inadequate watertight subdivision. It spelt certain mortality as well as the birth of a legend.

Recognising that perhaps the most vital safety provision aboard a ship, whatever its type or function, is adequate means of escape in an emergency, then, while disregarding the absence of actual discomfort from not being physically crowded, the lack of such provision amounts to a form of overloading. If she had been occupied to capacity – and fortunately she was not – the *Titanic's* lifeboats would only have had enough space for a third of her passengers and crew (1,178 people out of a total of 3,547), although the actual number of boats exceeded the minimum requirement stipulated by the Board of Trade regulations of the time.

As another common factor for the majority of the ships in these pages, it was the exigencies of war that dictated their operation in such an inappropriate fashion, filled to overflowing, in whatever role or application their controlling authorities dictated. To quote a correspondent, Björn Pedersen, who was referring to the madness of such practices: 'It is only during war [that] you place more than 4,000 people on board an old three-island steamer as [troops, prisoners] refugees or whatever.'

We may well question the extreme overloading of prisoners of war aboard the Japanese 'hell-ships' (see Chapter 6), in respect of the appalling conditions in which they were accommodated, as well as for the fact that the practice of using them as slave labour breached international conventions. But as to the prisoners' vulnerability through inadequate means of survival, in the event that the ships were sunk, we cannot so fairly criticise. Much the same was the case aboard Allied troopships, such as the *Queen Mary* already referred to, as well as aboard British ships transporting Axis prisoners.

With reference to the *Queen Mary* during her wartime collision, the urgent need to man up in readiness for the imminent invasion of Europe had necessitated that risks such as overloading and inadequate provision of life-saving equipment should be taken.

As far as British ships carrying prisoners were concerned, the conveyance of enemy captives to holding camps overseas was a matter of practicality rather than one of securing a forced-labour resource. Living conditions aboard them may also have been significantly better than on the hell-ships, but interpretation of the rules governing the treatment of prisoners of war would suggest that transporting them by sea where there was significant risk of exposure to violence could altogether have been an illegal practice, no matter which country was responsible. Realistically, none of these ships was entitled to registration for safe conduct clearance under the auspices of the International Red Cross, to be painted appropriately and with their function and intended route declared. Even if they had been, there is evidence, including for at least two of the cases described in these pages, that protected status and the adoption of internationally recognised protective livery were no guarantee of safety. Wantonly disregarded, vessels were attacked with impunity.

There is another factor that deserves reflection in this Introduction, being germane to the various circumstances that conspire to turn maritime accidents and incidents into tragedies. As already stated, the vast majority of the ship losses described in this book occurred during wartime. Of that total, a significant percentage fell as the victims of what, in modern parlance, could be called friendly fire – in that the human casualties of the attacks on these ships were either the national or allied compatriots of those who had carried out the attacks, all having been prisoners of one sort or another on board. It was not only Allied citizens or personnel who were regrettably killed in this way in the Second World War, for Axis prisoners of war similarly became the mistaken target. The *Empress of Canada* and, as related herein, the *Laconia*, for example, were both torpedoed by German U-boats. The loss of life which unfortunately resulted from these attacks was the unintended consequence of naval or air force crews doing no more than carrying out their military orders as part of the overall endeavour to win the war. As the ships concerned carried no markings whatsoever to reveal their true purpose, such friendly fire incidents were completely unavoidable.

However, continuing research in the post-Second World War period has revealed that this may not have been quite true in all cases. It is not the purpose of that statement to suggest that servicemen who launched fatal attacks on ships heavily loaded with humankind had either prior knowledge or information about the nature of their targets that should have aroused concern or countenanced caution as to whether or not to proceed. But, there is evidence that such intelligence *was* at the disposal of higher authorities who carried the wider responsibility for the conduct of military operations and that it was not, in all instances, passed on to the relevant personnel. It has been concluded that the dangers to captured service personnel through the sinking of unmarked ships, whose existence and function were often known about, were well understood.

Of course, these are all matters for speculation, no less so than are many other aspects of the circumstances surrounding these, the worst ever maritime disasters. If there is one thing above all else that the *Titanic* tragedy has taught us, it is that the passage of time does little to diminish the almost obsessive debate about every minute dimension of that appalling event. It is no different where the more controversial aspects of some of these other major shipping losses are concerned.

Just as we can speculate on the past, sometimes with reasonable confidence if the evidence seems to support our conjectures, so too we can wonder what the future may hold. Have we, through the aid of ever-more sophisticated technology, moved to the point where maritime disasters of this magnitude can no longer occur? Alternatively, are we, through over-dependence on such technology, allowing our vigilance to slip and unwittingly creating the circumstances in which there will be more catastrophic reminders of our continuing vulnerability on the sea lanes?

We can only hope that these horrors *are* a thing of the past and that in a hundred or so years time, around the beginning of the next century, mankind will not be paying its respects on the 100th anniversary of the loss of another passenger-carrying ship whose name has succeeded that of the *Titanic* as the acknowledged metaphor for maritime tragedy.

David L. Williams
2012

Author's Note

The reader will be aware that the casualty numbers quoted in many instances have been rounded to a whole, and that in other instances there are conflicting casualty numbers given by different sources. This simply reflects the circumstances in which these disasters occurred: when precise numbers of occupants were uncertain and when it was difficult, if not impossible, to make an accurate or reliable head count of the survivors. Governments and certain shipping authorities have typically preferred to give lower casualty figures, in an attempt to reduce the gravity of certain disasters. It should be noted, though, that even by the most optimistic calculations the toll of lost life in each of the cases described in the following pages exceeded that of White Star's *Titanic*.

The reader should also be aware that reports of incidents often did not declare whether the times given were in local time, GMT, BST or of any other time zone. This may have resulted in discrepancies. However, the timings between key events in the individual accounts related herein are correct.

1

FIRST TO SURPASS THE *TITANIC*

PRINCIPE UMBERTO (4/1909)

Navigazione Generale Italiana, Genoa, Italy

Italy's entry into the First World War against the Central Powers was opportunistic, driven neither as a defence against a direct hostile threat, nor as a response to a long-standing treaty obligation. The country's political leaders hoped that it would provide an expedient for the pursuit of its nationalistic, irredentist and imperialistic ambitions. Whatever the motivation, though, the Allies benefitted from a strengthening of their forces with around 1 million trained fighting men and a small but substantial modern navy.

War was declared on Austro-Hungary in May 1915 and on Germany and the Ottoman Empire that August. Over the next three to four years, the Italian war effort was to be dominated by the twelve battles fought along the line of the Isonzo (Soča) River near her north-east border, north of Monfalcone. The Italian navy and merchant marine also played an important role in support of the Allied effort, patrolling in the Mediterranean and transporting troops and supplies. A heavy price was paid in lost ships, not least those of the Navigazione Generale Italiana (NGI) company, four of whose vessels, among them two front-line passenger liners, did not survive.

The NGI was the longest-standing and principal shipping concern among the Italian-flag companies operating passenger services on the routes from Europe to North and South America. The company faced stiff competition in the early part of the twentieth century and to reinforce its dominance, the NGI ordered six new, broadly similar, modern liners in 1905 – three each for the two transatlantic routes. Built for the North Atlantic were three so-called 'Ducale' ships: *Duca degli Abruzzi* (1908), *Duca di Genova* (1908) and *Duca d'Aosta* (1909). For the Genoa–La Plata ports service there was a 'Regale' trio comprising *Regina Elena* (1908), *Re Vittorio* (1908) and the *Principe Umberto* (1909). They elevated the standard of accommodation in all categories and, with more powerful engines giving higher speeds, they reduced passage times on both routes. The run to Buenos Aires was cut to less than seventeen days. With comparable amenities, the ships were interchanged, as required, between the southern and northern services.

Though of modest size and dimensions compared with their counterparts operated by the likes of Cunard, White Star and Norddeutscher Lloyd, they were sleek-looking ships nevertheless, an impression emphasised by their long, low-profile superstructures surmounted by two black-and-white banded funnels. Each ship could carry in excess of 1,300 passengers in three classes, the majority as emigrants in steerage. While they may have been relatively insignificant when ranked against the likes of the illustrious *Mauretania*, *Olympic*, *Aquitania* and *Imperator*, one of their number, the *Principe Umberto*, was to gain a different kind of notoriety, when, as the victim of an Austrian U-boat, she was sunk with record loss of life. For more than twenty years it remained the worst ever maritime disaster.

For the *Principe Umberto* and her sisters, six largely uneventful years were to pass after they entered service, steadily maintaining a schedule of regular sailings, until Italy's involvement in the First World War brought all civil operations to an abrupt halt. Three of the six liners were taken up from early 1916 for employment by the Italian government as combined auxiliary cruisers and transports, carrying out patrols and ferrying troops to and from Thessaloniki and Libya. Up to April 1915, the Mediterranean Sea had been a relatively quiet area, but the Anglo-French Gallipoli campaign changed things dramatically with the arrival of Allied warships to bombard the Turkish coast and attempt to force through the Dardanelles Channel. Simultaneously, troopships began to ferry in fighting men, while hospital ships commenced the removal of casualties. It offered rich pickings for the Central Powers' submarines that began to infest the lower Adriatic and seas of the Aegean around the Greek islands.

Apart from its stalemate with the Austro-Hungarians at Isonzo, Italy also had been obliged to send an expeditionary corps, comprising three divisions, to Albania. This was in part to prevent enemy occupation of the ports along the Adriatic coast, which would have compromised the evacuation of the remnants of the Serbian army defeated in Montenegro. Italian ships first took these units to Brindisi and from there they were transferred to Corfu. After the rescue operation was completed in February 1916, Italian forces remained in Albania fighting a rearguard action in a bid to prevent a complete conquest by Austria and Bulgaria, and to support anti-Austrian partisans. Within months, though, it became necessary to withdraw these forces.

Following the inconclusive Fifth Battle of Isonzo in February 1915, the Austro-Hungarians had triggered a counter-offensive in the Asiago Highlands, in the province of Vicenza, and all available manpower was required to support the defence of the Italian positions. Variously known as the Battle of Asiago, the Trentino Offensive or the *Strafexpedition* ('Punitive' expedition), it began with an unexpected attack against the Italian front on 15 May 1916, preceded by an artillery barrage by 2,000 heavy guns. The objective was to advance to the plateaus of Lavarone, Folgaria and Asiago, beyond the valleys of Sugana and Lagarina, by isolating and dislodging the Italian 2nd and 3rd Armies on the western Isonzo, and the 4th Army defending the region of the eastern Trentino.

As with the five earlier battles of the Isonzo, the engagement secured only minor gains of ground, achieved at an enormous cost of combined casualties – 27,000 dead,

The *Principe Umberto* photographed at an unknown port prior to the First World War. (World Ship Society)

Another view of the *Principe Umberto* in a pre-First World War publicity card. (Mario Cicogna)

155,000 wounded and 65,000 either missing or taken prisoner – incurred over a period of less than one month.

While the Austro-Hungarian expedition had been checked, conveniently aided by a Russian offensive at Galicia, which created a diversion and forced the enemy to withdraw troops to strengthen resistance on that front, the fact that the Italians had been caught off guard had political repercussions. It also led to a demand for the troops in the Isonzo region to be increased by 400,000 to deter any future Austro-Hungarian incursions.

Thus, the scene was set for the return to Otranto of the 55th and 56th Infantry Regiments and other units still in Albania. Already, by May 1916, after valiantly holding the enemy at Monte Piana and at Sabotino – essential for the protection of the ports of Durazzo (Durrës) and Alessio (Shëngjin) – the Italians had been forced to abandon these positions. Although Otranto was only some 60 miles away across the Adriatic from Durazzo, the sea in this area was known to be very dangerous, both because of minefields and because Austro-Hungarian submarines based nearby at Kotor could easily attack convoys. Therefore, having decided against conveying the returning troops from Durazzo, the Italian forces withdrew from the port, destroying everything they could not take with them, and made for Valona (Vlorë), further south, from where the return to Italy was to be made.

A troop convoy was organised to sail from Valona on 8 June 1916. The convoy consisted of the former NGI ships *Principe Umberto* and *Re Vittorio*, the similar-sized *Stampalia* of La Veloce and the small passenger-cargo steamer *Jonio*. They were escorted by the Regia Marina destroyers *Insidioso* (Captain Amici Grossi), *Espero* (Lieutenant Fossati), *Impavido* (Captain Ruggiero) and *Pontiere* (Lieutenant Commander Mancini).

The Compagnie Sud-Atlantique passenger ship *Gallia* was the second worst U-boat victim in the First World War. When she was sunk on 4 October 1916 with 1,428 casualties, it was a loss of life almost as severe as on the *Titanic*. (World Ship Society)

The situation became increasingly critical in the hours approaching the convoy's imminent departure. Late on 7 June 1916, the Italian troops had encamped at Drasciovizza where they were attacked by Austrian aircraft. There were no injuries and the next day they entered the port where boarding commenced onto the ships moored at piers 1 and 2. The *Principe Umberto*, under the joint command of naval officer Lieutenant Nardulli and her mercantile master, Captain Sartorio, embarked 2,605 servicemen besides her crew. Included among them were the 55th Regiment's 1st and 2nd Battalions, along with companies 11a and 12a of the 3rd Battalion. Fully loaded, the convoy finally left Valona at 19.00 hours on 8 June.

Meanwhile, patrolling the area of the southern Adriatic, at the very point where the convoy was to cross, were two Austro-Hungarian submarines, one of which, under the command of Lieutenant Friedrich Schlosser, was the *U-5*, a Holland-designed vessel that had been constructed by the Whitehead Co. at Fiume.

Without realising it, the *Principe Umberto* bore down upon the *U-5*, forcing it to reduce speed and retract its periscope. Schlosser ordered the *U-5* to flank speed before turning his boat into a bow firing position. At a distance of 1,000m, two torpedoes were fired, aimed at the larger ships. In fact, the visibility was bad and the *U-5*'s attack was launched as much in hope as by calculation. One of the torpedoes narrowly missed the *Jonio* but, as the submarine made an emergency dive, a single loud explosion was heard.

The *Principe Umberto* had been mortally damaged, her stern almost destroyed, and she began to sink rapidly. The attack had taken place approximately 15 miles southwest of Cape Linguetta, the convoy's destination at Otranto barely 40 miles away. Although time was against them, as many as possible of the sinking ship's lifeboats were launched while the other troop transports rushed to the scene to try to render assistance. Even so, only a fraction of those aboard the *Principe Umberto* could be rescued, reportedly as few as 779 people. Besides the crew casualties, 1,826 servicemen had died. In the meantime, the destroyers, assisted by the small cruiser *Libia*, endeavoured to repel the submarines for fear of further attacks on the ships that were now dead in the water – but the U-boats had already escaped.

Despite the efforts of the other convoy ships, it was a desperate struggle for survival for those soldiers and crew members who, when so many others had been trapped inside the *Principe Umberto*'s hull, had somehow made it to the surface. Colonel Meneghetti, a 3rd Battalion officer and one of the survivors, described the scene:

> On the sea, dimly lit by the moon, the black shadows of those men fighting with death could not be seen; the silence of the calm sea was broken only by the desperate cries for help as they begged for their mothers or called the names of their wives and children.

Slowly, one by one, the voices were quelled until nothing more could be heard.

The figures for the people who perished vary considerably from report to report. The number of people that boarded the *Principe Umberto* and the number of casualties stated above, are taken from an article entitled 'L'Affondamento de *Principe*

Umberto' by Alfio Moratti and Amos Conti, which appeared in *Ricerche Storico* (No.106, October 2008). Another report states that 1,750 were killed, while yet another account gives the number as 1,948. Crew casualties may be included in this latter figure, but the preceding *Ricerche Storico* numbers relate only to army personnel and refer to forty-eight officer victims, with the remainder soldiers of lower rank.

In an instant, the *Principe Umberto*'s disappearance beneath the surface with approaching 2,000 souls had relegated the *Titanic* disaster to second place in the list of the worst ever maritime calamities. But the aftermath of the tragedy at least appeared to offer some hope for the future.

A year earlier, when the *Lusitania* had been torpedoed south of Ireland, killing 1,198 civilian passengers and crew, medals depicting Death selling the voyage tickets had been struck in both Germany and Great Britain, both cynically exploiting the terrible incident for propaganda purposes. Clearly, the German action implied a celebration of the torpedo attack – certainly that had been the case where some newspapers were concerned – but the medal's designer, one Karl Goetz of Munich, argued that it had been intended only as a satirical comment on the German government's allegations that the *Lusitania* had been carrying contraband, thereby rendering her a legitimate target. Those claims were subsequently proved to be correct, although there had been only relatively trivial quantities of materials aboard the *Lusitania*, and they were for manufacturing purposes rather than direct, hostile use as weapons or ammunition. The fact that the attack had been launched without warning, a breach of international law relating to maritime warfare, and that a vast number of innocent people had unjustifiably lost their lives, does not seem to have been considered. In the event, it was revealed that only forty-four examples of the German medal had

The *Lusitania* of Cunard Line was both U-boat victim and propaganda victim. (Author's collection)

been struck, whereas 300,000 of the almost identical British medal had been cast, financed by Mr Gordon Selfridge, the department store owner, to whip up hatred against Germany. The British response can only be viewed as a shallow deed in the extreme to seek to take advantage of mass slaughter in this fashion.

Such unsavoury practices, expressing self-congratulation for callous deeds with cruel disregard for the appalling consequences, were, it seems, a further indication of the downward direction of attitudes to the plunder of life during wartime. But not so with the *Principe Umberto*, even though she had been, without question, a valid military target. Even so, Austro-Hungary, also a signatory of the convention that stipulated 'Restricted' submarine warfare, had failed to ensure that its submarines acted accordingly by ordering the enemy ship to stop in order to search it prior to sinking it. That was, perhaps, an unrealistic expectation if all it achieved was a depth charge attack from escorting warships.

Whether or not it was in recognition of the horrifying loss of life caused by the *U-5*'s torpedo attack, or for some other benevolent reason, is not known, but shortly afterwards the Austro-Hungarian military authorities published an official postcard, widely purchased and mailed, that depicted the moment when the *Principe Umberto* was struck by the torpedo. Though inaccurate in its detail – the fatal torpedo in fact struck the ship at her aft end – its purpose appeared to be to raise money, possibly for a relief fund. Responsible for the publication of the card in this seemingly con-ciliatory, even apologetic gesture was the *Österreichen Flottenvereines zu Gunster des Kriegsfürsorgeamtes* along with the *Kriegshilfsburos* and the *Roten Kreuzes* (Red Cross). It is not known, however, whether any of the proceeds of the sales ever reached the families of the victims.

The reverse side of the *Principe Umberto* postcard (see image 5 of the plate section for the front side). (Mario Cicogna)

The 55th Regiment was based near Treviso and drew from towns in the surrounding region, notably Reggio Emilia. A little-known dossier, 'In Memoriam', listing all the missing people from the *Principe Umberto* attack, was compiled and published by the Municipality of Reggio Emilia in 1919. In addition, the Civic Museum at Treviso is jointly named after the *Risorgimento* and the 55th Infantry Regiment – in the latter case as a tribute to the victims of the *Principe Umberto* tragedy. Nearby, the 'Serena' army barracks at Dosson has a monument that likewise commemorates those who lost their lives when the ship was sunk.

The First World War came to an end on 11 November 1918. More than 9 million people had been killed over the four years and four months since it had started, many of them casualties of the war at sea. For the next twenty or so years there would be some respite, and there would not be another shipping disaster to rival the *Titanic* until after the second great war of the twentieth century had begun.

2

DISASTER IN THE MIDST
OF A MIRACLE

LANCASTRIA (6/1922)

Cunard White Star Line, Liverpool, UK

Winston Churchill, the wartime prime minister, described the evacuation of Dunkirk and the associated operations that rescued British servicemen from France in the summer of 1940 as a 'Miracle of Deliverance'. Operation Dynamo alone, the Dunkirk evacuation, secured the recovery of some 338,226 soldiers of the British Expeditionary Force (BEF) along with 27,935 Belgian and French troops, taking them to the safety of the United Kingdom.

In truth, Britain and France had been caught on the hop, lulled into a state of inertia by the so-called 'phoney war' and an unrealistic sense of confidence in the defensive protection afforded by the Maginot Line. In the event, they were overwhelmed by the onslaught of the German blitzkrieg ('lightning war'), from which they never recovered. The greatest miracle was the fact that any at all of the routed armies was able to get away and reach England's shores.

From August 1939, when Britain and France declared war on Germany following the invasion of Poland, a combination of BEF and French army units had taken up positions along the line of the French border with Belgium and Germany. But they made no move to engage what was then, very briefly, an inferior *Wehrmacht* (German armed forces). Even had they done so, there is little doubt that the tactics adopted would have led to a resumption of the trench warfare of twenty years earlier: the defence of a static frontline interspersed with set piece battles to try to secure more ground, a slow and costly process of attrition of both men and munitions. There was little appreciation at the time of the now modern concept of mobile warfare, typified by quantities of fast-moving mechanised divisions spearheading an assault, a form of land warfare that the Germans had fine-tuned as blitzkrieg.

When Hitler ordered his forces to launch their attack on the Western Front on 10 May 1940, the British and French were taken completely by surprise – not just by the nature and speed of the unexpected onslaught, but by the complete divergence of its direction from what had been anticipated and planned for. The Schlieffen Plan, upon which the French defensive strategy had been based, anticipated a southwards thrust towards and around the eastern side of the Maginot Line. The offensive launched by the Germans in 1940 took a quite different route and comprised two main elements: an attack on the Netherlands and invasion into Belgium, north of Liège, to draw the British and French forces west and northwards; and simultaneously an attack through the Ardennes to cross the River Meuse at Sedan before sweeping into northern France and advancing west to Amiens and the Channel. The Maginot Line, simply outflanked, was instantaneously reduced to an irrelevant anachronism as the opposing forces were trapped in a pincer movement. All that the ensnared Allied forces could do was fight a rearguard action as they retreated towards the coast; a heroic effort designed to buy time to permit a rescue operation to be organised. Launched on 26 May 1940, Operation Dynamo began the desperate task of removing the exhausted troops from the beaches of Dunkirk, utilising the hundreds of 'little ships' that had been mustered or volunteered to assist the rescue campaign by ferrying men through the shallows to the bigger vessels lying offshore.

After the cessation of the evacuation operation at Dunkirk on 5 June 1940, Prime Minister Churchill falsely gave the British public the impression that the BEF had been saved when, in fact, over 150,000 British troops remained trapped in France along with thousands of Belgian and French soldiers, besides countless civilians and other displaced people.

Those troops who had not been caught in the trap at the North Sea coast on the Belgian–French border were in full retreat, heading west. Some made for the ports along the central and western Channel, at Dieppe, Le Havre, Saint-Valery and Cherbourg, from where they were rescued in Operation Cycle, the second phase of the relief exercise, between 10 and 13 June.

Another 130,000 trudged on or made their way by whatever means of transport they could find to the French Atlantic coast, to the naval port of Brest and the docks of the great shipbuilding city of Saint-Nazaire. For them, the final, great emergency evacuation, Operation Aerial, masterminded by General Alan Brooke, got underway on 15 June. It continued for ten days until the mission's abandonment became unavoidable, as German forces completed their rout of France and the threat posed by the Luftwaffe to any shipping caught in the open near the coast became intolerable.

Just as the 'little ships' had performed shore-to-ship ferry duties at Dunkirk, taking men from the beaches out to the destroyers and cross-Channel ferries lying off shore, so in turn those larger craft were employed to transfer personnel to the many big transports, mainly former liners, which had been mustered and lay at anchor 5 miles out in Quiberon Bay. A sizeable fleet of troopships was commandeered for Operation Aerial, among them the three Orient Line ships *Ormonde*, *Oronsay* and *Otranto*; Canadian Pacific's *Duchess of York*; P&O Line's *Strathaird*; the *Arandora Star*; Cunard White Star's *Georgic*, *Franconia* and *Lancastria*; and two Polish ships, the *Batory* and *Sobieski*, along with three MoT transports.

The *Lancastria*, commanded by Captain Rudolph Sharp, had been on a cruise to the Bahamas when war broke out and, after disembarking her passengers, she was instructed to sail from Nassau to New York where she was immediately converted into a troopship. She was kept busy from the outset and was one of the vessels of a twenty-ship convoy engaged in the evacuation of troops and civilians from Narvik in Norway that May. Her next task saw her taking fresh reinforcements to Iceland to bolster the garrison there, after which she returned to Glasgow and then Liverpool, where it was anticipated her crew would get a well-deserved rest while the ship underwent a refit.

She arrived in the Mersey port on 14 June and was hastily disembarked, but there was to be no break, no matter how badly needed. Before the day had ended, the crew was recalled to the ship. The *Lancastria* had received orders to sail at midnight, first to Plymouth and then on to an unspecified destination. En route to Plymouth, Captain Sharp, on the bridge with Chief Officer Harry Grattidge, soon became aware that there were many other vessels of various sizes bound at speed in the same direction, heading south in the Irish Sea or emerging from the Bristol Channel. They deduced that something major was unfolding, although they had no idea then what it was. During that day, the order was given for the evacuation of Brest and Saint-Nazaire to commence by a single signal: 'PIP'. Ultimately, it was to be a successful operation, rescuing another 186,700 people, mainly troops but also civilian men, women and children, besides nurses and other auxiliary personnel. But it was achieved at a terrible cost.

From Plymouth, the *Lancastria* was ordered to Brest along with fleet-mate *Franconia*. They were to join HMS *Wolverine*, their escort, off the French coast. On reaching Brest, it was discovered that the Germans had already partially mined the entrance to the port and the two big ships had to rely on a French trawler to guide them through the Channel where it narrowed by the Roscanvel peninsula. During these manoeuvres, they came under attack from German aircraft and, though the bombs missed, the explosions severely damaged the *Franconia*, which was forced to retire. She limped back alone to Liverpool for repairs.

The *Lancastria*, seen in commercial colours prior to the Second World War, before she was converted into a troopship. (Tom Rayner)

Meanwhile, Captain Sharp resolved to take the *Lancastria* further south. While proceeding in that direction during the night, a group of seven cargo vessels, led in single file by the *John Holt*, was encountered. Bound for Saint-Nazaire, Captain Sharp joined the convoy, reaching the southern end of Quiberon Bay on the morning of 17 June. Numerous other troopships were already there, hove to offshore, all dangerously exposed and defenceless. Embarkation of evacuees began almost immediately. A naval transport officer gave the order to load: in essence the *Lancastria* was to take as many troops and refugees aboard as could be carried, disregarding the limits laid down by international law. This constituted a breach of the Ministry of Shipping instructions that her maximum permitted loading capacity of 3,000 people was not to be exceeded.

The *Lancastria* had a peacetime capacity, following her conversion into a two-class cruise ship in 1924, of 1,580 in addition to her 320-man crew. She had been modified and equipped as a troopship to permit 3,000 servicemen to be accommodated, in itself a not insubstantial increase. It was not long, though, before that number was well and truly exceeded, driven on by the desperate circumstances.

A shuttle of craft worked ceaselessly back and forth from the harbour quays. Largest of them were the destroyers HMS *Havelock* and *Highlander* aided by tugs, fishing boats and a variety of other small craft. As best they could, the purser and chief steward counted the evacuees as they swarmed aboard, clambering up scramble nets or entering through doors in the ship's side near the waterline. The decks were rapidly packed with soldiers, representing most of the army services that had been stranded in France: Royal Artillery, Pioneer Corps, Royal Engineers, RASC, RAOC, REME, the Royal Army Pay Corps, Royal Logistic Corps and so on. Around 800 RAF ground crew were billeted in No.2 hold, forward of the bridge. Members of the Royal Navy and Royal Marines were also taken aboard. While the destroyers brought the servicemen to the ship, tugs ferried civilians to the *Lancastria*, among them children with their parents, nuns, medical staff, and civic authority personnel. As they embarked, each was issued a Board of Trade lifejacket.

The number of people estimated to have boarded the *Lancastria* range from 4,000 to 9,000, with the more precise figures of 5,310 or 5,506 often quoted. It is claimed that when the count conducted by the purser and chief steward reached 6,000 they considered it pointless to continue, even though hundreds more were pouring onto the ship. Captain Sharp complained that his ship was becoming dangerously overloaded, but with the pressing need to get as many as possible away from France before it capitulated, he was urged to take more. Little did he know that France would fall that very day.

The urgency attached to this, the final phase of the BEF rescue operation, was amplified by news filtering through to Saint-Nazaire that forces led by General Erwin Rommel had made a rapid 150-mile incursion across north-central France, and had already taken the Channel ports of Le Havre and Cherbourg. His forces were within striking distance of the evacuation fleet and the beleaguered units attempting to hold a defensive line at Nantes. He could reach Saint-Nazaire within hours. Moreover, the remorseless Luftwaffe attacks on the anchorage were steadily intensifying.

By mid-afternoon on 17 June, the crew aboard HMT *Lancastria* were making ready to depart, her sea doors having been closed and the scramble nets hauled on deck to prevent any additional passengers from boarding. The senior officer aboard HMS *Havelock* indicated that, if she was full to capacity, the *Lancastria* should get underway. However, Captain Sharp signalled in reply, 'Can you route us, if we proceed?' He had no charts for the area and preferred to have an escort as he feared for the ship's safety if it was attacked by a submarine. In the event, he decided to wait for the *Oronsay*, judging that there would be greater protection if the two transports returned to England together.

Air attacks of varying intensity had been continuing throughout the embarkation operation. For the most part the large troopships had been shielded by the anti-aircraft fire from naval vessels. Earlier in the afternoon, around 14.00 hours, the Germans stepped up their aerial bombardment, sweeping low over Charpentier Roads to drop their bombs. The initial target was the *Oronsay*, which was hit on her bridge, destroying her compass and reducing the chartroom to a pile of debris. Fortunately, the ship's wheel and engine room telegraph remained serviceable, as did her radio room. The raid apparently over, the planes headed east. Back on the *Lancastria*, what seemed like the end of the attack was greeted with considerable relief, but it was to be just a short interlude, and when the attack was resumed it was the *Lancastria* that was in the bombers' sights.

As the air-raid warning sounded yet again, a Junkers Ju 88, one of a number from Kampfgeschwader 30, flew directly at the troopship and released her stick of bombs. It was 15.48 hours when the first landed directly on No.2 hold, killing all the RAF men inside and starting a furious fire. As the *Lancastria* was hit twice more she shuddered and bucked alarmingly. It was thought that No.3 hold had also been struck, rupturing fuel tanks below and releasing over 1,400 tons of oil into the sea, which gunners from Messerschmidt Me109 fighters subsequently tried to set alight to add to the ensuing carnage. One, perhaps two more bombs – there is some dispute as to whether three or four bombs found their target – hit the ship, sealing her fate. It was thought that one bomb went directly down the *Lancastria*'s funnel, to explode in her engine room. The fact that her entire engine room crew were not killed instantly suggests, however, that the bomb more probably exploded very close to the funnel.

The *Lancastria* immediately took on a list to starboard, before righting and then listing over to her port side while she also began to settle at the bow. Below decks, as many as 5,000 men were trapped. At least 4,000 who were unable to reach the open decks went down with the ship. In the sea another 2,000 were struggling to survive, shedding their kit and even their clothes to keep afloat, choking and gagging on the thick, slimy oil that coated the surface and hoping they would be spared from being shot by the machine guns of enemy planes or burnt in the fires they were starting with incendiaries. Others clung to the ship, slithering down her sides as she rolled over, waiting for the moment when they would have to take their chances and jump into the sea.

Rescue ships and other evacuation vessels headed to the scene to help pull survivors to safety. The trawler *Cambridgeshire* rescued 900, transferring them to the *John*

Holt, which only hours earlier had led the *Lancastria* to Saint-Nazaire. Some, a very brave few, managed to swim ashore; 460 and 600 were lifted aboard HMS *Havelock* and *Beagle*, respectively; and almost 1,500 were taken to the *Oronsay*, which became an emergency refuge and medical station, swelling the numbers already aboard her. Last to leave the horrific scene were the lifeboats of the Union-Castle Line's cargo ship *Dundrum Castle*. There were numerous burn cases requiring urgent attention and countless men suffering from exhaustion and the effects of oil ingestion. In total, officially, there were 2,477 survivors – a number that suggests the figures above reflect considerable duplication as the rescued were moved between ships.

Timed by watches that stopped working when they were immersed in the seawater, the *Lancastria* disappeared beneath the surface at 16.12 hours, not even thirty minutes from when she had been first hit. She sank some 5 miles south of Chémoulin Point in the Charpentier Roads, approximately 9 miles from Saint-Nazaire. Her wreck, still on the seabed in the position 47.09N, 02.20E, is marked to this day by a large red buoy.

The loss of life was so severe that, coming on top of the already grave reverses in France and the Low Countries, culminating in the retreat from Dunkirk, the British government determined to suppress news of the disaster. They did so by invoking the D-Notice (Defence Notice) system, a practice that, though not legally enforceable, sought to restrict the dissemination of information by requesting news editors not to publish or broadcast items on specified subjects for reasons of national security. The story was broken elsewhere, though, beyond the control of HM government, when the *New York Times* published its account of the tragedy. British newspapers followed suit by releasing the story in varying degrees of detail, but not until some six weeks after the event. As part of the effort to conceal the full horror of what had occurred,

The *Lancastria* sinking off Saint-Nazaire following the German air attack. (Crown Copyright)

survivors and the crews of the ships that had gone to their aid were prevented, under the threat of courts martial, from revealing what they knew. The official report of the inquiry into the loss of the *Lancastria* is subject to the Official Secrets Act and cannot be published until 2040.

The exact death toll of the *Lancastria* disaster may never be known for a number of reasons, among them the official prevention of disclosure. Based on the data it has gathered over the years, the HMT Lancastria Association has registered 1,738 deaths – although it holds the belief that the actual number killed is far in excess of this. Various sources place the casualty number at or above 3,000, although the basis for the calculation is not known. Others state that 4,800 or as many as 5,800 lost their lives in those desperate few hours on 17 June 1940. It is widely accepted, despite the lack of verification, that the death toll when the *Lancastria* was sunk was not less than 3,500, of which up to 1,000 could have been civilians.

Both to pursue the truth of the tragedy and to ensure that it is remembered, the Association of Lancastria Survivors (now the HMT Lancastria Association) was created after the war by Major Peter Petit. Since that time, the association has organised commemorations, pilgrimages to the wreck site, the erection of memorials and the continued petition of successive governments for the event to be properly honoured, the wreck site to be made a war grave and for the early release of official documents. Today, thanks to the French government, an exclusion zone has been placed around the wreck site to provide a measure of protection.

There are several memorials to the *Lancastria* disaster: one on the sea front at Saint-Nazaire, one at the National Arboretum, Alrewas, Lichfield, and one planned for Glasgow, the city where the *Lancastria* was built. The principal *Lancastria* memorial is in the St Katherine Cree church in the City of London, which has a commemorative panel in the stained glass window. It now displays the ship's bell, recovered from a military cemetery in France in 2005, which will be rung each year on 17 June.

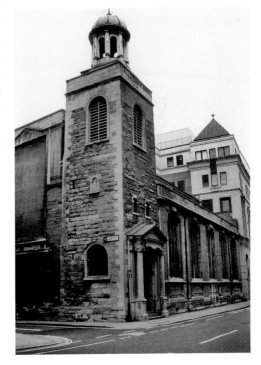

The St Katherine Cree church in the City of London, the home of the *Lancastria* memorial. (David L. Williams)

Part of the memorial display in St Katherine Cree church. (David L. Williams)

In the context of this book, it is fitting to close this account with words expressed by one of the HMT Lancastria Association members:

> With respect it's quite distressing that over the years a film like the '*Titanic*' glamor-izes death by drowning [aboard a ship] which was made to make money. It is worth remembering that those on the *Titanic* were in pursuit of pleasure whereas those on the *Lancastria* were losing their lives for their country. Survivors we have worked with don't want publicity – they just wish for recognition.

LENIN ex-*Simbirsk* (9/1909)

Black Sea Shipping Co., Sovtorgflot, USSR

Just over a year later, on 27 July 1941, a comparable tragedy occurred in the Black Sea, off Crimea, in the southern USSR. Like the *Lancastria* case, it too was subjected to an official blanket of secrecy that was only lifted sixty years later. This was the loss of the Soviet passenger-cargo steamship *Lenin* with a count of victims which, though it remains unconfirmed, ranges from 900 to 4,600 according to different reports. Despite the uncertainty about the gravity of the loss, for qualification for inclusion in this book, it was by any other standard a seriously grave occurrence. Besides which, the nature of this book's subject requires that there should not be a pedantic application of arbitrary rules, for there is no relativity to tragedy and the story of the *Lenin* certainly deserves to be recounted.

The facts of this shocking calamity were only declassified after persistent and penetrating research at the turn of the millennium by Sergey Alekseevich Soloviev, the academic secretary of Sevastopol's Military-Scientific Society. Having gained access to the files, he conducted a thorough study of the inquiry records and the testimonies of witnesses, and made copies of maps and photographs. His efforts revealed the unvarnished truth that had been concealed but suspected for so long: that the sinking had almost certainly resulted in the deaths of many thousands of people. The most realistic estimates suggested that the number killed was greater than the combined casualties of the *Titanic* and *Lusitania*.

The circumstances that brought the *Lenin* to her untimely end, the overrunning of western Russia, Belarus and the Ukraine by German forces in the summer of 1941 after the launching of Operation Barbarossa (the invasion of the Soviet Union) are explained more fully in the next chapter. Suffice to say here that the *Lenin* was part of an armada of ships, which, like those at Dunkirk and Saint-Nazaire, were involved in an evacuation, first from Odessa and later from Sevastopol and Yalta, of epic proportions. In total, through countless runs to Mariupol, Novorossiysk and Tuapse, under relentless German aerial bombardment, they managed to rescue millions of people.

The *Lenin* was built in Danzig (now Gdansk) in 1909 as the *Simbirsk*, one of five similar ships, entering service for Obshchestvo Dobrovolny Flota (Russian Volunteer Fleet Association) in the Far East on a route linking Vladivostok, Kholmsk and Yokohama, Japan. Her consorts were the *Orel*, *Poltava*, *Riazon* and *Penza*. After the First World War the *Simbirsk* was taken over by the Communist government, allocated to the Black Sea & Azov Shipping Co. and renamed *Lenin* in 1924, from which time she remained in regular Black Sea service, working between Odessa and Novorossiysk.

Early in 1941, the *Lenin* underwent a comprehensive refit and was painted in new colours. Her return to commercial service was short-lived, though, for that summer, under the command of Captain Ivan Semyonovich Borisenko, she was activated for auxiliary duties in support of the unfolding emergency at Odessa.

Her first refugee voyage, which commenced on 12 July 1941, took her from Odessa to Mariupol, in the Azov Sea, via Sevastopol and Yalta, a round trip lasting ten days. On the return leg she was attacked by German dive-bombers, which were driven off by her escort, the cruiser *Comintern*. Back in Odessa, the city was also being targeted in air raids and the civilian casualties were mounting. The *Lenin*'s master was ordered by the ship's owners to rapidly load cargo and embark passengers in order to make an immediate return to Mariupol.

The evacuation arrangements were under the control of the Navy Commandant's office ashore but in the rapidly deteriorating situation, it was a frenetic and haphazard process. Nobody was counted aboard the *Lenin* because it was understood that this was being done by the naval staff, while boarding cards were issued to blocks of passengers rather than to individuals. For example, one card (a single count) was allocated for all the adults of a family or a complete group of colleagues. Children were disregarded completely as far as the refugee count was concerned. Consequently, there is no way of determining precisely how many people in total boarded the ship. It was so crowded that every area of space, in the salons, companionways, the inside and open decks, even in the holds, was completely jam-packed. Besides the civilian evacuees taken aboard, who included local officials and their families, Captain Borisenko was also ordered to accommodate 1,200 Red Army reserves. Members of the crew also took aboard their families and friends in a bid to help them reach safety.

Unofficially, based on the recently uncovered proceedings of the court of inquiry and the contemporary cross-examination accounts of survivors, it has been estimated that, contrary to regulations, there were around 5,200 passengers in total on the *Lenin* when she sailed on 24 July. This is in marked contrast to her peacetime complement of 482 passengers and ninety-two crew. The *Lenin* was also carrying a valuable non-human cargo in the form of 400 tons of 'non-ferrous' ingots, along with bonds and hard currency from the vaults of the Odessa State Bank. After two days loading the ship, which itself must have caused enormous feeding and sanitary problems, the *Lenin* sailed at 22.00 hours on 24 July in convoy with the equally overloaded cargo ships *Voroshilov*, previously the *Brazilian Prince* of Furness Withy, and *Berezina*.

The outbreak of hostilities with Germany had necessitated the laying of defensive minefields to protect strategic points along Russia's Black Sea coast. For safe passage through these areas, a special system had been introduced for shipping movements. Navigation lights and beacons on shore, though not switched off altogether, were subject to a managed illumination schedule, knowledge of which, along with the positions of the clear channels, was restricted to a very few qualified pilots whose engagement became obligatory. Despite the obvious benefits of these measures, they were undermined by a poor communications system. In order to contact the operations duty officer ashore, pilots aboard the ships were required to transmit radiograms via naval ships, an irregular arrangement that could not be relied upon.

Photographs of the Russian passenger ship *Lenin*, the ex-*Simbirsk*, sunk by mine in July 1941, are few and of inferior quality, like the example shown here. (Boris Lemachko)

Appointed to the *Lenin* as her pilot was Lieutenant I.I. Svistun, a recent graduate of the Leningrad Higher Naval College, who, though qualified for the task, lacked practical experience. Initially, the convoy's progress was slow as the three bigger vessels were held back by two small, low-powered barges that had also been attached to the convoy. Later, after the barges were detached, the transports were able to speed up but a further delay occurred on 26 July when the ships were off Cape Lukull, between Pishchane and Andriivka, around 15 miles north of Sevastopol. The *Voroshilov* suffered a complete failure of her diesel engines, attributed to a hastily executed and ineffective repair. Already, it had been necessary for the convoy, which was hugging the Crimean coast, to take evasive action from repeated German air attacks and, concerned for the safety of the countless vulnerable passengers stranded aboard the *Voroshilov*, Captain Borisenko had the *Lenin* take her in tow to Kazachya Bay, 6 miles south-west of Sevastopol, where they arrived later that day.

The following day, the *Lenin* continued her voyage, bound for Yalta in company with fleet-mate *Gruzia* and escorted by the naval patrol boat *SKA-026*. Some reports suggest that the repaired *Voroshilov* also sailed with them. Late on 27 July, just before midnight, as she passed Cape Sarych, the *Lenin* was rocked by a massive explosion between holds No.1 and No.2 and she sank within ten minutes, taking the vast majority of her occupants with her.

Almost immediately all information and records relating to the disaster, both its circumstances and the numbers, names and personal details of the victims and survivors, were classified as secret. All official news agencies were instructed not to report on the event although this was not unusual for few, if any, other wartime shipping casualties had been given press attention.

It was claimed that the *Lenin* had been torpedoed by the Romanian submarine *Delfinius*, an unsubstantiated conjecture, which probably referred to an unsuccessful attack that had occurred earlier, during the *Lenin*'s previous relief voyage. The truth of the matter was that the *Lenin* had struck a Soviet mine as the result of a navigational error when the young pilot had altered the ship's bearing.

A better impression of the *Lenin* can be gained from this picture of her near sister, the Red Cross Line (C.T. Bowring) ship *Silvia*, the ex-*Orel*. (World Ship Society)

Lieutenant Svistun, who was among the approximately 643 survivors (forty-three crew and around 600 passengers), was duly arrested and tried by a military court. In accordance with the court's decision, he was executed by firing squad on 24 August 1941. Although his error had caused the deaths of thousands, it was a harsh punishment for someone who had been literally 'pitched in at the deep end' as a novice. This was recognised when, on 18 August 1992, a naval tribunal conducted by Russia's Black Sea Fleet Command recommended a posthumous pardon. It was a belated and sadly inadequate consolation for a young man who had been charged with a heavy responsibility beyond his capability. As Rear Admiral A.R. Azarenko commented: 'He would have made a navigator in a long time but Svistun was not appropriate for the role in peace, not to speak of wartime.'

The wreck of the *Lenin* today still lies 96m down, about 2½ miles offshore from the former presidential resort of Zarya and the dachas of the Soviet era at nearby Foros.

3

SAFE PASSAGE GUARANTEED?
(PART ONE)

Wartime hospital ships are afforded protection from attack under the Hague and Geneva Conventions, provided that they are appropriately declared, clearly marked and illuminated in accordance with recognised protocols, and are not used for any military purpose. These rules are particularly relevant where the opposing nations are signatories to the conventions.

Unequivocally, to attack a hospital ship was, and is, a war crime. However, because Article 4 of the Hague Convention outlined strict restrictions applicable to the operation of hospital ships, it permitted belligerents, as specified by the convention, the right to search a hospital ship if it was suspected of being operated in violation of these restrictions. If it was confirmed that the restrictions had been violated, the ship would be treated as an enemy combatant and could be lawfully attacked. To deliberately fire on or sink a hospital ship that was in compliance with the convention regulations would, though, be a war crime.

In summary, the essential elements of the convention provided that marked hospital ships were protected under international law and their protection could only be removed following a search by a belligerent in which irrefutable evidence of military use or carriage of contraband was discovered. Any other action was illegal. Written down on paper like this, there appear to be no ambiguities as to the safe conduct afforded to hospital ships; it is generally and widely accepted as being beyond question. Yet such was not always the case during either the First or Second World Wars.

In the First World War alone, no fewer than nine hospital ships were torpedoed without warning and sunk, although other losses caused by mine could not be regarded as blatantly and unlawfully aggressive actions. Twenty years later, after the outbreak of the Second World War, the disregard of the safe passage protection of hospital ships resumed. A Japanese submarine sank the Australian hospital ship *Centaur* off the Queensland coast on 14 May 1943 with the cost of 268 lives, 223 of the victims being medical staff. On 18 November 1944, RAF warplanes attacked and sank the German hospital ship *Tübingen* near Pola, and American bombers not only sank the Japanese hospital ship *Buenos Aires Maru* on 26 November 1943, but returned to the scene to strafe survivors adrift in the lifeboats. Besides these incidents, another case of breach of the convention resulted in a loss with human casualties of an even greater magnitude, placing it among the worst, if not *the* worst maritime disaster up to that time.

ARMENIA (1928)

Black Sea Shipping Co., Sovtorgflot, USSR

The Soviet-flag passenger motor vessel *Armenia* was one of a class of six ships built in the late 1920s in Russia and Germany (*Abkhaziya, Adzharia, Ukraina* and *Armenia; Krym* and *Gruzia*) completed for the services of the state-owned Black Sea Shipping Co.. They were designed by the Central Bureau of Merchant Marine Shipbuilding, Leningrad, as part of an intensive Sovtorgflot programme for the regeneration of the Soviet merchant fleet.

The design provided for a relatively large passenger capacity and substantial cargo stowage within a moderate-sized hull, for operation on intensive short-sea routes in areas where there were draught restrictions. The class was considered to be one of the most successful for work on ferry routes conceived by Soviet designers in a project team led by Ing. J.A. Koperżyńskiego. The placement of contracts for two of the six ships in Germany, with Friedrich Krupp, at the Deutsche Werft yard at Kiel, was purely a capacity-driven decision in order to have all six in service before 1930, rather than because of a need for foreign expertise. The heavy demand on the Leningrad shipyards at that time precluded the construction of more than four hulls in the allotted time span.

Each ship could carry 518 passengers in berthed accommodation, which was a step improvement on what was then available on older vessels still working the Black Sea routes. Some 462 deck passengers were also carried. Despite their shallow draught, all six were sturdy vessels with good sea-keeping qualities – but they were not built to withstand the impact of exploding bombs, torpedoes or mines.

On completion, all six ships entered service on the Ukraine and Crimea–Caucasus line, linking Odessa, Sevastopol and Batumi. At least one of the group also maintained an irregular sailing schedule, taking passengers and freight from Odessa via the Bosphorus to Beirut.

The *Armenia*, like her sisters, continued in commercial operation until 1941 when the launching of Operation Barbarossa, the German attack on the Eastern Front,

The Soviet-flag Black Sea passenger motor ship *Armenia*; one of very few photographs of the ill-fated vessel sunk with the greatest loss of life of any Russian vessel. (Infoflot)

Sister ship of the *Armenia*, the *Abkhaziya* was sunk at Sevastopol while serving as a hospital ship, another vessel whose protected status was not respected by German warplane crews. (Infoflot)

propelled the Soviet Union into the hostilities on the side of the Allies. Earlier, after having unsuccessfully courted Great Britain and France to form a defensive alliance against German aggression, the Soviet Union had entered a Non-Aggression Pact with Germany. Whether or not it was considered to be an adequate safeguard to protect Russia from Germany's rampant expansionism, it bought time to increase military preparedness – or so the strategists thought.

Events of 9 June 1941 were to show how vulnerable the Soviet Union had remained despite her planning. Germany launched a huge three-pronged armoured land offensive into the Soviet Union on an 800-mile front, sweeping across from Poland and Romania and immediately making huge gains as her armies pushed into Belarus and the Ukraine. The Soviet troops were forced back into Russia itself as Leningrad was rapidly encircled and even Moscow, with the seat of Soviet government at the Kremlin, was threatened.

Further south, the oil fields of the Caucasus were the key objective and a thrust towards Rostov and through the Crimea was to blaze a path, so it was planned, that would lead eventually to Baku and the vital oil installations in Adzharia. Army Group South's offensive was directed initially at Kiev, Pervomaysk and Odessa but compared to the Central and Northern Army Groups, it came up against stiffer resistance. Over the six months following the start of the Barbarossa campaign, the Germans and Romanians pushed forward relentlessly: taking Kiev on 19 September; encircling and capturing Odessa on 16 October. With the bulk of Crimea in their hands by the end of the year, the south-east front reached its furthest extent with the occupation of Novorossiysk.

It was in these circumstances that the *Armenia* and her consorts, all stationed in the area, were activated for auxiliary service, initially for the relief and partial evacuation of Odessa. Under the command of Captain V. Ya. Plaushevsky, the *Armenia* was mobilised on 8 August 1941 and taken over and equipped by the Black Sea navy as a hospital ship, along with the *Abkhaziya* and *Ukraina*. However, it is said that they did not fully comply with the requirements of the Geneva Convention, having perhaps had 45mm calibre guns fitted, along with some machine guns. Manned by 119 medical staff in addition to her regular crew, the *Armenia* was designated as the main vessel of this type for service on the Black Sea.

Painted all white with bold red cross emblems on her funnels and sides, as stipulated by the Hague and Geneva Conventions, she made fifteen runs between Odessa and Sevastopol. Carrying around 1,000 people on each trip, made up of the injured, hospital cases, invalids, the elderly and infirm, along with hospital staff badly needed for the growing number of treatment centres in the Crimea. There was no reason to believe that the German forces would not respect the safe passage protection that her status was supposed to guarantee.

After the fall of Odessa, the enemy's main targets became Sevastopol and Yalta. The evacuees earlier transferred to the Crimean capital now had to be moved again, further eastwards, to Novorossiysk and Tuapse. The evacuation of casualties from Sevastopol commenced in early November in parallel with the transportation into the city of fresh troops for its defences. The hospital ships, including the *Armenia*, were to operate in tandem with the troopships, among them the *Adzharia*, *Gruzia* and *Krym*.

Having earlier called at Sevastopol, the *Armenia* arrived at Yalta bound for Tuapse on 6 November 1941 on the first of this phase of mercy runs. There she embarked a huge number of people, variously put at from 5,500 to 10,000 but believed to have been actually of the order of 7,000. Crammed aboard her were wounded soldiers, civilian evacuees, the staff of the Central Black Sea navy hospital, along with the staff and patients from twenty-three other military and civil hospitals in the region. The order from Naval Command had been to take *all* medical personnel, injured and ill people from all of the hospitals in and around besieged Sevastopol.

One of the mysterious aspects of the *Armenia* case, which was to have a major influence on what was to transpire, was why the authorities insisted so many vulnerable people should be embarked on the *Armenia* alone when there were other hospital ships in the port. Given the desperate circumstances, with Odessa already fallen, Rostov close to being overrun and the whole of the Crimea threatened, every available ship was involved in getting the casualties out and, to bolster the defences, reinforcements in – but other hospital ships did have spare capacity.

When the *Armenia* was ready to sail, Russian Naval Command instructed her master to delay his departure until 19.00 hours at the earliest, when light was falling, or until escorts became available. For a reason that no one now can explain, Captain Plaushevsky ignored these orders. He did wait at Yalta through the night but the following morning, 7 November 1941, at 08.00 hours, he put to sea, bound for Tuapse in broad daylight and without a proper escort.

Less than four hours later, reports say at 11.25 hours, the *Armenia* was spotted off the coast near Gurzuf by Heinkel He 111H bombers of Kampfgeschwader 28, which immediately attacked. The planes had been armed for attacks on shipping and, besides dropping their bombs, they also carried torpedoes, which they unleashed at the *Armenia*. One hit the helpless ship at her forward end. With her bows and forepart blasted away completely, she sank almost immediately. A survivor, one of only eight picked up later by a naval escort vessel, timed the sinking at 11.29 hours, only four minutes after the assault had started. In such a brief interval, there was no opportunity to organise anything even remotely like a proper evacuation of the ship.

The German pilots had no excuse for their actions. They certainly could not have been mistaken about the *Armenia*'s function, for standing out brightly in the morning sunshine, her white hull and prominent red crosses would have been clearly seen: they chose deliberately to disregard the markings. An eyewitness who had watched the tragedy unfold from the shore later recalled:

> Hardly had the boat reached the open sea, when a group of German planes attacked it. It goes without saying that the Nazi pilots could see the big red crosses on the ship. Nevertheless, they started bombing the vessel. We could hear both bomb explosions and people's screaming.

Maybe Captain Plaushevsky had taken his chances that fateful day because he felt sure the Germans would not attack a ship operating under the protection of the Red Cross, but sadly his judgement failed him.

The catastrophic loss of the *Armenia* was then, and remains to this day, the worst ever involving a Russian ship. For just over three years it was the world's worst maritime disaster with an official figure of 5,000 casualties, although it is widely accepted that the actual number of dead was nearer to 7,000.

Every year, on 9 May, in honour of the victims of the tragedy, war veterans, ex-servicemen and local citizens lay wreaths on the water above the wreck, which lies at a depth of 472m.

GRUZIA (2/1929)

Black Sea Shipping Co., Sovtorgflot, USSR

Although the *Gruzia*, sister ship of the *Armenia*, was not a hospital ship, the account of her loss has been related here to follow the close chronology of events immediately following the *Armenia*'s loss. Unlike the *Armenia*, therefore, when she was sunk she was not under the protection of safe-passage status.

It was only a matter of days after the *Armenia* had been sunk (another disaster which was largely suppressed by the Soviet authorities) that Rostov was taken, on 21 November, while most of the Crimea fell to the Germans on 5 December. The exception was Sevastopol, which, completely surrounded, continued to hold out for almost six months. Russian landings on the Kerch peninsula on 26 December 1941, in a bid to relieve Sevastopol, were initially successful but in May 1942, driven back by superior German forces, the Russians withdrew and the city was finally occupied late that June.

The *Gruzia*, another ship of the *Armenia*-class. She was sunk as a troopship in June 1942 while transporting units of the Red Army into besieged Sevastopol. (Peter Tschursch)

During those six desperate months, at a huge cost in shipping losses, every effort was made to sustain the beleaguered city; taking in food, supplies and reinforcements and removing military casualties and those injured from the civilian population that had remained there. Among the vessels engaged in the relief of Sevastopol were the *Armenia*'s four remaining sisters (the *Adzharia* had been sunk at Odessa on 23 July 1941), notably the *Gruzia*.

In the final days of the city's valiant resistance, as enemy attacks on Sevastopol intensified, the *Gruzia* was to fall victim of the onslaught as she attempted to make another reinforcement run, ferrying-in 4,000 troops and 1,300 tons of ammunition. Under the command of Captain M.I. Fokin, who also held the naval rank of lieutenant commander, she had already survived a bombing attack en route to Sevastopol when an escorting destroyer had come to her aid, driving off her assailants. Claims were made that she was subsequently attacked and hit by torpedoes from Italian MAS boats during the night of 12 June, as she was approaching the Crimean port, but in fact it was German bombs that sealed her fate the following day.

In the entrance to the harbour, while unable to take evasive action at slow speed and in the restricted channel, aircraft swarmed onto her. One of the bombs dropped in the second wave detonated in the area of her forward hold, triggering immense explosions in the ammunition stowed there. Critically, her end came before she had been able to disembark the servicemen she was carrying and the majority of them were killed, along with most of her crew – yet another devastating shipping loss costing the lives of around 4,000 souls.

The *Gruzia* may not have been a hospital ship but the fact was that in the Crimean and Black Sea campaigns, it was quite evident that the Germans gave scant regard to the immunity afforded to vessels of that type anyway. Two more of the *Gruzia*'s class were sunk while engaged as hospital ships, the *Abkhaziya* and *Ukraina*, the former

Another view of the *Gruzia*, taken prior to the involvement of the Soviet Union in the Second World War. (Author's collection)

The *Ukraina* was another of the *Armenia*-class ships attacked and sunk while serving as a hospital ship, in her case bombed at Novorossiysk. With sister ship *Krym*, the *Ukraina* was recovered after the war and returned to service following salvage and repair. (Dr Piotr Mierzejewski)

having been sunk by Junkers Ju 87s just three days earlier within the harbour at Sevastopol. Up to then she had completed thirty-five brave but dangerous missions into the war zone and had ferried 65,000 civilians and 32,355 wounded servicemen – 9,500 of whom underwent surgery in her on-board theatre – to the safety of Novorossiysk and Tuapse. The *Ukraina* was bombed in the port of Novorossiysk on 2 July 1942. Other Russian hospital ships attacked or sunk were the *Chekhov*, *Kotovskij*, *Dnepr* (ex-*Cabo San Agustin*, sunk on 3 October 1941) and *L'vov* (ex-*Ciudad de Tarragona*). The latter ship was the only civilian vessel mobilised by the Soviets during the war to be decorated with the Order of the Red Banner.

So concerned was the Soviet Naval Command about the enemy's disregard for the protected status of hospital ships, it finally adopted a radically different policy for the operation of such ships. It concluded that painting them in the authorised colour scheme required to reveal their purpose and allow them to proceed about their business without harm, served only to expose them more vividly to those who had no intention of respecting their protected status. In effect, it turned them into more conspicuous targets. Therefore, it was decided that, for the remainder of the conflict, Soviet-flag hospital ships would no longer be painted as prescribed but instead rendered in concealment colours; either plain navy grey or in disruptive patterned schemes.

As a postscript to the loss of the *Gruzia*, attempts were made to salvage her wreck, first in 1949 and, on a second occasion, in 1956. When she was raised to the surface the first time, salvors discovered a large quantity of unexploded gas shells and bombs in her stern hold. Judged to be dangerously unstable, they prudently allowed the wreck to settle back onto the seabed. During the second attempt, the salvors worked under specific government instructions to recover the suspect ordnance, as its contents could be made use of in new chemical weapons. They were to be denied, however, for the *Gruzia*'s hull broke in two and it remains to this day, with its deadly cargo, on the floor of the Black Sea.

4

THOSE IN PERIL ON THE SEA

The next three chapters deal with extreme disaster cases that occurred while ships were transporting prisoners of war. The legalities of such practices was open to question insofar as the provisions of the Geneva Convention were concerned, particularly where the vessels engaged in these voyages were unmarked, thereby placing the occupants at risk of attack by friendly fire.

In recent times, there has been much discussion and reportage on the practice of 'extraordinary rendition', the abduction and illegal transfer of people from one nation to another, often for the purposes of carrying out discreet interrogation using torture techniques. The implication is that any movement of captives, either prisoners or illegal combatants, contravenes internationally agreed regulations pertaining to the conduct of hostilities. There is, however, a legally approved form of transfer known simply as 'rendition', the difference being that in the latter action, the change of jurisdiction may occur either after legal proceedings have taken place against those people being moved, or in accordance with the laws of international conflict. The Geneva Convention in particular provides for the humanitarian treatment of war prisoners of all categories and in all circumstances. Essentially, it is the adherence to these rules or otherwise that determines whether the action taken, whatever it may be (in the context of these accounts, specifically transportation by ship) is legally permissible or not. The rules stipulate that prisoners must be protected against any act of violence. Furthermore, the conditions of their detention, including during transit, lay down minimum standards for accommodation, food, clothing, hygiene and medical care. The deliberate denial of these conditions could be regarded as a war crime but, equally, failure through inadvertent exposure to a perceivable risk, such as when an unprotected ship is sunk while carrying prisoners, may reasonably be argued as also amounting to a breach of the provisions of the Geneva Convention.

Transportation of prisoners by sea was commonplace during the Second World War, practised not only by Germany and Japan but also by Great Britain, including aboard the *Laconia*, described here. Quite apart from its gravity, the *Laconia* case is now known for the controversy that surrounded it; a controversy that arose from the interpretation of a German naval directive, which instructed commanders of U-boats to leave the survivors of ships they had sunk to their fate rather than render them life-saving assistance. While in essence the affair focused on the degree of aid that the naval forces of belligerents should have reasonably afforded the survivors of attacked ships, and the fact that German Naval Command had challenged the offering of *any* help, it did not elicit deliberation on the equally serious matter of failure to adequately protect prisoners in the first place, in accordance with convention rules, by not exposing them to the risk of attack at sea.

LACONIA (1/1922)

Cunard White Star Line, Liverpool, UK

As the result of the successful campaign waged by British Commonwealth forces in North Africa through Operation Compass, from December 1940 through to February 1941, and in East Africa with the defeat of the Italians in Somaliland, Ethiopia and Eritrea, between January and April 1941 more than 230,000 Italian soldiers were taken prisoner.

Held in prison camps in Egypt, so many captives presented major difficulties, logistically, administratively and in respect of adequate food, drink and sanitation provision. There was also great concern about the retention of so many prisoners in such close proximity to the battlefront just across the border in Libya. Since the arrival of General Erwin Rommel as commander-in-chief of the Deutsches Afrika Corps there had been a real threat of him making an eastwards push to the Suez Canal to take strategically vital Alexandria and Cairo. A major thrust of sufficient magnitude in that direction could also have liberated huge numbers of hostile forces from the holding camps permitting the strengthening of the Axis position. For all these reasons, it became necessary to take action to mitigate the risks. This involved, on the one hand, negotiating and arranging prisoner exchanges with the Italians and, on the other, the dispersal of large numbers of prisoners to more secure locations in North America and Great Britain.

The first prisoner exchange took place in April 1942, followed by others that year and in 1943, but these only scratched the surface of the problem. Agreeing the transfer terms, a painstaking process, took a lot of time and the numbers involved were relatively insignificant, further diluted by the inclusion in the exchanges of non-military detainees. On three occasions, Italian ships were permitted to take personnel from Massawa, Eritrea, without a corresponding compensation of returned British captives. This was simply because the British occupation forces feared a massacre of Italians by the native population in reprisal for the treatment they had received since their territories had been seized in 1935.

In the absence of a real alternative, emphasis was placed on the transportation of Italian prisoners of war overseas as the best way to relieve the pressing situation. Resources were limited, though, and there was a reluctance to take ships away from more urgent war work to undertake these duties. Among the vessels requisitioned was the former Cunard White Star liner *Laconia* under the command of Captain Rudolph Sharp, who had been transferred to her after surviving the ordeal of the sinking of fleet-mate *Lancastria* off Saint-Nazaire.

The Cunard White Star liner *Laconia*, seen in the 1930s. (Basil Fielden)

On the outbreak of war, the *Laconia* had initially been converted for operation as an auxiliary cruiser manned by a naval crew, but she had been released for troopship employment in 1941. The *Laconia* and her sisters *Samaria* and *Scythia* constituted the first group of a five-ship class for Cunard's intermediate transatlantic services. Her peacetime accommodation, reduced in 1924 with cruise service in mind (an activity she spent much time engaged in during the 1930s) provided for a maximum of approximately 1,800 passengers in three classes.

In late July 1942, the *Laconia* was at Port Tewfik where she boarded a large complement, it is believed totalling 2,645 people. Strangely, given the orderly circumstances of the embarkation, there are now disputed versions of the number of people who sailed with the *Laconia*. After scrutinising documents from Cunard and in the Lloyd's collection at the Guildhall Library, London, as well as the accounts of surviving crew members, the figure of 2,645 is considered to be the most reliable; comprising 286 British military personnel, 1,793 Italian prisoners of war, 103 Free Polish guards and 463 crew. She also had a general cargo, which included skins, kapok and sisal.

The *Laconia* departed on 29 July 1942 bound for Liverpool, sailing southwards to go around Africa. En route, she made calls at Aden, Mombasa, Durban and Cape Town. By the time she left Cape Town on 1 September 1942, an additional eighty-seven civilian passengers had joined the ship, mainly women and children. The *Laconia* was armed but, as she had done from the outset, she sailed unescorted. She carried no markings on her plain grey-painted hull to indicate the nature of her human cargo and she had not been declared to the enemy, no doubt because, without agreed safe-passage protection, that may have invited interception.

The voyage home proceeded well until the evening of 12 September 1942, at which date, as she was steaming midway between Ascension Island and Liberia, she was intercepted by the German submarine *U-156*, commanded by Kapitänleutnant Werner Hartenstein. Two torpedoes were fired that hit the *Laconia's* starboard side in quick succession, the first at about 22.10 hours. One struck the ship amidships, the other near the aft hold, instantly killing many of the Italian prisoners who had been billeted deep in the bowels of the ship. The *Laconia* immediately listed to starboard and began to settle at the stern, her fate sealed.

At 22.22 hours, barely ten minutes after the first torpedo explosion, a Mayday signal was transmitted, 'SSS SSS 04.34 South/11.25 West Laconia torpedoed', followed by a request for urgent assistance. The position placed the stricken ship some 150 miles north-west of Ascension. It has been stated that neither this radio message nor the second, sent four minutes later, were received by Allied listening stations. Research has shown that cannot be so, for the Lloyd's War Loss Records state quite clearly that an un-named Royal Navy ship was alerted to search for survivors, as was the *Empire Haven*, a British cargo ship, which was nearest to the scene. What is more important is that the messages *were* picked up aboard the *U-156*, as revealed later in an exchange that took place between one of the survivors and the U-boat commander. Kapitänleutnant Hartenstein allegedly stated that, by making the call to the Royal Navy for assistance, the *Laconia* had in effect declared itself to be a naval auxiliary, confirming his belief that he had attacked, completely legitimately, an enemy troop carrier. On learning of the true nature of his target, he apparently questioned the sense of arming a ship engaged in such work, for had she not been carrying guns he would not have sunk her without challenging her first.

These observations are pertinent inasmuch as the *Laconia*, which was indeed an armed merchantman, forfeited her entitlement to protection from attack without warning, and, with it, the requirement that her occupants should be removed to a place of safety before she could be sunk. It may be felt that these are moot points, for there are countless testimonies from the Second World War of U-boats sinking unarmed cargo ships without any warning whatsoever. Equally, there is much evidence of vessels being stopped and searched before any hostile action was taken, along with the ensuing provision of food and water, a compass and directions to the nearest land to survivors in the lifeboats. It should be stressed that, in sinking the *Laconia*, Hartenstein was not guilty of any infringement of the accepted rules of submarine warfare.

The reader may consider that such deliberations seem strangely incongruous, or at least irrelevant, when two foes are engaged in conflict and each is bent on completely subduing the other by all means at its disposal in order to gain ultimate victory. Besides that, the commander of the attacking craft has an equal duty to protect his own vessel and the well-being of his own ship's company. By revealing a submarine's presence in order to act in accordance with the rules of engagement, risked exposing it to the danger of counter-attack – such was the delicate balance of conflicting considerations that confronted those that were waging war at the sharp end.

What followed the sinking of the *Laconia* suggests, though, that there could be a compassionate dimension to the war at sea; that, other than there being a callous disregard of the consequences of a torpedo attack, there were acts of great courage in keeping with the age-old spirit of the sea to mitigate the worst extremes of lost life. As the *Laconia* upended and disappeared bow first into the ocean, the *U-156* surfaced. It was approximately 23.20 hours. Following normal practice, the intention had been to try to take into custody any of the sunk ship's officers for the intelligence that might be extracted from them. The *U-156*'s crew instead greeted the scene with surprise at the number of people struggling in the sea, compounded when cries of '*aiuto*' were heard, the Italian for 'help'.

Although there had been adequate time to launch the *Laconia*'s lifeboats, some had been destroyed by the explosions while the ship's severe list had made it impossible to lower others on the port side. Many of the Italians who had survived the torpedoes were still penned-up down below and went down with the ship. Captain Sharp did not survive the sinking, either. For those in the sea, new dangers confronted them. They were hundreds of miles from land with inadequate space for all in the lifeboats and were now facing the additional hazard of sharks and barracudas attracted by the commotion.

Once the true nature of what had happened dawned on Hartenstein, he immediately initiated a rescue operation. He took some ninety survivors aboard his submarine and had the overflowing lifeboats shepherded together and connected by ropes so they could be towed towards land. At 01.25 hours on 13 September, the situation was reported to U-boat Command BdU (Headquarters) in Germany, and they were requested to summon more assistance. Despite concerns about Hartenstein's spontaneous rescue plan, Vice Admiral Dönitz duly ordered two more U-boats to break off from their patrols and divert to the scene, while the Vichy French were also requested to send surface ships to the area to take the rescued to safety ashore.

It may be judged that Hartenstein's actions were motivated exclusively by no more than a desire to save as many as possible of the Italian prisoners, soldiers allied to the German cause, but it is evident that his efforts in fact had a broader humanitarian stimulus. At 06.00 hours he transmitted an unencrypted radio message in English, which read: 'If any ship will assist the ship-wrecked *Laconia*, I will not attack providing I am not being attacked by ship or air forces. I picked up 193 men 04.53 South, 11.26 West – German submarine.' While he did not identify his vessel, he gave the true position in degrees of latitude and longitude whereas earlier, when he had communicated to U-boat Command, the position had been stated in accordance with the German navy's grid-reference system, as FF 7721 310 degrees.

For the next two and a half days, the *U-156* struggled to contain the situation as best it could. Dry clothing was provided and the survivors on board and in the lifeboats were fed with whatever rations were available. Medical attention was rendered to the sick and injured, some of whom were blast victims while others had shark bite and bayonet injuries – the latter no doubt inflicted by zealous guards who, despite the critical circumstances, had endeavoured to the last to prevent the Italian prisoners from escaping.

Late in the morning of 15 September, the *U-156* was joined first by *U-506*, commanded by Kapitänleutnant Erich Würdemann, and soon after by *U-507* under

Survivors from the *Laconia* on the topside decks of the submarines *U-156* and *U-507*.
(Oberleutnant z.S. Leopold Schuhmacher)

Korvettenkapitän Harro Schacht along with the Italian submarine *Comandante Cappellini*. Between them, they re-distributed the survivors to relieve some of the overcrowding. Then, with the lifeboats still in tow and their decks full of standing survivors, they set off for the African coast and the planned rendezvous with three French warships: the cruiser *Gloire* from Dakar, Senegal; the patrol vessel *Annamite* out of Conakry, French Guinea; and the frigate *Dumont d'Urville*, which had sailed from Cotonon, Dahomey (now Benin).

The following day at 11.25 hours, a patrolling American B-24 Liberator from Ascension Island spotted the four submarines with the cluster of lifeboats. Hartenstein signalled the pilot by Morse lamp to explain the situation and request assistance, and the four submarines draped Red Cross flags across their topsides to communicate that a rescue operation was underway. The bomber turned away, however, and the pilot, Lieutenant James D. Harden, who was unable to understand Morse code, radioed his base with a request for instructions.

The senior duty officer there, Captain Robert C. Richardson III, unaware of the events unfolding 150 or so miles to the north, feared that it might just be an elaborate German hoax to draw Allied vessels into a trap. The only information he had was that a troopship had been sunk and two cargo ships were searching for survivors. He believed, too, that the rules of war prohibited any combat vessel from flying or displaying the Red Cross, reinforcing his doubts as to the veracity of the request for assistance. For those reasons, he ordered the bomber to return and attack the submarines.

The relief felt by the U-boat officers when, an hour later, they saw the returning aircraft, expecting it to drop supplies into the sea, changed to horror when instead it began to drop bombs and depth charges on them. The aircraft made three passes, its bombs landing among the lifeboats and killing more of the survivors, while others straddled the submarines showering them with water and shrapnel. Without delay, the remaining lifeboats were cast adrift and the survivors on deck ordered into the sea as the U-boats executed crash dives to escape – the German and Italian commanders had no choice but to try to save their boats. As a result, many more of those who had escaped the sinking *Laconia* now lost their lives.

The precise number of casualties, like that of her complement when she set out, now seems shrouded in uncertainty, in part because of the subsequent dispersal of those who had survived. Figures for the survivors range from 975 to 1,111, meaning that between 1,621 and 1,757 people perished, the majority of them Italian prisoners, for it has been calculated that fewer than 400 of their number were rescued.

As a footnote to this aspect of the loss of the *Laconia*, the Lloyd's War Loss Card states that twenty-two boats got away and a total of 976 survivors could be accounted for, plus an unspecified number of high-ranking Italian officers who were taken away on the submarines.

In the dark and the ensuing chaos following the attack on the ship, as the struggle to evacuate the ship had unfolded, two of the *Laconia's* lifeboats had been overlooked. They drifted away, dependent on their own fortunes for salvation. Despite efforts to row it, one boat floated without direction for twenty-seven days before it finally made landfall on the coast of Liberia. By that time, fifty-seven of its sixty-nine occupants had died. Another boat was discovered after forty days on the open ocean, but the British trawler that came across it found only four people alive out of the fifty-two who had scrambled into it a month and a half earlier. All the dead had succumbed to injuries, exposure or starvation.

Those fortunate enough to be picked up by the three French warships on 17 September were taken to Casablanca and from there to a detention camp in the desert at Mediouna. The expectation was that, ultimately, they would end up in a prison camp in Germany for the duration. Luckily, though, liberation came within weeks following the Allied landings in North Africa. In the ensuing debriefings, not only was the heroic conduct of Werner Hartenstein revealed but some of the harrowing experiences of the sinking were also disclosed: the distressing scenes on the sinking ship, the nightmarish deaths of young children lost in the sea and the shark attacks on those who struggled for survival.

In the wake of the *U-156's* rescue attempts, Vice Admiral Dönitz issued his now infamous order to all U-boat commanders, officially known as the Triton Null signal of 17 September 1942 but better known as the Laconia Order, instructing them that in future 'no attempt of any kind must be made to rescue the crews of ships sunk'. Effectively, from that point Germany was to wage unrestricted submarine warfare. For this, Dönitz stood trial at Nuremberg charged with war crimes, with the so-called Laconia Order central to the prosecution's indictment. In his defence, Admiral Chester Nimitz, one of the United States Navy's most respected senior officers, pointed out that the US Navy's submarine force had applied the principles of unrestricted warfare from the very commencement of its engagement in the hostilities.

The *Empress of Canada*, a Canadian Pacific liner taken over for troopship duties, was a 'friendly fire' victim, lost while transporting Italian prisoners of war, in her case with the loss of 392 lives. (Arnold Kludas)

Though acquitted of the Laconia Order charge, Dönitz was found guilty of other crimes by the Nuremberg Tribunal and he was sentenced to eleven and a half years in prison.

The last words here concerning the *Laconia* go to two of the survivors, one of whom said, alluding to the American bomber's intervention: 'Truth *is* stranger than fiction, when you think that four U-boats and three enemy warships searched for survivors while our own allies bombed us.' Another reflected on the deeds of Werner Hartenstein. After hearing that he had been killed later in the war with his entire crew, like many others she was saddened by that news. She declared: 'He was a good man. He was doing his job when he torpedoed our ship but by rescuing us he showed great courage and humanity.'

RIGEL (8/1924)

Det Bergenske D/S, Oslo, Norway

Just over two years after the loss of the *Laconia*, another attack on a ship carrying prisoners, this time a vessel under the German flag, resulted in a death toll that surpassed that of the *Titanic* by a considerable margin. This was the sinking of the formerly Norwegian-owned *Rigel*, which had been seized by the occupying German forces after Norway was invaded in August 1940.

The *Rigel* was an unusual-looking vessel of moderate size – a motor ship lacking a traditional funnel like other pioneering vessels of this type which had been introduced in the early years of the twentieth century by the Danish concern, the East Asiatic Company. Requisitioned on 16 August 1940, the *Rigel* was assigned to *Wehrmacht* troop-carrying duties, first with her original Norwegian crew running the ship and still flying the Norwegian flag, but from 2 November 1944 under a German crew. Even then she carried a Norwegian pilot, Edvin Nicolay Dagsvik Mørch, and one female crew member was also Norwegian.

Though frequently exposed to the war hazards of air attack or collision with mines, as far as is known the *Rigel* experienced neither and so had an uneventful war. Until, that is, the closing months of the penultimate year of hostilities. It was earlier that year, on 14 January 1944, that the Red Army launched its northern offensive: lifting the siege of Leningrad before making a thrust north through Finland, across the Kola Peninsula. Breaking into the Lapland region of Finnmark in northern Norway, it opened up a new front aimed at disrupting German forces in the country and, eventually, dislodging them altogether.

On 7 October, the Soviet 14th Army, comprising Russian, Ukrainian and Belarussian troops, backed up by Serbian infantry and covered by a heavy naval barrage from the Soviet Northern Fleet, attacked the German positions on the Rybachy peninsula. A simultaneous amphibious landing to the west by the Soviet Naval Brigade was designed to outflank and encircle enemy forces. Aware of the danger, the Germans fell back into Norway. Implementing a scorched earth policy as they withdrew, hotly pursued by the Soviets, they left the town of Kirkenes a blackened shell, all but destroyed in a bid to create a fire-break beyond which they could establish new defensive lines. The battles continued as slow progress was made driving

The Norwegian cargo ship *Rigel*. (Björn Pedersen)

The *Rigel* seen under German control, embarking *Wehrmacht* troops at an unknown Norwegian port. (Erling Skjold)

the Germans south and, by 24 October, the Red Army had liberated a sizeable part of Norway's Finnmark province. Nevertheless, the Soviet advance was held up and the area of West Finnmark and North Troms became an inhospitable no-man's-land between the opposing armies, in which thousands of displaced civilians were forced to hide in caves and other makeshift shelters for safety in the harshest of weather.

The offensive cost the Red Army more than 20,000 in casualties and over the course of the fighting, which ebbed and flowed, despite their overall reverses, the Germans captured around another 100,000 Soviet and Serbian soldiers who were moved into prison camps on Norwegian soil behind the front line. There were camps at Hordaland, Florø, Levanger, Trøndelag and many other places, in all of which the conditions were appalling, offering little hope of survival for their inmates as the Norwegian winter set in. That was unless their compatriots could reach and free them in time.

Just as the British had feared that Italian prisoners in Egypt could have been reunited with their German allies, so too the Germans in Norway were concerned that captive Soviets should not be liberated to resume the fight against them. Therefore, it was decided to transport as many as possible to more secure holding camps further south and back in Germany and the *Rigel*, along with other ships, was pressed into the work of transporting the prisoners along the Norwegian coast to the area around Bergen.

In November 1944, prior to departure on the 26th of the month, the *Rigel* was berthed at Bodø where she embarked a large number of prisoners who had been moved there by sea and rail from other small ports in Nordland, where other German prison camps were located. There were 2,248 prisoners of war in total, mostly

Russian but also many Yugoslavs and, according to Norwegian records, a number of Czechs and Poles. Held in the ship's holds, they were guarded by 455 German soldiers who also had custodial responsibility for a further 103 prisoners aboard the *Rigel*. These latter were ninety-five German deserters from the Finland front and eight Norwegians who had been apprehended by the occupying authorities, most likely because they were resistance fighters. The final component of the *Rigel's* vast complement was the crew of thirty-one sailors with their German master. For such a small vessel of just 3,828 gross tons, it was a quite staggering number of human beings, 2,838 in all, to accommodate in such a limited space.

The *Rigel* sailed as part of a small convoy designated 410, bound initially for Trondheim. With her was the collier *Pregel*, formerly the Norwegian-flag *Korsnes*, and the naval escorts *V-6308* and *NT-04*. The freighter *Spree*, due to join the southbound convoy, lay at anchor in the Vefsnfjord, off Alsten island, some 15 miles west of Mosjøen.

Out in the Atlantic, to the west, a British naval patrol force was deployed as part of Operation Provident, its task to carry out air attacks against coastal convoys off Norway. The primary unit of the force was the aircraft carrier HMS *Implacable*, supported by two escort carriers, HMS *Premier* and *Pursue*, the light cruiser HMS *Dido* and six destroyers, HMS *Myngs*, *Scourge*, *Zephyr* and *Scorpion*, and HMCS *Sioux* and *Algonquin*. When convoy 410 was spotted on 27 November near Tjøtta in Helgeland, south-east of Alsten, sixteen of the *Implacable's* Fairey Barracudas attacked.

The *Rigel* received five direct bomb hits and she was also strafed by cannon fire, setting her alight. The naval escorts returned fire but were swiftly put out of action.

The burning prisoner transport *Rigel* and collier *Pregel* photographed from one of the attacking warplanes from the aircraft carrier HMS *Implacable*. (Erling Skjold)

The aircraft carrier HMS *Implacable*, seen post-war. (Crown Copyright)

The *Pregel* was torpedoed and, ablaze from end to end, she burnt out and sank near Førvik, whilst the *Spree* was sunk while still at anchor. The stricken *Rigel* was sinking fast, stern first. Her crew worked desperately to launch lifeboats but there was no time. They were forced to abandon their efforts and jump into the sea to save themselves. The *Rigel's* captain managed to beach her on the east side of Rosøya, south-west of Sandesjøen, although her stern end sank, part of it submerged to a depth of 35m.

Locals from Rosøya rushed to the scene to assist in the rescue efforts but they were largely in vain, for all but 267 of those aboard the *Rigel* had either been killed in the attack or had drowned. Only one of the Norwegian prisoners survived, Asbjørn Schultz.

The loss of the *Rigel* remains the worst ever maritime disaster in Norwegian waters. Whether or not such a tragedy could have been prevented had Germany, a signatory of the Geneva Convention, treated its prisoners differently – in particular those who were shipped in small, unmarked transports that were completely unsuited to the purpose – is open to debate. Yet in the final analysis, although the Italian prisoners aboard the *Laconia* were accommodated in considerably better conditions, there is little to distinguish these disasters from one another insofar as there had been a fundamental failure by both Germany and Great Britain to protect prisoners in their custody from acts of violence.

The *Rigel's* bow remained visible for many years after the war. In 1969, the remains of her casualties were finally removed from the wreck and laid to rest in the war cemetery at Tjøtta: a total of 1,011 graves, along with more than 7,500 other plots of fallen Russian prisoners of war. Six years later, the remnants of the *Rigel's* wreck were removed by the Høvding Skipsopphugging company.

As a lasting testimony to the *Rigel* tragedy, there is a memorial in the Minnehallen in the small town of Stavern, south of Larvik, which commemorates six of the Norwegian prisoners who were killed. Recognised among the tributes are two very junior seamen, mess boy Martinius Haugland and deck boy Morten Reidolf Larsen.

5

THE PRICE OF CAPITULATION

By mid-1943, Italy's position, both militarily and as a member of the Axis, had become untenable. The balance was finally tipped with the invasion of Sicily that July, followed, after the island had been secured, by landings on Italy proper. Benito Mussolini, deposed by General Pietro Badoglio and other formerly acquiescent government associates, was obliged to resign by King Victor Emanuel III and was then imprisoned. Although, on 12 September, he was abducted by German paratroopers and went on to form a puppet fascist government in the north of the country, the new administration led by Badoglio had already, four days earlier, agreed an armistice with the Allies. A month later, on 11 October, Italy declared war on Germany.

Despite this dramatic change of alignment, Italy had effectively surrendered. The ramifications of these momentous developments were to compromise the Italian troops who remained dispersed among those of their former ally in Albania, mainland Greece and the islands of the western Aegean and the Dodecanese.

The German attitude towards the capitulated Italians was certainly not one of regard for their erstwhile compatriots, nor did they see them as defeated neutrals or, immediately, as potential opponents who had switched allegiance. Instead, they were collectively viewed as traitors who deserved nothing better than death.

Strategically, Germany moved faster than the Allies to fill the vacuum created by Italy's collapse, recognising that the seizure by Britain of any of the outposts in Italian hands would seriously weaken its own overall position. Having suspected that Italy may seek such an accommodation, they had reinforced their presence in all these areas well before the armistice had been agreed. In the interim, before they declared war on Germany, the Italians found themselves in a dilemma, their relationship with both Germany and the Allies being ambiguous. Troops on the ground were ordered not to attack the Germans, provided the Germans did not attack them, but there was no specific instruction for them to retaliate should such circumstances arise. At the same time, Italian forces were also ordered not to 'make common cause' with either partisans or, should they assault any of their garrisons, with the Allies.

To complicate matters further, after taking over from Mussolini, Badoglio had consented, despite the armistice terms, to the unification of the Italian and German armies under German command. Intended as an act of appeasement, it had the effect of permitting the Germans to treat as a mutineer any Italian soldier who disobeyed their orders. Three days after the armistice had been implemented, a counter-order instructed Italian forces to regard their German opposite numbers as hostile and to resist to the fullest extent, with their weapons if necessary, any attempt made to disarm them.

The very same day, 11 September, the Germans issued an ultimatum to all Italian commanding officers in the field. It offered them three options:

1. To continue fighting on the German side
2. To fight against the Germans (and take the consequences)
3. To hand over their arms peacefully

They had until 15 September to reach their decision.

Attempts to negotiate a way out of the impasse stalled and the Germans determined to resolve the issue by force. The Italians were not comfortable with any of the choices that confronted them. Their orders were treated as having come from the king himself via Badoglio, and so to continue fighting alongside the Germans would have amounted to violation of his authority, but the Italians had no desire, either, to confront those with whom earlier they had shared common cause. As for surrendering their weapons, this too was unacceptable, as it would have violated both the spirit and intention of the armistice terms. The possibility of escape as a means of avoiding any of these unpalatable options had, in most cases, at least for those Italians on island bases, been denied them because all ships, both naval and mercantile, were ordered to make immediately for Brindisi where they were to be transferred to Allied control. The only ships unable to fulfil this command were those that the Germans had already seized.

In the event, the standoff between the German and Italian military was resolved in different ways in different places. The Germans launched Operation Achse to disarm the Italian army and takeover the territories they occupied. On Cephalonia and Rhodes, the Italian garrisons were attacked by ground and air forces, and forced to surrender. On Crete and elsewhere, they were compelled to relinquish their arms after offering little resistance. The result achieved was much the same with huge numbers of Italian soldiers taken into German custody, for example 40,000 in Rhodes, 21,700 in Crete and 12,000 in Cephalonia. All now hated, they were a huge drain on German manpower and resources, as well as a distraction at a time when the British had to be resisted.

On the directions of Adolf Hitler, they were to be transported back to the Reich for employment as forced labour in munitions factories and other industries. The conditions in which the captives were to be transported were considered irrelevant, despite the fact that Germany was a signatory of the Third Geneva Convention. The Fuhrer's instruction to local commanders was that they should disregard safety precautions, notwithstanding any losses of prisoners' lives that may occur. But the neglect went further, for the Italians were crowded in the filthiest and most unsanitary conditions; crammed into the dark and damp holds of antiquated, often unseaworthy freighters, the Italian prisoners must have felt the cold wind of fate blowing on them.

New forms of designation were contrived for the Italian prisoners as a means of legitimising Germany's disinclination to recognise, or apply, the rights granted to them under international law. To get round the provisions of the Geneva Convention, they were initially categorised as 'Italian Military Internees' (*Militär-Italienische Internieten*). Later, from the autumn of 1944, while engaged as forced labourers in Germany, they were redesignated as 'civilian workers' to remove the protection they were entitled to receive from the Red Cross.

The term 'hell-ship' is normally associated with the Japanese wartime practice of transporting Allied prisoners of war around the Pacific in the most unbelievable squalor and degradation aboard what, in most cases, could only be described as old rust buckets. This grim episode of Italian prisoner transportation demonstrates, however, that the Germans were equally and unquestionably guilty of the same actions.

Numerous ships were mustered to convey the Italian prisoners via mainland Greece back to Germany. According to the Italian article '*La Nave della Vergogna*' ('Ships of Shame'), at least nine of the ships were sunk en route with heavy loss of life. Of them, four suffered casualties on an extraordinary scale, in each case more severe than the death toll of the liner *Titanic*.

DONIZETTI (12/1928)

Tirrenia, Società Anonima di Navigazione, Naples, Italy

Constructed as one of Tirrenia Line's Musician class, the *Donizetti* served on trans-Mediterranean routes prior to the Second World War. On 16 October 1940, she was requisitioned by the Italian navy and employed as a troop carrier in the Aegean Sea. She was in Greece when the armistice between Italy and the Allies was declared on 8 September 1943. Seized by the *Kriegsmarine* (German navy), she was then manned with a German crew.

When she arrived at Rhodes on 19 September 1943, she was carrying a cargo of guns and ammunition, along with troop reinforcements to bolster the German garrison there under the command of Major General Ulrich Kleemann. The 40,000 Italian forces on the island had already been suppressed, attacked on 9 September and defeated within two days. Kleemann was now under instructions to evacuate these unwanted men from Rhodes as swiftly as possible.

The *Donizetti* was a passenger-cargo ship with little accommodation. Although she had earlier transported troops, they had been in modest numbers and, realistically, her holds had sufficient space for only 700 people. Nevertheless, on the morning of 22 September, under the co-ordination of Lieutenant Colonel Arcangioli, she embarked a large number of prisoners whose count is believed to have amounted to 1,835. They comprised 600 air force personnel, 1,100 naval ratings, fourteen petty officers and eleven commissioned officers. The number would have been greater, as high as 2,090, but Arcangioli, in challenging the German authority and acting on his own initiative, ordered the cessation of boarding when the number of prisoners

The Tirennia Line passenger-cargo ship *Donizetti*. (Mario Cicogna)

reached 1,600. He was fearful of the dangers that his countrymen could face ahead, as well as the intolerable nature of the conditions on the *Donizetti* for even a relatively short voyage.

Arcangioli's orders were immediately countermanded by the German officers present, but even they finally relented and called a halt to the embarkation before it met its quota. For the 256 men who were left behind to join the next transport, it was a fortunate escape. There was no embarkation list so those aboard the *Donizetti* were, for all practical purposes, anonymous.

That evening, when boarding was complete, the *Donizetti* sailed in company with the escort *TA10*, the former French coastal destroyer *La Pomone*, under the command of Oberleutnant Jobst Hahndorff. Bound for Piraeus, the two ships took a south-westerly course, staying close to the east coast of Rhodes, passing Lindos. By 01.10 hours on 23 September, they had reached Cape Prasso at the southernmost tip of Rhodes.

While they had been making their slow progress, the ships had unknowingly been heading into danger, for ahead of them were four Allied destroyers on patrol. They were the British ships HMS *Eclipse* under Commander Edward Mack and HMS *Fury*, which were patrolling the Scarpanto and Rhodes sea-lanes while, further north, engaged in similar duties sweeping the sea area between Stampalia and Amorgos, were HMS *Faulknor* in company with the Free Greek destroyer *Vassilissa Olga*.

A clandestine wireless station on Rhodes, still in the hands of the Italians, had apparently radioed details of the departing convoy to Allied command at Leros, which the British had briefly occupied from 15 September, requesting them to intercept the *Donizetti*. This information was relayed to Colonel Turnbull, head of the Armistice

The British destroyer HMS *Eclipse*, whose guns sank the prisoner ship *Donizetti*. (Maritime Photo Library)

Commission based on the island of Symi. Recognising the need to liberate the Italian prisoners, Turnbull's intentions were to order the seizure of the *Donizetti* and its redirection to Cyprus, but moves to save the ship were overtaken by events at sea.

Once the *Donizetti* and *TA10* had been picked up on radar, the *Eclipse*, the nearest warship, closed in, focusing attention on the larger of the two unidentified ships. When the target distance was within her range, the *Eclipse* opened concentrated fire on the *Donizetti* with extreme precision. Within minutes, the transport had gone, sunk without trace. There were no survivors from the prisoners, their German guards or the ship's crew.

The *TA10* was also pounded by gunfire but her commanding officer managed to run her aground on the Prasonisi Rocks, where some of her crew were able to get ashore to shelter in a ruined Italian coastal battery until rescue arrived. Partially submerged, with only her funnel, bridge and upper works visible, the stranded *TA10* was finished off on 25 September 1943 by Beaufighter bombers from 227 Squadron, Lakatamia, to prevent the Germans from salvaging her.

The *Eclipse*, along with the other Allied warships, left the area completely unaware, until some time later, of the grave consequences of her devastating bombardment.

SINFRA ex-*Sandhamn* ex-*Fernglen* (7/1929)

Compagnie Générale de Navigation à Vapeur (Cyprien Fabre Line), Marseille, France

On 20 October 1943, just under a month after the *Donizetti* was sunk, the French cargo ship *Sinfra*, formerly the Norwegian-flag *Fernglen*, was at Souda, Crete, embarking Italian prisoners. As the *Fernglen* she had been owned by Fearnley & Eger until sold by that company in 1934 to Sven Salén Rederi of Sweden and renamed *Sandhamn*. The Cyprien Fabre Line had then acquired her in 1939. Confiscated by the Germans, she had been operating latterly under the management of Mittelmeer Reederei GmbH with German officers and crew.

Crete had been captured in May 1941 and occupied by a mixed Axis force, with part of the island under German control and the easternmost prefecture of Lasithi under the jurisdiction of the 21,700-strong 51st Siena Infantry Division. In the wake of the armistice, these Italian troops were disarmed with little resistance and, for those who had elected not to continue fighting alongside the Germans in the newly formed Legione Italiana Volontaria Creta, evacuation to mainland Greece commenced.

Throughout the day on 20 October 1943, the *Sinfra*'s holds were steadily filled with an incredible number of prisoners, some 2,460 in total, joined by 204 German personnel, guards and crew. It was not as hot at that time of year as it might otherwise have been, but for the prisoners crammed within the hold's steel walls it was unbearably uncomfortable.

The *Fernglen* of Norwegian owners Fearnley & Eger became the ill-fated *Sinfra*, sunk by Allied aircraft in October 1943. (Björn Pedersen)

Shortly after the *Sinfra* set sail on its short voyage to Piraeus, when only 115 miles to the north, she was sighted off Souda Bay by a formation of Allied aircraft, US Army Air Force Mitchell B-25 bombers and RAF Bristol Type 156 Beaufighters. The aircraft immediately attacked and made short work of sinking the hopelessly exposed transport. Disastrously, the attack cost 2,098 lives, the majority of them Italian prisoners. The 566 people who were rescued from the *Sinfra* were a mixture of prisoners, guards and crew.

PETRELLA ex-*Capo Pino* ex-*Aveyron* ex-*Pasteur* (7/1923)

Compagnia Genovese di Navigazione a Vapore SA, Genoa, Italy

The general cargo ship *Petrella* had started life as the French-owned *Pasteur*, one of nine ships commissioned by the French government as part of a programme to restore the French merchant fleet following the heavy losses of the First World War. She passed successively to the Compagnie des Chargeurs Français, the Compagnie Navale de l'Oceanie, for service to New Caledonia, and then to Compagnie Générale Transatlantique (French Line) in 1928. Renamed *Aveyron*, she operated first on the West Indies service from Bordeaux and later from Nantes and Bordeaux to Algiers and Tunis in the North African colonies.

On 10 July 1941, the Vichy French government agreed to the sale of the *Aveyron* to the Compagnia Genovese di Navigazione a Vapore SA and she was renamed *Capo*

The French cargo ship *Aveyron* was sold by the Vichy French government to the Italians in July 1941. She was first renamed *Capo Pino* and later *Petrella*. (French Lines Archives)

Pino. Two years later, after the Italian capitulation, she was seized by the Germans at Patras and returned to service as the *Petrella* under the management of Mittelmeer Reederei GmbH.

The *Petrella* was allocated the task of transporting Italian prisoners from Crete to the Greek mainland, continuing with this work through the winter of 1943 into early 1944. Her final voyage began on 8 February, after having 3,173 prisoners crammed into every available space within her ageing hull. It is hard to imagine that such a small ship of only 4,785 gross tons could hold so many occupants, especially as 1,500 Germans also boarded her. Worse still, she was also carrying a cargo of guns, ammunition barrels and other war material, including 60,000 lengths of piping. In effect, her vast human complement was sailing on a bomb!

Lying in wait for the *Petrella* off Souda Bay was the British submarine HMS *Sportsman*, which put at least one torpedo into her. On 16 February 1944, Lloyd's List reported extracts from the Admiralty Mediterranean War Diary in which it stated, under 'Admiralty Enemy Losses 5632 – Report No.61', that in position 35.35N, 24.90E at 08.32 hours GMT on 8 February 1944, a British submarine had torpedoed an enemy cargo vessel believed to be the *Capo Pino* (at that time the ship's German name was not known). It went on to state that just under two hours later, at 10.15 hours, the ship sank after a huge explosion.

The ship had clearly not sunk immediately and it had taken the explosion to finish her off. After the torpedo hit the *Petrella*, the German guards kept the prisoners locked up below and shot at those who tried to break free. The majority were still behind bars when the ship's cargo detonated.

The submarine HMS *Sportsman* was responsible for sinking the prisoner transport *Petrella*. (Maritime Photo Library)

Information received later revealed that few of the many Italians survived the explosion, the most optimistic figure being 475. Also, as fate seemed to mete out justice for the cruel action of deliberately preventing evacuation of the sinking ship, only around 500 of the Germans were to be saved after it blew up.

With anything up to 3,700 casualties, more when the crew members who were killed are added to the count, it was the worst maritime disaster up to that time to occur in the Mediterranean. Just three days later, an even worse tragedy would eclipse it.

ORIA ex-*Norda IV* ex-*Sainte Julienne* ex-*Oria* (11/1920)

Fearnley & Eger, Oslo, Norway

One of the twenty-six Norwegian vessels that were interned in North and West Africa between 1940 and 1942 was the cargo ship *Oria*. She had sailed from Bordeaux to Casablanca in convoy on 10 June 1940, just prior to the fall of France. From Casablanca, the *Oria* proceeded to Port Lyautey (now Kenitra), Morocco, 25 miles north-east of Rabat. While in Port Lyautey, she was interned by the Vichy French regime, some accounts say on 22 June, others that it was on 11 September that year.

It must be presumed that the *Oria* remained under arrest in port for a year while the Prize Court deliberated, for she was not formally appropriated by the French authorities until 24 June 1941. Renamed *Sainte Julienne*, she was placed under

Another Fearnley & Eger ship lost during the Second World War was the *Oria*. Her loss remains the worst maritime disaster ever to have occurred in the Mediterranean. (Björn Pedersen)

the management of Société Nationale d'Affrètements. Under her new name she returned to Casablanca where, on 24 July 1941, she joined a convoy bound for Oran, Algeria, where she arrived unscathed three days later.

The next news of the ex-*Oria* dates from 22 or 24 November 1942. She had transferred at some time in the interim to German ownership as the *Norda IV*, yet another ship managed by the Mittelmeer Reederei GmbH concern based at Hamburg. On 25 November, still as the *Norda IV*, she left Marseille bound for Italy but within days she was again given her original name *Oria*, though she remained under German management with German officers and a Greek crew.

It seems that the *Oria* may have been unsuccessfully attacked west of Stampalia on 31 January 1944. Early that morning, the Dutch submarine *Dolfijn* fired three torpedoes at a ship that was thought to be the *Oria*, but they missed their target.

The *Oria* was only to survive for another thirteen days, though. At Rhodes on 11 February 1944, she embarked 4,046 Italian prisoners along with thirty guards and sixty other German soldiers. It is believed that the prisoners comprised forty-three officers, 118 petty or non-commissioned officers and 3,885 lower-ranked soldiers. It should be noted that other figures are given for the number of prisoners that boarded the *Oria* that day, with figures as different as 4,033, 4,062, 4,073 and 4,115 being quoted. The problem with trying to establish the exact number is that, as with all the other freighters engaged by the Germans for prisoner transportation, no effort was made to carry out a proper count or to list the prisoners by name. Besides, with such a large number affected and the differences being so small, it is really academic whether any of the figures quoted are or are not that precise.

The *Oria* left Rhodes at 17.40 hours that evening bound for Piraeus. The following day, she ran into a ferocious storm and became stranded on the Gaidaroneos Reefs at Cape Sounion, when barely 30 miles from her destination. Completely overwhelmed by the weather and at the mercy of the waves, the *Oria* was pounded to a wreck and few of her occupants were able to escape for there were no other ships in the vicinity to offer assistance or to perform a rescue.

When tugs finally arrived on the scene the following day, they were able to save only twenty-eight people: twenty-one prisoners, six Germans and a single Greek crewman. It was, and it remains, the worst loss of life to occur in the Mediterranean in the sinking of a single ship, with 4,100–4,200 deaths.

⋅→══◎═══⋅←

The disasters that befell the *Donizetti*, *Sinfra*, *Petrella* and *Oria* had collectively accounted for a huge number of casualties, among them 10,500 Italian soldiers, but it was part of a greater calamity inflicted upon the capitulating Italian forces. Of the 1,006,370 Italian troops who were disarmed by the Germans in September 1943, some 650,000 were interned in labour camps in the Reich, up to 50,000 of whom perished. Thousands more were massacred by their former allies, the most infamous case being the execution of the 4,500 men of the 33rd Acqui Division following their surrender on Cephalonia.

6

SLAUGHTER ON THE HELL-SHIPS

Following its pre-emptive strike on the United States naval base at Pearl Harbor, which caused the eruption of the Pacific War, the Japanese initially enjoyed major successes, taking swathes of territory in South East Asia and out into the Pacific Ocean. Its empire was rapidly extended west as far as Burma; and south to Malaya, Singapore, the Dutch East Indies (now Indonesia) and the Pacific islands. A vast expanse of ocean was occupied from Kitka in the Aleutians to the north, to Wake Island in the central Pacific, to the Marshall, Gilbert and Solomon archipelagos in the south-west and as far south as parts of New Guinea, barely 100 miles from Australia. Called the Greater East Asia Co-Prosperity Sphere (implying that the peoples of these overrun territories welcomed the invader, and would even share in the benefits of this colonial expansion as a positive experience), it reached its extreme limit in August 1942. Thereafter, first on the defensive and then on the retreat, the Japanese dug in in their bid to secure and retain gains by repelling the anticipated and inevitable Allied counter-offensive.

The wiser heads in the Japanese high command knew that Japan could not possibly compete with the industrial might of the United States and would soon be overtaken by their enemy's massive productive capability, whether it was in respect of tanks or ships or aircraft. As it was, the naval war of the Pacific came to be dominated by aerial combat and it soon became apparent that the most valuable assets held by either side were aircraft carriers and their planes, for over a long period they exercised the greatest influence on the course of the hostilities.

Although Japan briefly had more carriers than its opponents, the situation rapidly reversed both through combat losses, such as at the Battle of Midway, and because America's vast building effort just could not be matched. The declining number of fleet carriers at their disposal made it essential for the Japanese to construct airstrips on the occupied islands to turn them, in effect, into static 'flat-tops', work that required a great deal of manpower. Furthermore, Japan's widespread commitment of forces in the field, for the control and retention of the possessions it had taken in the early stages of the conflict, had denuded its domestic industries of essential manpower, particularly its shipyards and aircraft factories. The labour force needed both to keep these manufacturing industries producing essential war output, as well as to construct airstrips overseas, could not be drawn in sufficient numbers from within the Japanese population.

Japan had ratified the 1929 Geneva Convention, but had declined to sign it. Thus, it was not bound by the convention's provisions in respect of treatment of military prisoners, which essentially prohibited the transportation of prisoners of war between different lands, their employment on war-related work or exposure to any threat that risked loss of life. Nor was Japan disposed morally to respect prisoners' human rights because, in Japanese eyes, they were cowards for having surrendered. As captives, prisoners were regarded as a convenient labour resource and deserved nothing better than to be worked to death, filling the manpower gap created by Japanese workers enlisted into the military.

It was much the same for the native people under Japan's domination who, other than being freed from their previous colonial masters, were brutalised as slaves. In fact, under the rules of the Hague and Geneva Conventions, even though they were not always applied or enforced, the military enjoyed better protection than did civilians. The rights of civilians in occupied territories were ambiguous at best and non-existent at worst. In passing, those inadequacies were later to lead to the Universal Declaration of Human Rights in December 1948. Outlawing all crimes against humanity, it came too late for the subjugated populations in the Second World War, many of them natives, for whom there had been scant regard for their welfare by their former colonial masters.

To exploit the convenient human resource Japan had gained, though, necessitated moving them to the places where they were required, either in the Japanese homeland or on any of the myriad of small islands scattered across the south-west Pacific. With limited ships available to the Japanese for these purposes and motivated by oppressive capacity directives that emanated from central Transport Command in Ujina, Hiroshima, the infamous 'hell-ship' transport programme was unleashed.

It has been suggested that the term hell-ship could as reasonably be attributed to the Germans when they conveyed Italian prisoners in appalling conditions to the Greek mainland, but the extent of the Japanese use of hell-ship transports, as well as the degree of unimaginable squalor on board and the barbarous treatment of the occupants, was on an altogether different scale.

On the outbreak of war in the Pacific, Japan had only a relatively small number of ocean-going passenger ships that could be called upon to perform transportation duties. Though modern, they were generally small in comparison with the liners registered under other flags, with none bigger than 20,000 gross tons and only two of greater size then under construction. To make matters worse, the Japanese military commandeered a significant number of these ships for conversion into aircraft carriers. Indeed, structural features had been incorporated into their designs under the so-called 'shadow' programme both to permit and to expedite such modification. Those vessels that were not so converted were adapted for employment in other strategically important roles, commissioned as full Imperial Japanese Navy warships.

This strategy left little tonnage available for the transportation of either troops *or* prisoners, causing logistical difficulties for the Japanese throughout the ensuing conflict. Prisoners of war, civilian captives and native peoples were, in the pecking order, the lowest of the low and for them, generally, the most decrepit craft were assigned for their conveyance. In fact, the ships employed in hell-ship voyages were a mixed bag for, besides ageing freighters, they included some former liners taken from the French and occasionally even modern naval vessels. Ironically, having committed much of its passenger fleet for conversion into aircraft carriers, at least two, the *Chuyo*, ex-*Nitta Maru* and *Unyo*, ex-*Yawata Maru*, were respectively diverted to carry prisoners of war in November–December 1943.

For the most part, though, the ships engaged for the hell-ship voyages were run down and neglected cargo ships, many of them nearing the end of their useful lives. Not only were they invariably in a poor state of repair, but they were both unfit and unsuited for the carriage of people of any description; they had no proper accommodation spaces, no sanitation facilities and inadequate means of food preparation other than for a very small crew. Nevertheless, the intention was for them to take thousands of men cramped together in filthy, dark, damp and vermin-infested holds on long sea voyages in the tropics. Inevitably, many died en route in such conditions, overcome by tropical diseases or acute malnourishment while, for all, there must have been a sense of overwhelming despair at their chances of survival. Having determined that these men should provide a labour force to keep Japanese industries running, or to build strategically vital airstrips and railways across the empire, one wonders at the mentality that saw little value in keeping them fit and healthy so they would be able to work on arrival at their destination.

Another dimension of the hell-ship traffic should be elaborated on here, for it demonstrates that the crude means of conveyance of prisoners and the treatment meted out on them was not the result of local ignorance, but part of an orchestrated policy dictated by central command in Japan. This helps to explain why, in the context of these major disasters at sea, so many people were on these ships in the first place. The fact was that the hell-ship transports were methodically organised and controlled by the Japanese Shipping Transport GHQ based at Ujina in Hiroshima Bay. This body was the conduit for official signals and orders that had originated from the Transportation & Communications Division (T&CD), Imperial General Staff, Tokyo. It was from there that directives on space allocation were transmitted to the officers manning the ships that would perform the task.

The space per prisoner as originally set out in the Army Transport Service Regulations was 1 *tsubo*, or 9 gross tons (9m³), for three men. On 8 September 1942, T&CD issued its infamous *Unsenden 557* directive, which revised the space allocation, stipulating that, in future, 1 *tsubo* was to be adequate provision for nine men instead of three. This implied that a 9,000 gross ton ship could accommodate as many as 9,000 prisoners but, in practice, the restricted space in cargo ship holds made it unattainable. The solution was provided in a later regulation known as the Chomansai Policy, forwarded to Japanese officers and introduced in 1943. This called for the construction of suspended multi-tiered wooden, mezzanine-type decks in the spaces between all existing decks. By limiting the available headroom for each prisoner to barely 12in, the number of prisoners per *tsubo* could be substantially increased. Essentially, the imposition of these practices compelled prisoners to remain prostrate throughout long, slow voyages, apart from any period when guards allowed them out onto the open deck for exercise and fresh air. The rest of the time they were confined to the holds, restricted in their movements and obliged to perform all bodily functions where they lay among their fellow compatriots, regardless of the health consequences.

Although prisoner numbers on some of the ships increased to a level that is difficult to comprehend, fortunately, the loading excesses which the Imperial General Staff were encouraging were never reached.

Besides the hellish conditions on the ships, prisoners confronted another hazard – the possibility that their ship might be torpedoed by a friendly submarine. None of these vessels carried any markings whatsoever to communicate the true nature of their function or their 'cargo'.

The first hell-ship sailing took place as early as 10 January 1942, when the *Argentina Maru* sailed from Guam to Japan with 800 prisoners of war. At first, before the Allies had gained the initiative, these vessels sailed with impunity, crawling their way across the South and East China Seas at speeds that rarely exceeded 10 knots. They seldom encountered hostile forces until Admiral Chester Nimitz launched an intensive and unrestricted submarine warfare offensive from June 1942. Within two years, it had crippled the Japanese merchant marine with 1,100 ships sunk, representing up to 4.8 million gross registered tons, or 56 per cent of the total strength.

The first serious loss of a hell-ship, only the second of many that were to be sunk, was that of the *Montevideo Maru* on 1 July 1942, torpedoed west of Luzon by the USS *Sturgeon*, at the cost of 1,053 Allied lives. There was worse, far worse, to come. At least seven Japanese hell-ships were lost with casualties of more than 1,000, but of those there were four whose victims each numbered in excess of the lives lost when the *Titanic* sank.

TANGO MARU ex-*Toendjoek* ex-*Rendsburg* (2/1926)

Hamburg Amerika Line, Hamburg, Germany

RYUSEI MARU ex-*Mabuhay II* ex-*Havo* ex-*Bra-Kar* (3/1911)

M. Matsumoto, Japan

The *Tango Maru*, a cargo ship operated by Nippon Yusen Kaisha, had started her life as the Hamburg Amerika Line's *Rendsburg*. She had been seized by the Dutch at Tanjong Priok in October 1940 and renamed *Toendjoek*. In March 1942, after the outbreak of the Pacific War, she was scuttled to block the harbour entrance at Tanjong Priok, creating only a temporary obstacle because, that August, she was salvaged by the Japanese and, following repairs, re-entered service under the flag of the rising sun as an auxiliary transport.

On 24 February 1944, the *Tango Maru* was in Surabaya where she embarked around 3,500 Javanese labourers (*rōmusha*) and several hundred Allied prisoners of war as a forced labour contingent. They were to be taken to the Moluccan islands of Ambon and Haruku to work on the construction of airstrips, supplementing the existing work-force, whose numbers had been alarmingly reduced by high death and sickness rates.

The convoy that the *Tango Maru* was to join included another freighter, the *Ryusei Maru*, originally the *Bra-Kar* of the Fred Olsen Co., which was transporting over 6,600 people, including 1,244 Japanese soldiers belonging to various army units, 2,865 Indian troops and 2,559 Indonesian coolies. The *Ryusei Maru* was the smaller of the two ships, yet her complement was far greater and the troops were packed into even less space than that allocated to the Javanese natives and prisoners of war. The

The Nippon Yusen Kaisha-managed steamer *Tango Maru* was not the first hell-ship to be sunk, but hers was the first such loss to suffer a worse death toll than the *Titanic*. She was originally the Hamburg Amerika Line's *Rendsburg*, as seen here. (World Ship Society)

The *Ryusei Maru* first entered service as the Norwegian-flag *Bra-Kar*. (Knut Klippenberg, Fred Olsen)

conditions aboard the *Tango Maru* were bad enough but it takes little imagination to appreciate that matters were far worse in the confined spaces of the *Ryusei Maru's* holds. Indeed, it is difficult to conceive how so many men could have been loaded onto such a small ship and still be expected to survive.

When the convoy departed at around 15.20 hours it took an easterly course along the southern coast of Madura to enter the Java Sea north of Bali. Thereafter, it would cross the Flores Sea and Banda Sea, a 1,000-mile voyage that would take eight to nine days to complete. Escorting the transports were two minesweepers, numbers *W-8* and *W-11*, and an auxiliary sub-chaser *No. 5 Takunan Maru*.

Already vectored into the area via the Lombok Strait, due to intelligence obtained from Ultra decryptions, were two American submarines, the USS *Raton* commanded by Lieutenant Commander James W. Davis and the USS *Rasher* under the command of Lieutenant Commander Willard R. Laughon. Their orders were to carry out a sweep in the vicinity of the Raas Strait north of Bali, as a Japanese convoy was expected in that sea area some time during the evening of 25 February.

The submarines made radar and visual contact at around 17.30 hours, but it was after sunset before there was an opportunity to get into a satisfactory attack position. By then, the convoy was approximately 160 miles east of Surabaya, 50 miles due north of Bali, with only two escorts remaining to protect the transports, the third having detached earlier. The *Rasher* moved ahead of the convoy and, taking advantage of the diminishing light and rough seas, prepared to launch a surface attack. Conveniently, one of the escorts moved from its position parallel to the transports sides, exposing the *Tango Maru's* port beam. Exploiting to the full the escort's error, four torpedoes were fired from the *Rasher* at 19.43 hours, three of which hit the target with such devastating effect that five minutes later the *Tango Maru* was gone. From under the water, more explosions were heard as her boilers detonated.

The submarine USS *Rasher* sank three ships, each of whose casualties exceeded those of the *Titanic*: the *Tango Maru*, *Ryusei Maru* and *Teia Maru*. (United States Navy)

Caught between searching for the attacker and making a run for it, the Japanese convoy broke up in disarray, leaving the highly vulnerable *Ryusei Maru* at the mercy of her underwater foe. Briefly hidden from view by reduced visibility as rain squalls swept over the sea, she lasted an hour and a half longer. Just as the escorts were returning to screen either side of the remaining transport, the *Rasher*, now reloaded, fired four more torpedoes. It was 21.27 hours. Seconds later, the *Ryusei Maru* was hit three times in a textbook-perfect spread along the length of her hull. Six minutes after the explosions, she too had sunk beneath the water.

The attack accounted for a huge loss of human life, in excess of 3,000 native labourers, prisoners of war and crew from the *Tango Maru*, and 4,998 soldiers, *rōmusha* and crew from the *Ryusei Maru*. When, four months later, the USS *Rasher* dispatched the troop transport *Teia Maru* with the loss of 2,665 of her occupants, she acquired the dubious distinction of having caused the greatest ever number of casualties in three torpedo sinkings. Only the Russian submarine *S-13* exceeded this total, in her case from sinking just two ships.

KOSHU MARU ex-*Teishu Maru* (11/1937)

Chosen Yusen Kaisha, Jinsen, Japan

While the hell-ships making their way north to Japan were also falling foul of Allied submarines, the worst sinking incidents continued to occur in the sea area of the Dutch East Indies. Native labourers and prisoners of war were continuously being shipped from Java and Sumatra to the Celebes and other smaller islands across the Java Sea. In all cases, they were destined for working parties to continue construction of new airstrips or to carry out repairs on those that were already completed. For those lucky enough to make it there and back unscathed, it was tough, punishing work while subjected to the hardest and cruellest treatment.

In late July 1944, the airfield at Macassar on the Celebes was in need of restoration and 1,513 Javanese natives were embarked upon the small army transport *Koshu Maru* at Batavia (Jakarta). Besides the native workforce, another 540 passengers also boarded the ship. At the same time, supplies and materials for the airbase were loaded in the little remaining hold space left after her large passenger complement had been accommodated.

Along with another transport, the *Shinai Maru*, and the escort vessels *Keinan Maru*, an auxiliary minesweeper, and *Hayabusa Maru*, a net layer, the *Koshu Maru* set sail from Batavia on 29 July. The saying goes that the speed of a convoy is the speed of the slowest ship and that certainly was the case on this occasion, for the maximum speed was little more than 7 knots, exacerbating the dangers faced by the five-ship convoy.

After travelling around 650 miles without incident, on 2 August the convoy arrived at Kotabaru, a port on Laut, a small island off the south-eastern tip of Borneo. The next day, the convoy resumed its voyage. The *Hayabusa Maru* was left behind, replaced by the torpedo boat *Kisasagi*, a far more appropriate escort vessel (although her presence did little to prevent what was to follow). As the convoy was crossing the Macassar Strait, 90 miles south-west of Cape Mandhar, in the early hours of 4 August, it was spotted by the submarine USS *Ray*, commanded by Lieutenant Commander William T. Kinsella, which was patrolling the area. Taking aim on the *Koshu Maru*, four torpedoes were fired. Three of them slammed into the cargo ship, one amidships in the vicinity of the engine room, the others striking the holds in the vessel's forepart. The *Koshu Maru* instantaneously broke in two, her structure unable to withstand the force of the massive explosions, and she sank within minutes. Many of her occupants were killed by the missile blasts; as many or more went down with the ship. The loss of life amounted to 1,540, of whom 1,239 were Javanese, along with 273 of the passengers and 28 members of the ship's crew and gunners.

JUNYO MARU ex-*Sureway* ex-*Hartmore* ex-*Hartland Point* ex-*Ardgorm* (12/1913)

Baha Shoji Kaisha, Japan

By far the majority of Allied submarines operating in the Pacific, the China Sea and the waters of the Philippines and Dutch East Indies were American, but it was to be a British submarine, HMS *Tradewind*, that was responsible for the costliest sinking of a Japanese hell-ship. This terrible incident, which accounted for the loss of 5,620 innocent lives, occurred on 18 September 1944. The ship concerned was the *Junyo Maru*, an ageing freighter that had been built in Scotland thirty-three years earlier as the *Ardgorm* and had seen service under three other names before the ship was finally sold to Japanese owners in 1926. A survivor of the loss of the *Junyo Maru* later said of this dreadful incident, echoing the sentiments of this book: 'Four times as much death as the *Titanic* but a thousand times less well known.'

By the time the *Junyo Maru* arrived at Batavia in the autumn of 1944, she was in a seriously run-down and dilapidated state. Everywhere aboard her there was rust and the evidence of neglect and overdue maintenance. Her holds contained residues of cargoes carried on previous voyages – coal, cement and sugar – with few signs of cleaning.

By March 1943, the Japanese military headquarters at Bukiltinggi, Sumatra, which relied on access to the rest of the empire through the port of Padang, was becoming increasingly isolated because of Allied submarine activity in the Indian Ocean. To provide it with access to the Malacca (Melaka) Strait on the island's opposite coast, the Japanese authorities initiated the construction of a 220km railway line linking Muare (Muara), Sumatera Barat (a terminus on the existing West Sumatra line) to Pakan Baroe (Pekanbaru) on the Siak River. Tens of thousands of Javanese forced labourers were drafted into gangs to construct the line along with, from 1944 onwards, in excess of 5,000 Allied prisoners of war and Western internees. The task confronting them was difficult in the extreme as the line passed through swamps and jungle. The conditions of the work camps in which the men were held offered meagre shelter and there was inadequate sustenance, while medical care was non-

The cargo ship *Ardgair*, seen here, was the sister ship of the *Ardgorm*, which later became the *Junyo Maru*. Both ships were built at Port Glasgow by the Robert Duncan shipyard. (Glasgow University Archives)

existent. The construction of the line was achieved at the cost of an estimated 70,000 lives. The *Junyo Maru*, commanded by Captain Uranosuke Yoshihara, was to feature in the transportation of men conscripted into this grim environment.

After discharging at Tanjong Priok, Batavia, the *Junyo Maru* embarked a huge number of prisoners and natives overnight on 15/16 September 1944. In total, it is estimated that from 6,526 to 6,607 people boarded the *Junyo Maru*, the majority of them 4,320 Javanese so-called 'contract labourers'. The other occupants were 506 Ambonese and Menadonese native prisoners, and 1,781 Allied prisoners of war and internees, mainly Dutch but also British, American and Australian. The latter had been held in the former barracks of the Dutch 10th Infantry Battalion (KNIL) in Batavia. Apart from captured soldiers, they included civilians, crew members from Dutch merchant ships and members of the disbanded *Staadswacht*, the former city guards. Many of these prisoners had been induced to join the railway work party with promises of pay, better food and living conditions but the reality that awaited them was to be treated as slaves. Marched to the station at Senen, they were then taken by train to the docks at Tanjong Priok. Amazingly, there were only 100 Japanese to guard so many prisoners.

Aboard the ship, there was inadequate room in the holds for so many people – even allowing for the construction of wooden intermediate decks that provided only the most restricted space. With insufficient headroom to sit, the men were forced to lie down. Those fortunate enough to board the ship last remained on the open deck but, despite being in the open air, they blistered in the intense heat while their comrades suffered in the unbearably oppressive conditions below. Despite their selection as 'healthy' for the purposes of the work party, many of the men were suffering from

Artist's impression of the hell-ship *Junyo Maru* by the Japanese artist Kihachiro Ueda. The few photographs that show the *Junyo Maru* are of extremely poor quality. (Kihachiro Ueda)

HMS *Tradewind*, the Royal Navy submarine that sank the *Junyo Maru*. (Royal Navy Submarine Museum)

dysentery and malaria. No water was provided for either drinking or washing and, before the ship had gone far, there were deaths from exhaustion, the victims' bodies crudely cast into the sea without ceremony.

Accompanied by two escorts, described by survivors as corvettes but in fact sub-chaser *No. 8* and minesweeper *W-9*, the *Junyo Maru* sailed on Saturday, 16 September at 15.00 hours. By the morning of 17 September she was in the Souda Strait heading for the Indian Ocean. Her speed was only 8 knots, permitting the faster escorts to constantly circle around the overloaded transport. In the afternoon, the weather deteriorated as temperatures fell drastically and the men were obliged to huddle together for warmth, especially those on the *Junyo Maru*'s outer decks. Throughout the day the west coast of Sumatra remained in sight.

On Monday 18 September, the day dawned with extremely high temperatures and humidity as the weather changed completely. That afternoon, just before 16.00 hours, the ship was shaken by two violent explosions as torpedoes slammed into her starboard side amidships. They had been fired by the British submarine HMS *Tradewind*.

Hours before, aboard the *Tradewind*, whose high-power periscope was not functioning and whose radar was defective, smoke had been sighted on the horizon by Lieutenant P.C. Daley RNVR, using her low-power periscope. Since April 1944, the *Tradewind* had been attached to the 4th Submarine Flotilla of the Eastern Fleet, based at Trincomalee. Under the command of Lieutenant Commander (later Captain) Stephen L.C. Maydon, she had left Trincomalee on 8 September with orders to interrupt the flow of supplies, fuel and provisions reaching the occupied Dutch East Indies. Because some of her equipment was unreliable, the *Tradewind* was moved as close to the target as possible on the surface before submerging at a distance of around 3,000m, despite picking up the escorts' asdic echoes. The target was zig-zagging, so Maydon manoeuvred his vessel into an attacking position. The *Junyo Maru* was barely 5 miles from the shore, due west of Mukomuko, midway between Bengkulu and Padang. At a range of around 1,750m, four torpedoes were fired, timed at 15.51 hours, each separated by a fifteen-second interval. Just under two minutes later, two explosions were heard.

Debris flew through the air as the *Junyo Maru* immediately began to sink. The Japanese master called for order, announcing that the ship's engines had failed, but the Japanese crew and guards made to abandon ship without waiting for his command, leaving the prisoners to the mercy of the sea. Men clambered over each other as they scrambled to get out of the holds. In the absence of life-saving facilities, many jumped into the sea but most remained aboard the sinking ship – the Javanese, for the most part unable to swim and paralysed with fear, clung to the ship's rails. As the *Junyo Maru*'s stern rose up before she took the final plunge, hundreds of them held on until their strength failed before dropping, one by one, into the sea and on top of each other inflicting serious injuries. In the water, men called out for help, among them some of the Japanese crying 'Toclong Nippon'.

After twenty minutes, the *Junyo Maru* disappeared into the ocean with a thunderous roar. Bengkulu on Sumatra's west coast was by then between 6–8 miles (10–12km) distant, beyond even the strongest swimmers. Half an hour after the *Junyo Maru* sank, the escorts, which had attempted to depth charge the escaping *Tradewind*, returned to the scene to pick up survivors but effort was concentrated on Japanese personnel and the crew. Most of the captives were left to drown.

Just as there are doubts about the precise number of people who boarded the *Junyo Maru*, so too there is speculation about how many survived. Some reports claim there were 723, others nearer to 880. What is not disputed, though, is that an estimated 5,620 died; over 4,000 of the Javanese native workers and around 1,520 of the other prisoners, the majority of Dutch nationality.

In his interrogation in May 1947, Yoshiaki Matsushita, who had been the *Junyo Maru*'s chief officer, offered the Japanese version of the events. Insisting that it was the only time that the *Junyo Maru* had carried prisoners and that they had been treated well and provided with adequate life-saving gear, he offered his recollection of the ship's complement as well as the number of the victims. According to him, there had been 3,871 natives, 2,200 prisoners of war, sixty Korean and Japanese guards, and a crew of eighty-one aboard the *Junyo Maru*: a total of 6,212 people. Three rescue sorties had been undertaken after the torpedo attack, on 18, 19 and 20 September, in the course of which a total of 1,569 survivors were recovered. Consequently, the death toll by his reckoning had been 4,643 (1,448 POWs and 3,182 Indonesian natives, plus 9 of the crew and 4 guards), a view not supported in the testimonies of Allied survivors. The All Japan Seamen's Union, in contrast, believes the casualty figure was 5,649.

By 4 October the *Tradewind* was back in Ceylon, neither her master or crew having even the remotest inkling of either who or what had been in the holds of the ship they had sunk or what the consequences of their attack had been. In fact, it was not until twenty-four years later that Captain Maydon discovered the truth about the ship he had despatched on 18 September 1944.

As for the relatively few survivors, they were destined to continue to Padang and to graft on the construction of the railway track, as had been intended. Only ninety-six of them remained alive when the line was finally completed on 15 August 1945 – ironically, the very day that Japan surrendered.

ARISAN MARU (6/1944)

Mitsui Sempaku Kaisha, Tokyo, Japan

If the *Junyo Maru* was the worst sea disaster for the Dutch, then the *Arisan Maru* loss was the worst to affect American citizens.

The *Arisan Maru* was a modern, standard design cargo ship completed in 1944, one of some 130 vessels of the type. She remained under the control of her civilian owners, Mitsui Sempaku. On 11 October 1944, while berthed at Manila, she embarked 1,782 American and other Allied prisoners of war from camps across Luzon, along with 50–100 Allied civilians of various nationalities, all confined in the cargo holds. It was said that 600 were destined for the Kwantung Army in Manchuria but for what purpose is not known. The cargo holds, where three tiers of wooden platforms just 3ft apart had been constructed, were cramped to put it mildly. There was no cargo – quite literally the ship had no room left!

The *Arisan Maru* sailed after dark with a destroyer escort but, though destined ultimately for Japan, she first sailed south to Pelawan where she anchored off the coast for ten days to avoid American air attacks. For those trapped in her holds it was ten days of living hell. As there had been on the *Junyo Maru*, there were countless men suffering from dysentery and malaria but no medicine of any description was dispensed. Finally, on 20 October 1944, she returned to Manila where she joined the Takao-bound MATA-30 convoy.

Convoy MATA-30 comprised four transports, an oil tanker and six freighters, plus the research vessel *Ryofu Maru*, escorted by three destroyers, the *Harukaze*, *Kuretake* and *Take*. There was also the *Kurasaki*, a fleet supply ship and the 'kaibokan' or ocean escort *SC-20*. The seventeen-ship convoy set sail on 23 October 1944 but it

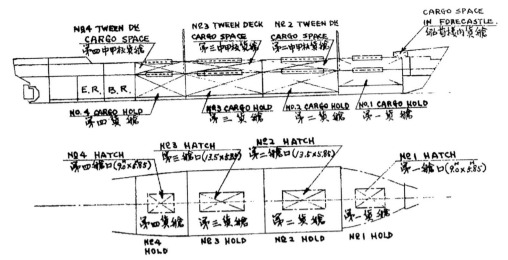

Elevation and plan of the Japanese Class 2A standard ship design, of which the *Arisan Maru* was an example. The hold space, intended for general cargo, became the accommodation spaces for thousands of American prisoners of war. (Author's collection)

headed directly into a submarine-infested area in the Bashi Strait, around 200 miles north-west of Cape Bojeador, Luzon. Two packs of American submarines, a total of nine boats in all, had been alerted to the convoy's approach and at 06.00 hours on 24 October, the Japanese destroyers began to intercept radio signals transmitted from the waiting enemy subs.

After some deliberation, the naval escort decided that the best move was to break up the mixed convoy and release the faster-moving ships to permit them to attempt to make for Takao alone. The *Arisan Maru*, barely capable of 10 knots, was not one of them. While the other ships scattered, even though many still met their end from torpedoes fired by the swarming submarines (all but two of the cargo ships, the tanker *Kikisui Maru* and the three other transports), the slow-moving *Arisan Maru* was left to her fate.

At about 05.30 hours that day, torpedoes from the USS *Shark* (Commander Edward N. Blakely) slammed into the starboard side of the *Arisan Maru*, striking her amidships and at the stern. The vessel broke in two, both sections remaining afloat for a short time, but it was to no avail for the prisoners struggling to escape the ship, only nine of whom survived.

The Japanese guards cut the rope ladders into the forward hold and closed the hatches on another, trapping the prisoners inside. Escape became possible only when the guards' preoccupation turned to their own survival. Some of the prisoners managed to reach the deck where they set about reattaching the ladders and lowering them into the holds so that others could get out, but for most it was already too late.

The ship disintegrated so rapidly – suggesting a critically weakened structure – that many were still trapped below when the *Arisan Maru's* severed parts sank. For those who had made it topside the situation was little better, for the limited quantity of life-saving equipment, including the few lifeboats, had already been taken by the Japanese. Some prisoners attempted to swim to the destroyers, by then standing by, but those who made it were beaten off by poles wielded by the naval crew and left to drown.

The Japanese Prisoners of War Information Bureau, formed in 1941 as part of the Japanese Army Ministry (subsumed into the PoW Research Network in March 2002), which assumed the task of compiling details of the prisoners lost aboard hell-ships, listed 1,778 casualties from the 1,782 it claims boarded the *Arisan Maru*, but this does not seem to take into account non-military passengers. It is known that a few Allied survivors were picked up by the cargo ship *Haro Maru* (aka *Hokusen Maru*) and taken to Taiwan, while five more survived in the sea until rescued by a Chinese junk, eventually, with the help of partisans, making it to an American airbase. They had found of all things an empty and abandoned lifeboat and survived aboard this until discovered drifting on the open sea. Nevertheless, the majority of the *Arisan Maru's* prisoners did not make it. Already emaciated and weakened by starvation and illness, they lacked the strength to keep alive and either drowned or succumbed to exposure or thirst.

The number who actually died when the *Arisan Maru* was sunk, not including any crew or Japanese military who were lost, was probably more of the order of 1,820. Of these, the vast majority were Americans and the *Arisan Maru* disaster remains the greatest cause of lost life at sea of American citizens ever.

Depth-charged by the *Harukaze* and *Take*, the USS *Shark* was also lost with her entire crew, none of them ever aware that the victims of their torpedo attack had been for the most part their fellow countrymen.

⋯⊱═◉═⊰⋯

Like so many other hell-ship sinkings, the *Arisan Maru* was an example of a major loss of life by friendly fire. Given that this was one of the most extreme and well-documented instances of the use of Ultra intelligence (from the British Ultra-secret system) for the interception and decryption of Japanese naval signals, as a means of aiding the submarine offensive, it begs the question: why was nothing done to avoid attacking those ships known to be carrying prisoners? While the intelligence relating to ship types and numbers and what was aboard them was fairly accurately known, it does not seem to have been relayed to submarine commanders whose orders were to attack convoys, not specific ships.

In his book *Death on the Hellships*, Gregory Michno is unequivocal in his comments:

> A number of these ships were sunk with full knowledge that there were Allied captives aboard. We not only killed our own, we often knew we were doing it.

It appears certain that the Allies knew which convoys were carrying prisoners.

Concerning the intercepted radio intelligence relating to Japanese shipping movements, Michno amplifies the scope of what was known beyond the ships' identities, having ascertained much more from the wartime decrypts that have now been made public (between 1978–88 in the USA, and 1999–2004 in the UK). He has been able to reveal that they encompass a great deal more information: 'The number of prisoners, their points of embarkation and debarkation [sic], the dates of arrival (and departure) and the methods of communication and transportation.' Having made such criticisms, Gregory Michno also argues, as a balance to the observations above, that these incidents occurred during wartime, in the thick of a particularly intensive and aggressive conflict:

> The Pacific War was a struggle between completely incompatible antagonists. It was a war without mercy. If any innocent parties got in the way they would have to suffer. It is harsh, and indubitably heartless, especially when looked at through a fifty year cushion of time. War is hell, and hell is relative. The fatal Ultras were sent. Axis and Allied died together.

As a final comment on friendly fire, the question has to be asked: why did submarine commanders themselves, given they had a choice of targets between an old, slow rust-bucket of a cargo ship and a modern heavily armed naval escort, choose to fire their torpedoes at the former, especially given the potential risks to Allied personnel of sinking unmarked freighters? Few of the hell-ship sinkings gave any real advantage to the Allied war effort that could justify such slaughter and Allied submarine commanders must surely have deserved both the right to know what, potentially, they were attacking and to decline from making such an attack if in doubt. Would it not have been better to use their 'fish' against those modern and heavily armed Japanese escorts, which were continuing their hostile engagement of Allied forces? In the final analysis, given that there may or may not have been irrefutable evidence as to whether or not a particular enemy ship was a prisoner transport, the deciding factor should surely have been the value to the war effort: the sinking of an ageing and militarily worthless cargo ship with limited capacity for war materials, against the cost of thousands of innocent lives.

7

THEY WERE EXPENDABLE

As already stated, the Japanese had sacrificed a potentially valuable troop transportation fleet by committing the majority of its best ships suitable for these duties for conversion for other auxiliary duties and, in particular, into aircraft carriers. Thus, they was increasingly obliged to turn to small, slow cargo ships to carry army units to the many outposts of the empire that required defending following their invasion and seizure in the early stages of the conflict. The ships designated for these voyages were completely unsuitable for the task, necessitating the accommodation of soldiers in adapted holds that lacked natural light and ventilation, and had little in the way of sanitary facilities. In many respects and, in many cases, they were little better than the hell-ships employed for the conveyance of prisoners of war. Indeed, in defence of its hell-ship practices, the Japanese authorities declared after the war's end that it had treated prisoners no better and no worse than it had treated its own military personnel; its soldiers had received no preferential treatment, as if to say that brutality to its own justified brutality to others.

Like the hell-ships, these highly vulnerable, slow-speed army transports were exposed to the same risks: attack from any of the many US submarines, which controlled the sea areas of the war zone from the summer of 1942 onwards, and which could attack with diminishing risk; and, later in the Pacific War, by the Allied warplanes, which dominated the skies as the military offensive closed in on Japan proper. The fact that Japan also lacked adequate numbers of escort vessels and, furthermore, was unwise in its allocation of the limited resources it had, served to contribute to the predicament of its army transports, increasing their exposure to danger.

A commentator on Japanese wartime naval policy, Enoki Koichi, speaking with regard to the strategic value, or lack of it, afforded to Japan's transport ships, has summarised the policy as follows:

In the southern front, Japan sent troops on cargo ships to defend occupied positions, 1,000 or more soldiers in a cargo ship of only 3,000 gross tons capacity as underdeck stowage. But a lot of soldiers were lost under the sea because the ships were sunk by US submarines. The Imperial Japanese Navy could not defend Japanese merchant ships transferring resources as well as ships ferrying army soldiers, besides also providing a screen for the capital warships. The IJN had not concerns to defend merchant ships anyway. The Grand Fleet thought a merchant convoy was a good bait to draw the United States Navy into naval engagements. The IJN fleet commanders did not sense that freighters had much higher value than battleships.

Central to Japan's war strategy was the possession and retention of a ring of Pacific Islands as a defensive line to keep the Americans at a safe distance from the Philippines, South East Asia and the Dutch East Indies – its most vital acquisitions. The plan was to transform the western Pacific into a Japanese-dominated lake behind a chain of heavily fortified bases established along a line of islands, from Wake Island down to the Marshalls and Gilbert Islands, through to the Solomons and the Bismarck Archipelago. Such a strategy depended upon having a high degree of mobility in the deployment of its forces, and a comprehensive transportation and escort capability. The fact was, though, that in its war preparations, Japan had not made adequate provision for these requirements, quite apart from its tactical weakness in underestimating the importance to the war efforts of freighters, auxiliaries and transports. Britain, whose circumstances were in some respects similar, paid a great deal more attention to this critical dimension of the war at sea.

Arising from such blinkered and distorted thinking, exacerbated as the turning fortunes of the Pacific War necessitated repeated repositioning of its defensive perimeter and, consequently, more and more movements of troop reinforcements to bolster beleaguered island outposts, a virtual bloodbath resulted as the growing Allied submarine menace picked off defenceless transports almost at will. A huge number of Japanese army personnel lost their lives in what is collectively the greatest count of ship sinkings, each of whose individual victims exceeded those of the *Titanic*. Whatever we may think of Japan's aggressive war and the atrocities it committed during the war years, from a detached point of view, its flawed transportation practices amounted to it committing military suicide.

In an endeavour to extract more details from the records about these ships and their activities, researchers working over the years since 1945 have pieced together the logs of many transport voyages; the make-up of their complements; how they met their end; and the numbers of their survivors, the latter grimly meagre in the majority of cases. For some vessels, though, there remains only the barest of facts to recount in recording their demise as losses that rank among the world's very worst maritime disasters.

The misfortunes that befell Japanese troop transports in effect tracked a parallel course to the nation's overall reversals in the campaigns of the Pacific, as the tide of war turned against Japan. There were many serious losses, many more than are recorded here. These that follow happen to be the very worst, but all of them together amounted to a massive and, for Japan, fatal loss of military personnel. It was a loss that they could ill afford, let alone an appalling loss of life in purely human terms.

TEIYO MARU ex-*Saarland* (2/1924)

Teikoku Sempaku Kaisha, Japan

The former German-flag passenger-cargo ship *Saarland* of Hamburg Amerika Line was sold to the Japanese government in 1940 and renamed *Teiyo Maru*. On 28 February 1943, she was outside Rabaul harbour, New Britain, having sailed there two months earlier from Shanghai via Truk Atoll as part of the fourteen-ship convoy No.35 of the Number 6 Go Transportation Operation, carrying members of the Japanese 6th Infantry Division. That convoy had originally been destined for Guadalcanal but was redirected to New Guinea to bolster the defences there, after the decision had been made to completely withdraw from Guadalcanal as defeat in the Solomon Islands loomed.

At Rabaul, the *Teiyo Maru*, under Captain Ishisaka Takezo, assembled with six cargo ships to form a new amphibious convoy under Operation 81 to take troop reinforcements to the Lae and Salamaua area of New Guinea. The *Teiyo Maru* embarked 1,923 troops of the 51st Division and loaded a large quantity of equipment, including 100mm cannons, field guns, various road vehicles, landing craft, collapsible boats, rowing boats and 1,500m³ of other assorted war supplies before the convoy departed that night at 23.30 hours.

In a rare event, the convoy was escorted by a veritable armada of naval vessels, principal among them the destroyers *Shirayuki*, *Asahio*, *Arashio*, *Tokitsukaze*, *Uranami*, *Shikinami*, *Yukikaze* and *Asagumo*, a force under the command of Rear Admiral Kimura Masatomi whose flag was in the *Shirayuki*. The convoy was divided into two columns; the *Teiyo Maru* was in the starboard column along with the freighters *Shinai*, *Aiyo* and *Kenbu Marus*.

The convoy took a north-west course, along the northern coast of New Britain. Later, it turned west and then south through the Bismarck Sea as it headed for the

Hamburg Amerika Line's passenger-cargo liner *Saarland* was taken over by the Japanese in 1940 and renamed *Teiyo Maru*. (World Ship Society)

Dampier Straits, between New Britain and New Guinea. The timing was unfortunate for the convoy found itself caught up in what became known as the Battle of the Bismarck Sea, which commenced on 2 March. From 08.00 hours that morning, when north-north-west of Cape Gloucester, the ships came under aerial bombardment from American and Australian B-17 Flying Fortress bombers. The cargo ship *Kyokusei Maru* was sunk and the *Teiyo Maru* received light damage but was able to proceed.

Her luck soon ran out, though, for on the following day, as Allied aircraft intensified their low-level bombing and strafing runs, the convoy vessels, including the *Teiyo Maru*, were picked off one by one. After surviving eleven near misses she was sunk by four bombs and two torpedoes when she was around 40km east-south-east of Cape Cretin. Engulfed in flames, she disappeared at 17.30 hours on 3 March at the cost of 1,882 of her troops. Also killed were seventeen of her crew and fifteen gunners; a total of 1,914 dead.

Apart from the *Teiyo Maru*, the Japanese lost the *Oigawa*, *Aiyo*, *Shinai*, *Taimei* and *Kenbu Marus*, representing a further acute depletion of the equipment it was also attempting to land. The engagement also cost the Japanese the destroyers *Asahio*, *Arashio*, *Tokitsukaze* and *Shirayuki*.

KAMAKURA MARU ex-*Titibu Maru* ex-*Chichibu Maru* (3/1930)

Nippon Yusen Kaisha, Tokyo, Japan

Two months later, the *Kamakura Maru*, a pre-war luxury liner of Nippon Yusen Kaisha (NYK) serving the Orient–California route, fell victim to an Allied submarine with even greater loss of life. In her case, her occupants were Imperial Japanese Navy (IJN) personnel with around 1,000 oil production specialists. Her full complement of 2,500 or so passengers included 150 females, almost certainly 'comfort women', as they were known. Embarkation took place in Manila, the *Kamakura Maru* having arrived there on 26 April at the end of a ten-day voyage from Kobe, Kure and Sasebo. The ship also had a 176-strong crew. Her holds were filled with ammunition and heavy vehicles to replenish the Japanese forces in East Borneo.

At 05.20 on 27 April 1943, the *Kamakura Maru* left port, completely unescorted, bound for Balikpapan. Just before midnight the same day, she was sighted in the Sulu Sea, south-west of Naco Point on the Philippine Island of Panay by the USS *Gudgeon* commanded by Lieutenant Commander William S. Post. The submarine pursued the transport, which was zig-zagging on a southerly course, making 18 knots. At 01.04 hours on 28 April, with the target some 3,200 yd distant, the *Gudgeon's* torpedoes were fired. Two struck the *Kamakura Maru's* starboard side, one in the region of her No.4 hold, the other in her auxiliary machinery department. The explosions set off fires astern as a frantic attempt to evacuate the stricken ship got underway. Unlike so many of the small freighters used as transports, the *Kamakura Maru* did have a healthy provision of lifeboats, but the effort to abandon

One of Japan's largest and most luxurious ocean liners before the outbreak of the Pacific War was Nippon Yusen Kaisha's (NYK) *Kamakura Maru*. (Nippon Yusen Kaisha)

ship was brought to an abrupt end just twelve minutes later when the ship upended to sink by the stern.

Many of the Japenese transports sunk in torpedo attacks, not all of which were ageing, neglected and obsolete cargo ships, had broken up so rapidly after they had been hit that it prompted the conclusion there must have been either a fundamental weakness in the structure of Japanese ships, or the high explosive used in American torpedoes was particularly devastating.

Half an hour after the *Kamakura Maru* had disappeared, aware that the transport had not had an escort, the *Gudgeon* surfaced to find a number of lifeboats, floating debris and many survivors in the sea. Their chances for survival depended on friendly ships reaching the scene in good time. As it was, it took until 2 May when the *Kamakura Maru* was reckoned to be overdue at her destination before a search for survivors was organised. Even then, rescue ships found 28 members of the *Kamakura Maru*'s crew and 437 of her passengers alive. Despite this, a total of 2,211 people had perished.

LIMA MARU (4/1920)

Nippon Yusen Kaisha, Tokyo, Japan

In early 1944, the MOTA-02 convoy was organised to take army units and their equipment from Moji to Takao. There were three transports, the *Rakuyo*, *Nanrei* and *Lima Marus*, and nine auxiliary supply ships. Prior to departure at 12.30 hours on 7 February, the *Lima Maru* boarded around 2,900 soldiers of the Japanese 19th Brigade. The convoy was relatively lightly escorted, given its size; present were the merchant auxiliaries *Toyo Maru No.3* and the *Kyoei Maru No.5*, the latter serving as a submarine chaser. With them were two regular naval vessels, patrol boat *No.38* and the torpedo boat *Sagi*.

By this time in the Pacific War, American submarines were patrolling close to the main Japanese islands. The convoy had not progressed far before it was inter-

cepted off the west coast of Kyushu by one of these patrols. On 8 February at about
22.45 hours, when the convoy was some 30 miles south-east of the Goto Archipelago,
the *Lima Maru* was singled out by Lieutenant Commander Charles O. Triebel aboard
the USS *Snook* and torpedoes were fired at the heavily loaded transport, two of
which struck with destructive impact.

The *Lima Maru* exploded and sank with frightening speed, and the majority of the
men accommodated in her holds were unable to escape. The number of casualties
was upwards of 2,765, meaning that fewer than 150 of the 19th Brigade survived.
The *Snook*, which six hours earlier had damaged the *Shiranesan Maru*, survived depth
charges dropped by the convoy escorts. It appears that the other convoy ships also
escaped unharmed, making for Kagoshima, Kyushu, to take refuge.

The loss of the *Lima Maru* was confirmed when the United States Navy's code-
breakers working in the Fleet Radio Unit at Melbourne, Australia, intercepted and
decoded a radio message transmitted to that effect.

Convoy MOTA-02 apparently resumed passage to Takao on 12 February 1944,
calling at Keelung en route and arriving at its destination on 21 February.

Japanese records give the position where the *Lima Maru* sank as 31.05N, 127.37E;
Lloyd's War Loss Records, compiled in October 1947, give the position as 32.18N,
129.20E.

Reflecting the worsening situation in the Pacific, in September 1943 the Imperial
Japanese Navy and Imperial Japanese Army jointly agreed that revised defensive
positions should be established and strengthened along what was described as Japan's
'absolute zone of national defence'. The zone had been moved westwards in recognition of the reverses that Japan had already suffered. Its new boundary extended
north from the Indonesian Archipelago through Western New Guinea (Irian Jaya)
and around the Philippine Islands to the Caroline and Mariana Islands, and from
there as far as the Ogasawara Islands and the Japanese homeland. Its airbases were a
vital constituent of the new protective perimeter.

Later, in February 1944, another Japanese transport was sunk with massive loss of
life, torpedoed east of Formosa by the US submarine *Trout*. The ship concerned was
the motorship *Sakito Maru*, one of Nippon Yusen Kaisha's 'S'-class cargo ships (a total
of six modern twin-screw cargo liners, which entered service from 1939).

SAKITO MARU (1 / 1939)

Nippon Yusen Kaisha, Tokyo, Japan

Japanese troops that had been serving as the garrison force at Haicheng, north of
Dalian in Liaoning province, and who were to strengthen the new defensive line, left
their training area near Liaoyang on 19 February 1944 and from there entrained for

Pusan. They comprised the 18th, 38th and 50th Regimental Combat Teams (RCT), collectively the reorganised former 29th Division of the Kwantung (Guandong) Army, which had been based in China since it mobilised in August 1937. By early 1944, Japan's military held the view that much of northern China was fundamentally secure and they felt confident that reductions of army strength there could be absorbed in order to transfer men to various Pacific islands, where the hyper-extended line of defensive positions was coming under increased strain and required reinforcement. Heavy air strikes against the Gilbert Islands heralded an imminent Allied offensive.

From Pusan the troops were ferried across the Yellow Sea to Ujina, where they boarded the *Sakito Maru*, *Aki Maru* (another NYK ship), and a third, unidentified vessel. The *Aki Maru* and the third ship carried the 38th and 50th RCT, while the *Sakito Maru* took aboard around 4,000 soldiers of the 18th RCT. She also loaded eight of the 29th Division's tanks.

The ships left Ujina on 26 February 1944, escorted by the destroyers *Asashimo* and *Okinami*, bound for Guam where they were expected to arrive on 8 March, after a call en route at Saipan. On 29 February, as the small convoy was passing approximately 625 miles east of Formosa, it came under attack from the American submarines *Rock* (Commander John J. Flachsenhar) and *Trout* (Lieutenant Commander Albert H. Clark). The escorts opened fire on the submarines with their guns and the *Rock* was damaged. Meanwhile the *Trout*, exploiting the distraction, launched torpedoes at the transports, damaging the *Aki Maru* and sinking the *Sakito Maru*. Breaking off the action against the *Rock*, the destroyers turned their attention to the *Trout*, which it is believed was sunk by depth charges from the *Asashimo*, although there was a suspicion she could have been hit by one of her own electrically propelled torpedoes.

Returning to the location where the *Sakito Maru* had been sunk, north-east of Saipan, the *Asashimo* and *Okinami* rescued all the survivors they could find from the sea, a collective total of 1,720. However, of the *Sakito Maru*'s total complement,

The modern cargo motor-ship *Sakito Maru*, one of six ships of the NYK 'S'-class. (Nippon Yusen Kaisha)

more than 2,200 had perished. The surviving infantrymen were conveyed to Saipan where, after reorganisation and re-equipment, all but 600 men of the 1st Battalion proceeded to Guam where they arrived in May 1944. There they joined the 38th RCT who had reached Guam on 4 March. Meanwhile the 50th RCT, aboard the *Aki Maru*, had been diverted to Tinian.

YOSHIDA MARU No. 1 (1 / 1919)

Yamashita Kisen Kaisha, Kobe, Japan

The TAKE-1 convoy, which sailed from Shanghai to Mindanao in the Philippines, Halmahera and Western New Guinea with urgently needed troop reinforcements, suffered four transports sunk and 4,290 soldiers killed during the course of its passage, which lasted from 17 April to 9 May 1944. Of them, the worst loss for numbers of victims was that of the *Yoshida Maru No. 1*.

Much of the vast oceanic area of the south-west Pacific was inadequately defended and the revised Japanese defensive policy called for the movement of combat units from China and Manchuria to reinforce key positions. Shipping shortages made it difficult to implement these essential troop movements, largely as a result of the Japanese navy's ill-conceived anti-submarine warfare practices, which had placed a low priority on the protection of merchant ships exposed to submarine attack.

The fact that the details of each troop convoy's composition, routes and ports of call were also being routinely transmitted with little caution as to the possibility that messages were being deciphered, added to the high attrition rate. To put these shortcomings into perspective, they cost Japan over ten per cent of the strength of its merchant navy in February 1944 alone. This was despite the fact that the military authorities had introduced changes to its convoy practices from around that time, in March 1944, primarily by assembling larger convoys, permitting the allocation of a proportionately greater number of escorts.

To protect the TAKE-1 convoy, which set out with fifteen ships, the 6th Escort Convoy Command was appointed under Rear Admiral Sadamichi Kajioka in his flagship, the minelayer *Shirataka*. The other naval units in the command were the destroyers *Asakaze*, *Shiratsuyu* and *Fujinami*, the frigate-type ocean escorts *Kurahashi*, *CD-20* and *CD-22*, the minesweeper *W-2* and auxiliary minesweeper *Tama Maru No. 7*, the sub-chasers *CH-37* and *CH-38*, and the gunboats *Uji* and *Ataka*.

The convoy's four transports, one of which was the *Yoshida Maru No. 1*, were carrying the Imperial Japanese Army's 32nd and 35th Divisions; a total of 20,000 men destined for Manila. From Manila, units were to be onward shipped to bases in the Marianas and Carolines, while others were to proceed to Western New Guinea. After the troops had embarked with their equipment, the convoy sailed from Shanghai on 17 April but even before it left port, the Allies were in possession of full details of the convoy thanks to Ultra decryptions. Continuing intercepts allowed the Allies to follow its progress and guide waiting submarines into its path.

When the convoy had reached the area north-west of Luzon on the morning of 26 April, the USS *Jack*, commanded by Lieutenant Commander Thomas Dykers, was waiting. Despite being sighted and attacked by defending aircraft, after taking temporary evasive action the *Jack* was able to restore contact with the convoy with little impediment. Attempts were made to take up an attack position after dark but the Japanese escorts were effective in keeping the *Jack* at a distance. Unable to get closer, the submarine fired nineteen of its torpedoes from long range and, despite the speculative nature of its attack, it was rewarded with a successful outcome. To compensate for his inabililty to penetrate the convoy, Dykers had concentrated his missiles on the core of ships clustered together in the centre, in the hope that at least one would find a target. As it turned out, the single torpedo victim was the transport *Yoshida Maru No.1* carrying an entire regiment, some 3,000 soldiers of the 32nd Division. Reluctant to stop to pick up survivors because of the ever-present submarine threat, not one person from the *Yoshida Maru No.1*'s entire complement was saved by the escorts.

Even as TAKE-1 was at sea, and partly influenced by the loss of the *Yoshida Maru No.1*, the Imperial General Headquarter's plans for the proposed reinforcement of the islands of the Central Pacific were abandoned. Instead, all the surviving troops, around 12,784 soldiers, were to be taken as more ships became available to Western New Guinea and the eastern Dutch East Indies, both of which were under imminent threat. When the TAKE-1 convoy sailed from Manila on 1 May, resuming its voyage south, it was bound for Manokwari to augment the Japanese garrison there at Halmahera on the Vogeltop Peninsula. However, en route on 6 May it was attacked for a second time, in the Celebes Sea by the USS *Gurnard*, losing the three remaining troop transports – the *Amatsusan*, *Taijima* and *Tenshinzan Marus* – and another 1,290 troops. As a consequence, the Japanese 32nd Division was reduced from nine to five infantry battalions, its artillery battalions down from four to one and a half. Equally, the six infantry battalions of the 35th Division were reduced to four, again with the loss of much of their artillery.

TOYAMA MARU (6/1915)

Ono Syozi Gomei Kaisha (Taiyo Kisen Kaisha), Osaka, Japan

The next major Japanese transport loss, the *Toyama Maru*, occurred on 29 June 1944. The *Toyama Maru*, an old 7,000 gross tons freighter, was requisitioned to carry units of the 44th and 45th Brigades, a total of 4,330 soldiers, as part of convoy KATA-412 bound from Moji to Keelung.

There were twelve merchant ships in the convoy, the *Toyama Maru*, the *Shokei Maru* and ten unidentified ships. Escorting them were five naval vessels, which rendezvoused with the merchant ships off the entrance of the Inland Sea between Kyushu and Shikoku. They were the minelayer *Niizaki*, the auxiliary minesweeper *Shonan Maru No.16*, the auxiliary patrol boats *Ryusei Maru* (not the ship described in Chapter 6) and *Chikuto Maru*, and the auxiliary net-layer *Shinto Maru No.2*.

The *Toyama Maru*, another small freighter sunk with heavy loss of life while employed transporting Japanese troops. The photograph, taken on 1 July 1922, shows her in the Narrows at Vancouver, British Columbia. (World Ship Society)

The convoy made a call at Kagoshima from where it sailed on 27 June, and all proceeded well until two days later. While crossing the Nansei Shoto, off Taira Jima, an island midway between Kyushu and the Ryukyus Group, the USS *Sturgeon*, under Lieutenant Commander Charlton L. Murphy Jr, on her eleventh and last war patrol, attacked the convoy. Torpedoes struck the *Toyama Maru*, the only ship of the convoy to be hit, which sank in flames taking 3,730 of her occupants with her. Just 600 soldiers were rescued.

NIKKIN MARU ex-*Hokusei Maru* ex-*Canadian* ex-*Golden West* ex-*West Ivan* (1/1920)

Nissan Kisen Kaisha, Kobe, Japan

The very next day, almost 600 miles north-west of the *Toyama Maru*'s last position, another Japanese army transport was sunk with heavy loss of life: the *Nikkin Maru*, a former American ship built at Seattle in 1920, seized by the Japanese in 1941 and placed under the management of the Nissan Kisen company.

Although unescorted, the *Nikkin Maru* was, like other Japanese merchant vessels, equipped with anti-submarine weapons, essentially depth charge launchers. She was engaged in ferrying more than 3,200 men of the 23rd Army from Korea to Japan as part of the programme of troop transfers to the Pacific front from Manchuria. The 23rd Army had been formed in June 1941 and placed under the control of the China Expeditionary Army based in Guangdong Province. Latterly, it had been deployed as a garrison force to deter expected Allied landings in China, but the need for increased military forces in the Pacific was regarded as having overriding importance.

At the time when the *Nikkin Maru* was in the Yellow Sea passing to the west of Mokpo, Korea, the American submarine USS *Tang* under the command of

Lieutenant Commander Richard H. O'Kane, was patrolling the sea lanes between Dairen (Dalian) and Kyushu in the full knowledge that troop transports were regularly making the crossing to Japan.

When the unescorted *Nikkin Maru* was sighted, the *Tang* attempted a surface attack on the cargo ship with two torpedoes, both of which missed. The submarine crash-dived to avoid depth charges but when she resurfaced she gave chase to the doomed merchantman, closing to within 750yds. A single torpedo was then launched, which struck the *Nikkin Maru* amidships and blew her in half.

There was no time to evacuate the ship and the majority of the troops on the *Nikkin Maru* – the official figure is 3,219 – perished. It has not been possible to ascertain whether there were any survivors. The USS *Tang* sank two more Japanese vessels, the cargo ship *Taiun Maru No.2* and the oil tanker *Takatori Maru No.1*, in the same vicinity the following day, but it is not known whether they were engaged in the rescue of men from the *Nikkin Maru*.

YOSHINO MARU ex-*Kleist* (3/1907)

Nippon Yusen Kaisha, Tokyo, Japan

The convoy MI-11, which sailed from Takao, Formosa for Miri, Borneo on 29 July 1944, comprised seventeen merchant ships, a mixture of eight cargo vessels, five oil tankers and four troop transports, one of which was the *Yoshino Maru*, formerly the German-flag *Kleist* of Norddeutscher Lloyd, which NYK had acquired in the 1920s. Despite Imperial General Headquarters' intention to provide more escorts, there were only six naval ships to guard the convoy, the most powerful of them the destroyer *Shiokaze*. The others were the minesweepers *W-28* and *W-39*, the 'kaibokan' *Shimushu*, the sub-chaser *CH-55* and the auxiliary gunboat *Kazan Maru*.

Another former German ship transferred to Japan; the *Kleist*, seen here, became the *Yoshino Maru*. (World Ship Society)

The *Yoshino Maru* had earlier been employed as a naval hospital ship. In convoy MI-11 as a transport, she was carrying more than 2,400 soldiers, along with naval gunners and her crew.

By 31 July, the convoy had entered the Luzon Strait where it encountered an American submarine wolf pack consisting of the USS *Parche*, *Steelhead* and *Hammerhead*. In the early hours, the tankers *Koei Maru* and *Ogura Maru No.1* were sunk by torpedoes from the USS *Parche* commanded by Lieutenant Commander Lawson P. Ramage. An hour later, at around 03.40 hours, more torpedoes hit and sank the *Yoshino Maru* some 100 miles north-west of Cape Bojeador, Luzon, with the cost of 2,495 lives: 2,442 troops, 18 naval gunners and 35 sailors from her crew. Also lost was her cargo of ammunition. Some reports say the *Yoshino Maru* was sunk by the USS *Steelhead* commanded by Lieutenant Commander David L. Whelchel, others that it was the *Parche*, but both submarines could have been responsible in the massed attack.

The *Yoshino Maru* had barely disappeared when the rout of the convoy was completed by the *Steelhead*, which damaged the cargo ship *Dakar Maru* and sank the transport *Fuso Maru*, while the *Parche* added the cargo ship *Manko Maru* to her tally. These additional losses cost the Japanese much valuable supplies, ammunition and fuel, along with a further 1,600–1,700 human casualties.

TEIA MARU ex-*Aramis* (10/1932)

Messageries Maritimes, Marseille, France

TAMATSU MARU (1/1944)

Osaka Shosen Kaisha, Osaka, Japan

Japan's appalling summer of heavy shipping losses continued unabated, and the next convoy to be targeted by the increasingly unavoidable Allied submarine fleet was HI-71, a large concentration of transports and supply ships that constituted part of the Sho Operation plans for the defence of the Philippines. Its route would take it from Moji, bound for Mako in the Pescadores Islands and Manila, after which it was projected to continue onto Singapore. The convoy assembled off Mutsure Island on 8 August 1944 prior to moving to Imari Bay, where final embarkation and cargo stowage were completed.

Among the convoy's eleven ships were the naval oiler *Hayasui* and two mercantile tankers, a food storeship and no fewer than seven transports, including the *Awa*, *Teia*, *Tamatsu* and *Mayasan Marus*. Appointed as the convoy commander was Rear Admiral Sadamichi Kajioka who had earlier commanded the ill-fated TAKE-1 convoy, now with his flag aboard the destroyer *Fujinami*. Also screening the convoy was another destroyer, the *Yunagi*, the escort carrier *Taiyo*, which had been launched as the NYK luxury liner *Kasuga Maru*, and five ocean escorts: the *Hirato*, *Kurahashi*, *Mikura*, *Shonan* and *CD-11*.

The *Teia Maru* was the former French-owned liner *Aramis* of Messageries Maritimes, which had been commandeered at Saigon on 12 April 1942 under the Right of Angary, a prerogative of belligerents that allowed them to requisition neutral merchant vessels within their territorial jurisdiction. In practice, she was chartered to the Imperial Japanese Navy by her owners who received compensation. Like the *Kamakura Maru*, she was later assigned to mercy voyages; exchanging internees and diplomatic personnel with the British and other Commonwealth powers.

The *Tamatsu Maru* was a modern cargo motor-ship, which had only been completed seven months earlier. She had been adapted as an auxiliary landing craft depot ship. Hers was to be a spectacularly short career.

The convoy departed Moji at 05.00 hours on 10 August and arrived intact at Mako five days later. After two days in port, the voyage to Manila resumed. The *Tamatsu* and *Teia Maru*, along with the other transports, were carrying units of the Japanese 26th Division for the defence of the Philippines. The importance of the convoy, already better defended than most Japanese convoys, was demonstrated by the augmentation of its screen with additional escorts: the destroyer *Asakaze* and the ocean escorts *Sado*, *Etorofu*, *Matsuwa* and *Hiburi*.

Despite having a total of thirteen naval ships watching over it (although *Asakaze* and *Yunagi* were later detached to escort the tanker *Eiyo Maru* back to Takao), American submarines were still able to attack the convoy with apparent ease. The weather conditions were not ideal, the convoy having steamed through a typhoon, but on 18 August, when it was 150 miles west of Cape Bolinas, Luzon, the first torpedoes

The Messageries Maritimes passenger liner *Aramis* became the *Teia Maru* when taken over by the Japanese. (Cie. des Messageries Maritimes)

were launched. The USS *Rasher* of Lieutenant Commander Henry G. Munson had already, late that day, sunk the carrier *Taiyo* and the oiler *Teiyo Maru*. At around 23.00 hours, her attention was turned to the transport *Teia Maru*. Making a surface attack and using radar to set the range and bearing, three torpedoes were fired that struck the former passenger ship's starboard side with devastating effect in way of No.2 hold, amidships and aft, setting her alight. Men crowded onto her decks attempting to launch the lifeboats as escorts tried to close in to rescue survivors, but the *Teia Maru*, which was developing an increasing list, suddenly exploded some thirty minutes after the attack and rapidly sank, taking with her many of those on board.

The *Teia Maru* was the second largest merchant ship sunk by the Americans during the Second World War. There is speculation as to the exact number of people she was carrying, ranging from 5,222 to 5,478, the majority of them members of the military plus 427 civilians. The records show that 2,316 troops, 275 civilian passengers, 20 guards, gunners and lookouts, and 54 crew lost their lives: a total of 2,665. Nevertheless, the rescue of almost 3,000 others was no mean achievement in the circumstances.

For convoy HI-71, the American assault was far from over, continuing through that night into 19 August. Splitting the convoy into two groups did little to hinder the submarines, as *Rasher* claimed two more hits – among them the *Awa Maru*, which was beached near Port Currimao. Other submarines participated in the taking of spoils, among them Lieutenant Commander Gordon W. Underwood's *Spadefish*, which was on its first wartime patrol. Around 03.30 hours, two of her torpedoes were fired into the *Tamatsu Maru*. Mortally damaged, she rolled over and sank with alarming speed, taking 4,755 men with her, the ship's entire complement. She sank north-west of Luzon, barely 40 miles from the site where *Teia Maru* had gone down.

An impression of the *Tamatsu Maru*, another Japanese cargo ship that became a wartime auxiliary. Like the *Akitsu Maru* and *Mayasan Maru* she was converted for service as a landing craft depot ship, but her hold capacity was also exploited for troop transportation. (Kihachiro Ueda)

The remnants of convoy HI-71 straggled into San Fernando as the escorts tried to drive off the American submarines. From their point of view, it had been a good night's work; their onslaught having cost the Japanese five ships sunk, including a valuable escort carrier and two tankers with their vital cargo of oil, three ships damaged and more than 7,000 troop casualties, with lost crew at a total of 7,546.

AKITSU MARU (1 / 1942)

Nippon Kaiun Kaisha, Tokyo, Japan

MAYASAN MARU (12 / 1942)

Mitsui Sempaku Kaisha, Tokyo, Japan

Three months later, troop-replenishment convoy HI-81 assembled in Imari Bay, Kyushu in readiness to sail in two parts to Manila and Singapore, calling at Mako in the Pescadores en route. Escorted by the destroyers *Etorofu*, *Tsushima*, *Daito*, *Kume* and *Shonan*, the escort carrier *Shinyo*, the former German passenger liner *Scharnhorst*, the escort destroyer *Kashi* and seven 'kaibokan', there was a total of ten merchant ships, a mixture of supply ships, oilers and transports. In some cases, reflecting the depletion of the Japanese merchant marine and the reducing number of vessels available for auxiliary service, certain of these ships had twin functions, notably the *Akitsu Maru*: officially a landing craft depot ship but, fitted with a flight deck and carrying twenty Japanese army aircraft, redesignated as a flight-decked amphibious assault ship. Responsible for the convoy was Rear Admiral Sato Tsutomu of the Eighth Convoy Escort, whose flag was aboard the destroyer *Etorofu*.

Less than twenty-four hours after the convoy sailed on 14 November 1944, it was attacked by the USS *Queenfish* (commanded by Commander Charles E. Loughlin) when 60 miles west of Nakadori-Shima where it had anchored overnight. Just before midday, two of the *Queenfish*'s torpedoes hit the *Akitsu Maru* on her port side, one

A rare view of the *Akitsu Maru*, which gives the impression of a full aircraft carrier conversion. In fact, she had limited capability. With just a rudimentary hangar and no aircraft lift, it was thought she was unable to recover planes after they had taken off from her flight deck. (Author's collection)

An impression of the *Mayasan Maru*. She was taken over for auxiliary service as a landing craft depot ship prior to being torpedoed and sunk while engaged in transporting troops. (Kihachiro Ueda)

amidships, the other in her aft end. The ship immediately began to list before it exploded and sank.

The *Akitsu Maru* had embarked men of the 64th Infantry Regiment and other Japanese army units at Moji. It is not known how many of these soldiers were rescued but the records show that 2,046 of the *Akitsu Maru's* complement lost their lives. The auxiliary landing craft depot ship *Shinshu Maru* dropped depth charges in a bid to sink the *Queenfish* but her efforts were in vain. Having been requisitioned on completion as a wartime auxiliary, and as a result of her loss in convoy HI-81, the *Akitsu Maru* never entered commercial service as intended.

At this point, it seems that the HI-81 convoy turned north and, on 16 November, it anchored for a second overnight stop near Cheju (Jeju) Jima, off the Korean coast. While there, another convoy, MI-27, with its seven supply ships and five escorts, joined HI-81 and the combined convoys sailed as one when they left at 08.00 hours on 17 November bound for the Chusan (Zhoushan) Islands, Qundao, 90 miles south-east of Shanghai.

During the morning a lone B-29 reconnaissance plane spotted the convoy. Fruitless efforts were made by the *Shinyo's* Nakajima B5N 'Kate' aircraft to drive off or destroy the B-29, but as evening was setting in the attempt to repel the interloper was abandoned for the day. The convoy, however, came under renewed submarine attack, the undersea craft doubtless guided to the targets by directions relayed from the American surveillance plane.

Singled out was the *Mayasan Maru*, which was carrying a diverse assortment of passengers – a total complement of 4,387 military personnel besides her crew – plus a vast array of equipment. The majority of the troops were infantry of the Imperial Japanese Army's 23rd Division, along with men of the 23rd Division's artillery regiment. There were also infantry and engineers of the 72nd Division. The equipment included 'Maru-Ni' explosive motorboats along with personnel of the 24th Sea Raiding Battalion who would operate them, landing craft, a vast quantity of ammunition and 204 horses. Another 740 troops were destined to join the Southern Army to compensate for losses that had been sustained in New Guinea. Also embarked aboard the ship were a number of specialist engineers and technicians with expertise in water purification, weapons repair, aircraft maintenance, wire communications and wooden boat building and repair. Finally, the *Mayasan Maru* was also carrying a large number of boy or young graduate soldiers who had undergone specialist training in communications as well as in tank, heavy artillery, field artillery and anti-aircraft warfare.

At 18.15 hours, torpedoes from the USS *Picuda* of Lieutenant Commander Evan T. Shepard hit the *Mayasan Maru*, which promptly sank, so rapidly in fact that within three minutes she was gone. The casualties were inevitably heavy: a total of 3,536 crew and troops. Also lost was all of the equipment and all of the horses.

EDOGAWA MARU (5/1944)

Nippon Yusen Kaisha, Tokyo, Japan

As mentioned, in parallel with convoy HI-81, another troop convoy, MI-27, had been forming at Moji destined for Miri in Borneo. Comprising nine merchant vessels, there were four oil tankers and five freighters, at least three of the latter carrying troops but none of them with a greater number than the *Edogawa Maru*, another Class 2A standard ship, whose complement included 2,173 troops, the majority from the 19th Sea Raiding Battalion and its base unit. Another 200 of the soldiers were young graduates from military schools specialising in weapons, tank warfare, signals and artillery. The ship also carried a comprehensive cargo of munitions and military vehicles, along with 150 horses and 200 dogs.

Two of the ships, the relatively new tankers *Kyokuun Maru* and *Enkei Maru*, were detached from the convoy soon after it sailed at 16.00 hours on 15 November 1944, both suffering mechanical problems.

After detouring along the Korean coast in a bid to avoid American submarines, convoy MI-27 joined convoy HI-81. Together they entered the Yellow Sea on 17 November where, some 100 or so miles south-west of Cheju (Jeju) Island, they encountered a four-boat wolf pack, the USS *Peto*, *Picuda*, *Spadefish* and *Sunfish*, the latter commanded by Lt. Cdr. Edward E. Shelby. Around 22.00 hours, one of the *Sunfish*'s torpedoes hit the *Edogawa Maru* in the region of her No. 2 hold. The crippled ship caught fire but despite the damage she remained afloat and even though her occupants were exposed to considerable risk she was not abandoned. Meanwhile, the attention of the *Sunfish* was turned to other convoy vessels and hits were scored on the *Seisho Maru*, a former American ship, which eventually sank with the loss of 448 lives.

In the early hours of the next day, the *Sunfish* resumed her attack on the *Edogawa Maru* and after another of her torpedoes struck the hapless transport she rapidly sank. Of the huge number of men aboard her, 2,114 were killed, 1,998 of the troops and

116 members of her crew. Also lost was the ship's entire cargo and all the livestock. The remnants of convoy MI-27 and HI-81 sought shelter at Shanghai. Submarines continued to harry the combined convoy, which was making little to no progress. It may be considered that the *Akitsu*, *Mayasan* and *Edogawa Marus* were their most important 'kills', but the biggest prize was probably the aircraft carrier *Shinyo*, sunk by the USS *Spadefish* an hour before midnight the previous day.

HISAGAWA MARU (1944)

Kawasaki Kisen Kaisha, Kobe, Japan

In total, the Japanese suffered well in excess of thirty major troop transport losses at a cost of more than 50,000 servicemen, besides the dead from their mercantile crews. It can only be described as a bloodbath. How deaths on this scale were communicated to families or the Japanese nation at large, if at all, is anyone's guess. The British concern about the effect on the nation's morale if the *Lancastria* disaster had been made known publicly is already documented, but this level of mortality and frequency of loss was of an altogether greater magnitude.

As far as the accounts of those losses described in these pages are concerned, this chapter ends with the disaster that befell the *Hisagawa Maru* on 9 January 1945. The *Hisagawa Maru* was a recently completed cargo ship ordered by Kawasaki Kisen Kaisha, now better known as the 'K' Line. She was assigned to convoy MOTA-30, which sailed at 07.15 hours on 1 January 1945 from Moji bound for Takao. The *Hisagawa Maru* was carrying a large contingent of troops from the 19th Infantry Division's 3rd Transport Unit, in excess of 3,500 men. With her in convoy MOTA-30 were four oil tankers, two cargo ships and another troop transport, the *Anyo Maru*. Their escort was five 'kaibokan' ocean escorts, the CDs *26, 36, 39, 67* and *112*.

Eight days out, in Tunghsiao Bay, the convoy ran into a concentration of submarines vectored into its path. Within two hours, five of the convoy ships had been destroyed or damaged and abandoned. The following day, 9 January, the remaining ships were separated into two groups: the *Meiho Maru* and *Daiga Maru* headed for Keelung, while the *Rashin Maru* with the *Hisagawa Maru* and three escorts travelled through the Formosa Strait towards Takao.

Allied aircraft now took their turn to assault the convoy and at 09.15 hours they scored bomb hits on the *Hisagawa Maru* damaging her so severely that she fell behind. The decision was taken for the five ships to head for Mako in the Pescadores to regroup and receive repairs, but just before 13.00 hours the *Hisagawa Maru* was subjected to another aerial attack, which finished her off. She sank 25 miles south-west of Tainan, Formosa. There were 2,283 casualties among the troops, before counting any crew victims.

Eight months later, on 14 August 1945, the Second World War at last came to an end. Before that, another six ocean-going merchant ships were to fall victim to the war at sea, each suffering greater casualties than the *Titanic*. Of these disasters, five occurred in the European theatre, specifically in the Baltic Sea.

8

SUFFER LITTLE CHILDREN

TSUSHIMA MARU (1914)

Nippon Yusen Kaisha, Tokyo, Japan

On 18 September 1940, the British liner *City of Benares* was some 600 miles out into the Atlantic Ocean, bound for Montreal, having left Liverpool five days earlier. She was making a special voyage under the Children's Overseas Reception Board (CORB) programme, in which British children were evacuated overseas for the duration, in this case to Canada, to keep them safe from the Nazi threat.

The CORB initiative had been conceived as part of the greater evacuation plans designed to get children away from major British cities that were expected to become the focus of German aerial bombardment. But the CORB plans, involving the taking of children abroad to Australia, New Zealand and South Africa as well as Canada, were greeted with a mixed reaction. Understandably, for those who could afford the cost, the removal of their children to a place of safety provided a welcome relief from anxiety. However, at government level it was seen as sending an undesirable signal to the Germans; hinting of surrender and anticipated capitulation.

As it turned out, the CORB programme was to be short-lived. On that bleak winter's night, alone on the vast inhospitable expanse of the grey ocean, the *City of Benares* was attacked and sunk by the *U-48* and seventy-seven of her ninety young charges were killed: the worst loss of children's lives at sea in a single incident up to that time. Earlier, on 30 August, as a hint of the dangers, the *Volendam* with 335 children aboard had been torpedoed in the mid-Atlantic while bound for Halifax, Nova Scotia. The crippled ship remained afloat and was towed back to Liverpool. There were no casualties but it was enough to ring the alarm bells. The CORB arrangements were suspended completely, never to resume, and all other planned sailings were cancelled. No other country after that time dared risk the lives of its young citizens by exposing them to the possibility of submarine attack. That is, with the singular exception of the Japanese.

Four years after the *City of Benares* was sunk, the Ryukyu Islands, the southernmost part of the Japanese archipelago, was threatened by the Allied advance. The island-hopping campaign embarked upon by US forces up until then had been slow and costly in lost lives. As the Allies had assumed a dominant position both at sea

The *City of Benares*, an Ellerman Lines passenger-cargo ship built in 1936. When she was sunk during a CORB evacuation voyage in September 1940, it was the worst case of children's lives lost at sea prior to the sinking of the *Tsushima Maru*. (Ellerman Lines)

and in the air, the decision was made to shorten the march on Tokyo by invading Okinawa, an assault that held huge psychological implications for the Japanese, for it would be the first foreign landing on their own soil, which was bound to be met by a fanatical resistance.

The prospect of such an invasion was greeted with alarm by the civilian population of Okinawa; a dread fear intentionally magnified by the Japanese military and the civic authorities. In the former case, it may well have been thought that reprisals could be anticipated in return for the brutal behaviour towards the native populations of the vanquished Pacific and Far Eastern territories, which Japanese troops had been guilty of over the previous two years. Equally, it could have been the intention, by appealing to the inbred Japanese national ethos, to encourage all to fight to the death in defence of their sacred homeland to prevent the island from being taken.

On the contrary, the scaremongering served only to trigger a suicidal panic, particularly among the young women who feared rape and molestation, and hundreds of them threw themselves off the clifftops onto the rocks below, preferring death to submission. The Americans dropped thousands of leaflets prior to launching their assault, explaining their conciliatory intentions towards the civilian population, but their reassurances largely fell on deaf ears. In the event, it may have been that the suspicions about how the civilian population would be treated were to some extent justified for, when the invasion came, there were 100,000 non-military casualties.

The people of Okinawa had particularly acute concern for the welfare of their children, should their island be attacked and occupied by the enemy. Earlier in the conflict, when American strategic bombing had commenced, targeting Tokyo and other major Japanese cities, thousands of school-age and younger children had been evacuated to rural areas in much the same way as had happened in Britain when Operation Pied Piper had been launched in 1939. Such a choice was not available to the citizens of Okinawa, for nowhere on their relatively small island could be considered safe, besides which, their concerns had as much to do with the circumstances that would prevail if and after the island fell. Evacuation by ship to the main Japanese islands was the only option open to them. So, in the summer of 1944, eight months before the Okinawa offensive was launched, planning commenced for child-evacuation convoys to take several thousand children from Naha to Kagoshima. It is not known exactly how many of these convoys were planned and arranged, or even how many occurred.

Given that the Japanese were entitled to negotiate safe conduct clearance for selected ships in order to secure their greatest protection, specifically for their precious passenger compliment during the 300-mile passage, it is surprising to discover that no such effort was made. It certainly was not because the Japanese were unfamiliar with those practices, having already participated in a number of diplomatic exchange missions with the *Asama*, *Tatsuta*, *Kamakura* and *Teia Maru*, as well as with the chartered Italian liner *Conte Verde*, taking Allied prisoners, civilian detainees and diplomatic staff to Lourenço Marques (Maputo), Mozambique and Mormugao, Goa.

Of course, there may have been a dimension to this particular initiative that was reminiscent of the reaction to the British CORB programme. Winston Churchill himself had regarded the overseas evacuation of British children as sending a defeatist signal to the Germans, and it could have been the case that the Japanese government felt similarly. While, in this instance, such a convoy would be allowed to proceed regardless, the nature of its purpose and, hopefully, therefore, its existence would remain unknown, ensuring its security so long as an application for safe passage status was not sought from the US government.

To have left the arrangements like that, in assembling a small convoy of solely merchant ships, while it still carried risks, would have been the least hazardous course of action. However, to perhaps provide some reassurance to the anxious parents (though again this is pure speculation), a naval escort was attached to the convoy. Where a group of small and innocuous merchant vessels may have been able to slip through the tightening American net unnoticed, the presence of warships was certain to stimulate an altogether different level of interest in the convoy, which is exactly what transpired. Besides which, American submarines operating at periscope depth, attacking legitimate targets, could hardly have been expected to segregate the benign from the threatening.

In late August 1944, the *Tsushima Maru*, an old passenger-cargo liner, along with two other, more modern cargo ships, the *Gyoku Maru* and *Kazuura Maru*, assembled at the port of Naha, Okinawa to form the convoy NAMO-103, which would sail to Nagasaki and then on to Moji. The three ships had arrived at Naha on 19 August

The passenger-cargo ship *Tsushima Maru* was built for Nippon Yusen Kaisha in Scotland in 1914 at the Russell shipyard at Port Glasgow. (Nippon Yusen Kaisha)

as part of convoy No.609 from Woosung (Wusong), China, with 3,339 soldiers and 900 horses of the 62nd Infantry Division who were to reinforce Okinawa's defences. From the American point of view, had Ultra decryptions provided them with these details, they would have been rightly justified in regarding these ships as a threat that needed to be neutralised.

It is not known whether only the *Tsushima Maru* boarded passengers, but among her occupants was a large number of the children who were to be evacuated to the Japanese main islands for safety. Her total complement was 1,612: comprising 826 children, many of a tender age; 741 adult passengers, including some school teachers and parents who were accompanying the youngsters; and 45 crew members.

The accommodation for the evacuees aboard the *Tsushima Maru* was basic at best; primitive and crude at the worst. Reflecting her earlier use as a troop transport, her cargo holds had been adapted to create what were euphemistically described as 'cabin areas', or 'cabin spaces'. Survivors' accounts reveal how, after they had clambered aboard up steep stepladders at the stern and descended into the depths of the holds, they found they had been partitioned to segregate the school evacuees' quarters from those allocated to family evacuees. Whoever was fortunate enough to be billeted in the precious few first-class cabins in the main superstructure (enough for only eight passengers in peacetime) is not recorded.

In the holds, the schoolboys were instructed to sleep on the lower bunks with the girls above them on the upper levels. The depth between the levels was so small that the children constantly hit their heads on the boards directly above them and they had to learn quickly to be cautious in their movements. How grown men, the soldiers who had been conveyed previously, had managed to squeeze into such restricted spaces is beyond comprehension. Food was served to the evacuees in their sleeping quarters and it was said that they engaged in communal singing before they settled down on the night of their departure.

Escorted by the destroyer *Hasu* and the gunboat *Uji*, the NAMO-103 convoy departed Naha at 18.35 hours on 21 August 1944. The ships adopted a protective formation with the *Tsushima Maru* and *Kazuura Maru* positioned 1,000m apart at the heads of the convoy and 600m ahead of the *Gyoku Maru*, which was flanked by the *Hasu* and *Uji*. Given what the *Tsushima Maru* was carrying, it would surely have been better for her to have been placed between the two escorts. Certainly, the convoy's leading merchantmen were the most vulnerable to torpedo attack and because their existence had not been communicated via the Red Cross in Switzerland, none of the American submarines in the area was aware that the *Tsushima Maru* was carrying evacuees or, of greater significance, that over half of them were, in fact, of school age.

All went well until late on 22 August. Patrolling the sea area of the Ryukyu Islands a short distance north-west of Akuseki-Jima, Kagoshima prefecture, was the USS *Bowfin* with Commander John H. Corbus at her helm. The ships of the convoy were picked up on the *Bowfin*'s radar and she was manoeuvred into position ready to launch a night attack on the surface. At 22.12 hours, torpedoes were fired at the largest target, the *Tsushima Maru*, hitting home with devastating effect. Fatally damaged, she sank soon after with almost no opportunity to launch lifeboats or organise a proper evacuation. Many aboard her died in the bunks where they slept, while those who were able to make it from their cabins to the upper decks were cast into the sea. The naval escorts did not permit either of the other ships to stop to rescue

Responsible for sinking the *Tsushima Maru* was the American submarine USS *Bowfin*. (United States Navy)

Exterior view of the Memorial Museum to the *Tsushima Maru* disaster at Naha, Okinawa. (Tsushima Maru Memorial Museum)

An interior view of the *Tsushima Maru* shrine and exhibition centre. Besides being a focal point through which the relatives of the *Tsushima Maru*'s many child victims can channel their grief, the memorial also promotes better understanding between different nationalities and pursues a commitment to peaceful international relationships. (Tsushima Maru Memorial Museum)

survivors as the *Bowfin* continued her uninhibited attack, firing numerous additional torpedoes, for neither the *Hasu* or *Uji* made any attempt to drive her off or sink her with their depth charges.

It was only some time later, after the *Bowfin* had left the area having presumably exhausted her ammunition, that the *Hasu* and *Uji* returned to the scene, by which time few of those who had been left to the mercy of the cold sea were still alive. Between them they were able to rescue only fifty-nine children and twenty-four adults. It is believed that the *Tsushima Maru's* entire crew perished.

The attack on the *Tsushima Maru* had cost at least 1,529 lives; 767 of them, more than half the total, being those of the young evacuees.

As in other cases, those aboard the USS *Bowfin* had no idea until over twenty years later of the calamity that had unfolded in the aftermath of the torpedo attack. In contrast, for the families of victims back in Okinawa the tragedy had a deep and profound impact. It is hard to comprehend the overwhelming grief and sadness that was felt collectively at the loss of so many children. It truly left an entire community in deep mourning, an experience that perhaps only the port of Southampton could relate to, having been the home of 549 victims from the crew of the *Titanic*. It was said of that huge loss that in some streets not a single house had been spared from losing a father, son or brother.

Neither have the passing years dulled the pain felt by the people of Okinawa at the sacrifice of so many young lives. Their bereavement continues, now focused through a specially built memorial and museum in Asahigaoka Park, with its Kozukura Tower cenotaph, in Wakasa, Naha. Not only does it act as a place of reflection, but it is also a centre promoting international peace. There are also monuments to the *Tsushima Maru* on Akuseki-Jima and in Tokyo, in the grounds of the Zojoji Temple. Films have been produced and books written in Japan about the *Tsushima Maru* incident, but in the West little is known about this, one of the most appalling ever disasters at sea.

To this day, annual ceremonies of remembrance also take place over the site of the wreck, which was positively identified on 12 December 1997 in a mission carried out on the request of relatives by the Japan Agency for Marine-Earth Science & Technology Centre (JAMSTEC), using Dolphin 3K deep-sea detection equipment. Since it was located, 870m down, no attempt has been made either to recover the ship or any of the artefacts or personal belongings from within it. The wreck of the *Tsushima Maru* has been left undisturbed as it was found, a grave and shrine to the dead on the ocean floor.

9

SAFE PASSAGE GUARANTEED?
(PART TWO)

URAL MARU (3/1929)

Osaka Shosen Kaisha, Osaka, Japan

It is not known for certain whether the cargo-passenger ship *Ural Maru* was operating as a hospital ship, painted in the recognised colour scheme and thus entitled to immunity, when she was sunk on 27 September 1944, but that would appear to be the case. Certainly, between 13 October 1937 and February 1938 she had functioned in that role, after she had been requisitioned and converted by the Imperial Japanese Army for service during the second Sino-Japanese War. Later, too, after a period operating as an armed transport, she returned to hospital ship duties in February 1943, when she was definitely repainted in accordance with the international regulations: white overall with prominent red crosses on her sides and funnel.

Despite that, she had been attacked and bombed by US Army Air Force B-17 Flying Fortresses off Guadalcanal on 3 April 1943, while evacuating wounded soldiers. The incident provoked a war of words between Japan and the Allies. When the Japanese complained about this – the latest of what it claimed had been a number of attacks on its hospital ships – they were reminded that they were equally guilty of the same disregard for the immunity from hostile action of protected vessels. As already stated, the Japanese submarine *I-177* had callously sunk the Australian hospital ship *Centaur* on 14 May 1943, with the loss of 268 lives.

It is likely, given the extreme bitterness of the conflict in the Pacific Ocean, and despite such recriminations, that in fact neither side was abiding by the spirit, let alone the letter of the Geneva regulations pertaining to the conduct and treatment of hospital ships. Hence, even if the *Ural Maru* was appropriately coloured on 27 September 1944, it would have made little difference.

What can be stated, indisputably, as far as the *Ural Maru* is concerned, whatever her category, was that there were hundreds, even thousands of wounded troops aboard her when she sailed from Singapore in convoy SHIMI-10 at 13.00 hours on 5 September 1944. Moreover, additional troop casualties were taken on board during the voyage after calls were made at Kuching and Miri in Sarawak (Borneo). This is known because it was documented in a first-hand account of the voyage written by an Indian National Army Cadet, Ramesh S. Benegal, who was travelling aboard the ship with nine other cadets, representing Azad Hind (the Provisional Government of Free India), bound for Japan.

Convoy SHIMI-10 was a fairly large convoy made up of twelve merchantmen and three auxiliary escorts, all of them adapted minesweepers. All told, there were around 2,500 people aboard the *Ural Maru* in addition to her crew. Apart from the wounded Japanese soldiers, there were accompanying nurses and medical staff, and many Japanese 'comfort women' – sex workers who had been providing favours to the troops in the field and who were returning home for 'a rest'. Besides the *Ural Maru*, there were at least five supply ships and four tankers. There was also a former Dutch ship, the *Imaharu* (ex-*de Klerk*). The escorts were the auxiliary minesweepers *Choun Maru No.6*, *Choun Maru No.7* and *Toshi Maru No.2*.

At 05.30 hours on the morning of 8 September, the convoy reached Kuching where it stayed for almost two days, sailing again at midnight on 9 September. A day and a half later, just after midday, it reached Miri, Sarawak. When the convoy departed Miri at 15.00 hours on 15 September, it had been reconstituted and redesignated as MIMA-11 (also referred to as MIMA-16). The convoy had been augmented with five more mercantile oil tankers plus the fleet oiler *Kamoi*, making eighteen ships in total. The minesweeper escort had been detached and replaced by three 'kaibokan', the *CD*s *8*, *25* and *32*, and the sub-chaser *CH-28*.

Bound initially for Manila, before proceeding to Takao and on to mainland Japan, the convoy stayed close to the coast with frequent stops made at small anchorages. Aboard the ship, the ten Indian passengers had been perplexed and embarrassed to discover that they had been billeted in the same space as the sex-workers. Indeed, they were in bunks situated immediately above these ladies. What made matters worse, in the words of Ramesh S. Benegal, was that 'they behaved with a complete lack of inhibition and often shocked us'.

While at sea and during stopovers, boat drills and practice in the donning of life-jackets were carried out with relentless, almost paranoid, frequency. Indeed, at one port of call, all able-bodied people were instructed to test their cork lifejackets by jumping into the sea from the ships' sides to ensure that they learnt how to don them correctly.

At 08.07 hours on 27 September, when approximately 150 miles due west of Masinlok, Luzon, the submarine USS *Flasher*, under the command of Lieutenant Commander Reuben T. Whitaker, fired torpedoes at the *Ural Maru*, at least one of which hit the ship in the engine room, leaving a gaping hole in the ship's bottom.

Aboard the *Ural Maru*, there was pandemonium as the passengers struggled to get off the ship, which assumed an immediate and rapidly worsening list. Dense smoke, piercing sirens and blood-curdling screams testified to the gravity of the damage and that the explosion had already killed and maimed many. The ship's loudspeakers announced that the *Ural Maru* was to be evacuated, which further contributed to the panic, causing the lifeboats to be rushed; the majority of them were lowered incorrectly and under-filled. Several even upended, tipping their occupants into the sea before they disappeared beneath the waves, denying the stranded victims the means of escape.

Mitsui's *Ural Maru*, sunk en route to Japan with war injured, was also carrying ten Indian nationals of the independence-motivated Azad Hind, who were destined to be trained as aviators. (Mitsui-OSK Lines)

As the *Ural Maru*'s bow submerged and her stern rose higher until the ship was almost vertical, the steep incline of her decks made it difficult to stand up. Trying their best to keep their feet, those who were able to leap overboard swam to reach any floating object that would support them until help arrived. Luckily, rafts with rope loops, stowed on deck, had floated free. The injured and incapacitated down in the holds, especially those who had been stretchered aboard, did not stand a chance. Among those who jumped into the sea were nine of the Indian cadets. The tenth, who had unwisely returned to his cabin, was never seen again.

The *Ural Maru* turned over gracefully and slipped into the sea, no more than ten to twelve minutes after the torpedo explosion, watched aghast by those who now awaited rescue. But it was not to come – at least not soon enough for most of them. The *Flasher* had kept up her attack on the convoy, damaging the tanker *Tachibana Maru*. Two hours after the *Ural Maru* sank, another American submarine, the USS *Lapon*, torpedoed the *Hokki Maru*, which also sank after a fruitless attempt to take it in tow. During this time, the escorts gave no attention to the *Ural Maru*'s survivors but steamed off in pursuit of the submarines, which were an enduring threat to the rest of the convoy.

For three and a half hours, the survivors clung to the rafts, drifting helplessly. When a gunboat came into view, they waved and shouted frantically to get its attention but it steamed off. When, later, a second warship appeared it approached the rafts and hopes were once more raised, but loud hailers informed the survivors that they would have to wait and for a second time they were abandoned when it steamed away. Minutes passed and explosions were heard in the distance. Finally, the escorts returned and the castaways were hauled aboard.

It was only then that the full gravity of the disaster became apparent, for it was discovered that fewer than 150 had been rescued, mostly men and only a small number of women but, miraculously, all nine of the Indian cadets. Around 2,400 had died.

After transfer to an oil tanker, the survivors were landed at Mindoro in the Philippines and eventually reached Japan via Manila some time later. There the Indian cadets were trained as pilots at the Imperial Japanese Air Force Academy at Tokyo. After his return to India at the end of the war, Ramesh S. Benegal rose to the rank of air commodore of the Indian Air Force.

⋆⇒◉⇐⋆

Besides hospital ships, safe conduct protection during the Second World War was also granted to another group of ships: those deployed for the repatriation and exchange of prisoners and internees, as well as the distribution of Red Cross food parcels destined to inmates of prisoners of war camps. Designated as 'cartel ships', they did not have the same status as hospital ships, nor were they subject to the same restrictions. Each voyage undertaken was performed strictly in accordance with unique conditions, negotiated between the opposing nations under the brokerage of the protecting power, Switzerland, including strict adherence to a pre-declared course. Equally, they did not wear hospital ship colours but were painted in one of several approved schemes that were, in some respects, similar. For instance, some displayed prominent crosses on their sides and funnels but they were painted white rather than red, in some cases within a blue disc. Others had the words 'Diplomat' or 'Protected' painted on their hulls.

So vital was it to precisely adhere to the agreed exchange formalities that it led to an apparently bizarre episode that took place on one such ship, the *Arundel Castle*, during a British-German prisoner exchange on 9 September 1944. When it was discovered, after the *Arundel Castle* had sailed from Gothenburg bound for Liverpool, that a number of escaped British and Norwegian prisoners who were not part of the manifested list had managed to stowaway on board, the captain ordered them to be arrested and locked up while he had the ship turn back to port. The unfortunate POWs were handed over to the Swedish authorities to be returned to Germany for continued incarceration in whatever *stalag* they had managed to break out of. It seemed harsh but any deviation, no matter how insignificant, could have compromised the *Arundel Castle*'s protected status as well as future exchange efforts.

Given such absolute observance of the rules that governed every aspect of the highly unusual operation of these so-called 'Mercy Ships', it might be reasonably concluded that this at least was a group of ships that were guaranteed freedom from intervention or attack. But not so. One case serves to show that even these vessels were vulnerable, despite the fact that they were appropriately painted, brightly lit at night, sailing strictly to a pre-determined course and, without escorts, completely alone. This is the case of the *Awa Maru*, which came to be known as the '*Titanic* of Japan'.

AWA MARU (3/1943)

Nippon Yusen Kaisha, Tokyo, Japan

Negotiating the agreements for the exchange of captive personnel, though protracted, had generally been successful, for there was clearly something positive to be gained by either party. Such exchanges took place, for example, between Britain and Italy, Britain and Germany, the USA and Germany, and the USA and Japan, and for many they spelt the end of long periods of wearying and worrisome detention in the hands of the enemy. However, obtaining agreements for the collection and distribution of Red Cross supplies proved more difficult to achieve as it meant that one belligerent's vessels, possibly essential to their war effort, had to be removed from auxiliary service and placed at risk with little to be derived from the exercise other than an enhancement to that country's humanitarian reputation.

Arising from rumours and first-hand accounts relayed to intelligence personnel from escaped prisoners and survivors of hell-ship sinkings (see Chapter 6), the American government was especially concerned about the welfare of its citizens, both military and civilian, detained in Japanese camps. Aided by the neutral Swiss government as the intermediary, a proposal was made to offer guaranteed safe passage to nominated Japanese ships, to permit the collection and trans-shipment of Red Cross supplies for Allied prisoners of war and civilian internees held throughout the Far East. The Japanese hinted at a willingness to co-operate, provided that the consignment could be collected from Soviet territory (Japan was not then at war with the Soviet Union).

The *Awa Maru*, a wartime view taken while she was operating as a military transport. (Nippon Yusen Kaisha)

Once all the details had been settled and co-ordinated by the American Red Cross, five lend-lease freighters then building in Portland, Oregon, were hastily completed and loaded before sailing to Nakhodka, east of Vladivostok, in December 1943. There the supplies were discharged into warehouses for collection by Japanese vessels.

At this juncture, the operation stalled, undermined by Japanese anxieties, and the relief supplies remained locked away at Nakhodka until November 1944 when the Japanese steamer *Hakusan Maru* finally arrived to collect them for return to Kobe. Two more ships were then identified as the transports that would convey the Red Cross consignment (that which remained after part of the supplies had been diverted to prisoners held in camps in the Japanese home islands). They were the *Hoshi Maru*, a freighter of similar size to the *Hakusan Maru*, and the *Awa Maru*, an almost-new motor-ship completed in March 1943 that had been ordered as an express passenger-cargo liner by Nippon Yusen Kaisha. Her intended employment had been the passenger and mail run to Australia but, as a wartime auxiliary, she entered service instead as a high-speed army transport.

Of the two ships, the *Hoshi Maru* was the first to make her humanitarian drop, after her exact departure date and the precise course she would follow from Kobe to Shanghai had been agreed. The ten-day round trip was completed successfully and without incident. For the *Awa Maru* it took longer to reach a settlement. The Japanese wanted to be confident that the safe passage arrangements for both her outward and homeward voyages were definite and unambiguous. She would be passing through significantly more hostile waters in the heart of the combat zone where Allied submarines were known to be particularly active – the East and South China Seas, and the Java Sea.

With concurrence on all the details of her course and schedule, the *Awa Maru* was demilitarised and repainted green overall with prominent white crosses on her hull, on both sides of her funnel and on the horizontal surfaces of her hatch covers. For night running, she was to be illuminated by special spotlights erected around her decks and the crosses on her funnel would be highlighted by an outline of lamps. She finally departed Moji, at the northern end of Kyushu, under the command of Captain Hamada Matsutaro, carrying 2,000 tons of supplies, on the afternoon of 17 February 1945.

In the prelude to the *Awa Maru*'s departure, beginning ten days before she sailed, COMSUBPAC (Commander Submarine Force, US Pacific Fleet) transmitted a signal to all submarines on patrol specifying in detail her ports of call, the dates of arrival and departure, and the course plot she would follow. The signal, broadcast three times on each of three successive days, also exhorted all boats to allow her to pass unmolested.

On the morning of 20 February, the *Awa Maru* arrived at Takao, Formosa (Taiwan). She left the following day, heading for Hong Kong, where she arrived on 22 February after noon, sailing again on the morning of 23 February. The next call was Saigon (arrival 25 February; departure 28 February), then Singapore (arrival morning of 2 March; departure 8 March) and finally Batavia (Jakarta) where her outbound voyage concluded on the afternoon of 10 March. A scheduled call at Surabaya was not made.

It was reported that while in Batavia, the *Awa Maru* took on 2,500 tons of crude oil but as it would have been difficult to stow such a commodity aboard her, besides being such a small amount, it is more likely that it was bunker oil to replenish her fuel supplies. She also embarked oil technicians and civilians, who were to return aboard her to Japan, as well as some military personnel. During the eight days she was in port, COMSUBPAC and COMSUBSOWESPAC (Commander, Submarines, South-West Pacific) again broadcast, three times on three consecutive nights, the particulars of the *Awa Maru's* return course and sailing schedule, once more stressing in the strictest terms that she was not to be attacked.

After departing Batavia on the morning of 18 March, the *Awa Maru* proceeded to Muntok on Banka Belitung where more Red Cross parcels were offloaded the next day. She remained at Muntok for four days before continuing to Singapore, arriving there for the second time on 24 March. There she embarked more oil and electrical technicians, relatives of diplomats and Japanese government colonial officials (administrators, intelligence staff, logistics and supply personnel and their families) who were stationed in Singapore, and many other civilians (those fortunate enough or who had been able to exert sufficient influence to be allowed to take passage). Many thousands more Japanese citizens, like countless others dispersed around the vast area of the occupied territories, who, acutely aware that the fortunes of the war were rapidly turning against them and were desperate to return to their homeland, remained behind on sailing day.

This artist's impression of the *Awa Maru* also shows her in naval grey paintwork while designated as a fast military troop transport. (Kihachiro Ueda)

By that time, the *Awa Maru* was carrying no military personnel, all those who had come aboard her at Batavia having disembarked at Muntok or on arrival at Singapore. It was as well, for there were many more people aboard the *Awa Maru* in total than she had been designed to carry in commercial service, which was just 137 in first class! The official number of people who sailed with her when she made her departure from Singapore, at 10.00 hours on 28 March 1945, was 2,071, including her 148-man crew and skipper.

The *Awa Maru*'s return non-stop voyage was to take her via the South China Sea to Moji where she expected to arrive on 4 April. Five days later, on 1 April, she reported her noon position as 23.20N, 117.27E, placing her north-east of Swatow (Shantou, Guandong), entering the Formosa Strait and just 1,200 miles from safety. It was to be the last message ever transmitted from her.

The weather was foggy with visibility below 200m. Patrolling in that sea area was the USS *Queenfish* under the command of Charles E. Loughlin. First contact with the *Awa Maru* was made by radar, but it wasn't long before she was sighted visually in the gloom. According to subsequent testimonies, it was concluded that the ship sighted was a Japanese destroyer because she was low in the water and had a small radar signature; further to this, she was making a good 17 knots and was not following a zig-zag course pattern.

Turning the *Queenfish* around to bring his stern tubes to bear, Loughlin ordered four torpedoes fired at a distance of around 1,100m. The time was 23.30 hours. All four torpedoes struck the target and within two minutes the *Awa Maru* had gone, sinking to a depth of 60m in the position 24.41N, 119.12E. According to the official figures of the Japanese government, the devastating attack had dealt a swift death to 2,055 of her complement: her captain, 147 members of the crew and 1,907 passengers.

A single survivor was pulled from the sea by the crew of the USS *Queenfish*, a steward named Shimoda Kantaro who, under questioning, revealed the identity of the ship that had been sunk. This horrific news was immediately communicated to Vice Admiral Charles Lockwood, COMSUBPAC, who in turn had it relayed to Fleet Admiral Chester W. Nimitz, CINCPACFLT (Commander-in-Chief US Pacific Fleet), and Fleet Admiral Ernest J. King, CNO.

Commander Loughlin was ordered to report directly to Guam where he was relieved of his command and arrested to stand trial by general court martial. Before leaving the scene, however, the *Queenfish*, assisted by another submarine, the USS *Sea Fox*, scoured the area for more survivors – none were found.

It is not known for certain whether, in fact, there were more survivors of the *Awa Maru*, or, if there were, how they were rescued, but the official figures suggest that sixteen people somehow escaped death that terrible night. Although the wording of the *Queenfish*'s log implies that Shimoda Kantaro was the only survivor, it could simply mean that he was the only survivor rescued by the submarine. One unsubstantiated account of the circumstances following the sinking states that there *were* other survivors in the water who preferred death to capture, but to suggest that victims were left to drown for such reasons is questionable. The code of the sea dictates otherwise.

Commanded by Charles E. Loughlin, the USS *Queenfish* carried out the fatal attack that sent the *Awa Maru* to the bottom in the Formosa Strait. (United States Navy)

The Lloyd's List issue of 13 April 1945 reported that the United States State Department had made an announcement two days earlier advising that: 'at about midnight on 1 April a vessel was sunk by submarine action at a position approximately 40 miles from the estimated, scheduled position of the *Awa Maru* which was travelling under Allied Safe conduct.' It added that the Japanese News Agency had stated, prior to the announcement of the sinking, that the Japanese government had been obliged to ask the US government through Switzerland, the protecting power, for information concerning the vessel as it had received no news. That July, in another bulletin, Lloyd's List reported that on 29 June the United States had officially acknowledged responsibility for the sinking of the *Awa Maru*. The cable indicated a willingness to consider indemnity, but only when the war was over. In the event, none was ever made.

Unlike the German attacks on hospital ships, the United States' breach of a protective mandate had been admitted, but it may seem callous by today's standards when, in none of the communications with Japan subsequent to the *Awa Maru*'s loss, was there any hint of contrition, apology or commiseration to the families of the victims. After all, those who were killed, while they were citizens of a country with which the United States was at war, were certainly not combatants.

In the ensuing court martial, Commander Loughlin was charged with 'culpable inefficiency in the performance of duty and disobeying the lawful order of a superior', but he was only found guilty of 'negligence in obeying orders' for which he received a reprimand in the form of a Letter of Admonition. This did not affect his sea-going career for he commanded at least two more ships, including the cruiser USS *Toledo*, and it did little to hinder his upward progression as a United States Naval officer. By the time of his retirement in 1977, he had been promoted to the rank of rear admiral.

One senses that not only was the American action in sinking the *Awa Maru* an extremely grave error – for there appears to have been little, if any, contemplation of the possibility that the target ship could be the vessel sailing under safe conduct protection – but it may be thought that Loughlin's punishment for failing to obey orders that emanated from the highest level of the US government fell short of what was appropriate. Quite apart from the moral issue of the case itself, it is not known how many other, later Red Cross runs were lost because of his actions, at the expense of the well-being, even survival, of countless other American prisoners of war.

Certainly, there are unanswered questions that suggest the *Awa Maru* tragedy may have been avoidable. There appears to have been no connection made, for example, between the vessel encountered and the one which, less than twelve hours earlier, had broadcast her position; nor does there appear to have been any deliberation regarding the absence of other 'blips' on the submarine's radar screen, which could only have meant that the target ship was sailing alone. Having said that, it would be wrong here to condemn Commander Loughlin for sinking the *Awa Maru*; he is entitled to the benefit of the doubt that it was an unintentional violation of a ship's protected status, and to take a different view would seem unreasonable. He had been obliged to make snap decisions in a hostile environment, fraught with dangers.

Equally unjustifiable, though, are the mistruths that have been allowed to circulate in the years since, in effect to support the exoneration of Commander Loughlin, if not to justify his actions. It has been suggested that the *Awa Maru* was carrying contraband in breach of the safe conduct agreement and that she was ferrying military personnel. Neither is correct and the record should be set straight. Indeed, the claim during Loughlin's trial, as the basis of his defence, that the carriage of contraband aboard the *Awa Maru* had forfeited her right to safe conduct clearance was ruled as immaterial because no restrictions had been imposed as to what the *Awa Maru* was permitted to carry. Similarly, the allegation that she was carrying so-called military passengers has been refuted as false on more than one occasion by reference to the ship's passenger manifest, retained after the withdrawal from Singapore. Others claim, wrongly, that she deviated from her declared course.

It has been claimed too that in the *Awa Maru*'s holds there was a fortune in gold and platinum bars and a huge quantity of industrial diamonds, again equally irrelevant. The fact is that in salvage efforts in 1977, 1980 and 1986 all that was recovered was a lot of victims' personal effects and a large number of antique Chinese ceramics and porcelain pieces.

In total disregard of such irrefutable evidence, false claims and statements about the ship's function and a contraband cargo have nevertheless persisted: a disservice to the *Awa Maru*'s victims. An example of this is contained in a San Diego, California, newspaper article in November 1986 pertaining to the possible salvage of 'an estimated five billion dollars in treasure' from the wreck. The article, summarised in a Reuters cable, states: 'The freighter [*Awa Maru*], posing as a hospital ship, was carrying war loot from Japan to Manila when it was hit by torpedoes.' Quite apart from the other errors (despite Captain John Bennet, said to have been the USS *Queenfish*'s navigating officer, being mentioned as a member of the salvage team), the un-named correspondent had even got the ship's direction and route wrong!

As a reminder of the *Awa Maru* disaster, as well as that of the *Tsushima Maru* (see Chapter 8), there is a monument in the form of a simple black marble tablet in a quiet, tree-shaded corner of the grounds of the Zojoji Temple in Tokyo.

10

NO ROSES ON THEIR GRAVES

Operation Hannibal, the evacuation of Germany's eastern territories and the lands seized in northern Poland, which took place over the winter of 1944/45, was the greatest seaborne rescue in history. It involved upwards of 800 ships[1], comparable to the 880 at Dunkirk (although that figure includes many of the so-called little ships), ultimately rescuing as many as 2.5 million people, both military and civilian refugees, in contrast to the 366,161 evacuated from north-west France between 27 May and 5 June 1940. It was triggered by the increasingly desperate necessity to save those threatened by the advancing Red Army as the tide of the war on Germany's Eastern Front turned unstoppably against them.

The huge tank battle of Kursk in July–August 1943, the greatest ever mechanised engagement between two armies, proved to be pivotal as far as the outcome of the war in eastern Europe was concerned. Thereafter, as the Red Army's offensive to drive the invaders out of Russia gathered momentum, the *Wehrmacht* was on an irreversible retreat. It was a slow capitulation initially characterised by stubborn resistance as Hitler implored all German servicemen never to surrender, to defend every inch of ground. Confronted by an overwhelming opposition whose strength of numbers and quantities of equipment was steadily growing, however, it was evident, to some at least in the German high command, that defeat was inevitable.

Adolf Hitler had assumed the position of Supreme Commander-in-Chief of the German forces and disregarded the repeated warnings he received, from his experienced Generals Guderian and Gehlen, that a Soviet offensive into East Prussia and Pomerania was imminent from as early as the autumn of 1944.

While there had been some effort to evacuate refugees from the area before the end of that year, the crunch came on 13 and 14 January when the Third Byelorussian Front, under General I.D. Charnyakhovsky, and the Second Byelorussian Front, under Marshall Konstantin Rokossovsky (a combined force of 1.5 million troops),

---

1   In his book *Unter Nehmung Retting*, the author Fritz Brustat-Naval lists 494 merchant ships as having been engaged in Operation Hannibal and gives the figure of 790 for vessels of all types. Charles W. Koburger, in *Steel Ships, Iron Crosses and Refugees*, states that 1,080 merchant ships were involved, but this figure may, in fact, refer to the combined total of both naval and merchant vessels. It may, too, have included small fishing craft that are invariably listed separately in shipping registers. Undoubtedly, many small, local craft were used to convey passengers from shore to the bigger ships at anchor.

attacked East Prussia; the Third towards Pillkallen (Dobrovol'sk) and the Second towards Elbing (Elblag). Already, the Red Army had taken much of the Baltic States of Estonia, Latvia and Lithuania and in the south it had driven the Germans out of Belarus (Byelorussia) and the Ukraine.

The new offensive was slow at first, hindered by extensive minefields, anti-tank obstacles and an intricate network of fortifications, while the 3rd Panzer Army fought tenaciously to halt the advance. Despite suffering heavy casualties, the Russians had captured Tannenberg (near Stebark, Poland) by 21 January and Allenstern (Olsztyn) and Insterberg (Chernyakhovsk) the following day. Elbing was reached on 23 January and by the end of the month the Russians had got to the shores of the Vistula Lagoon (Zalew Wiślany Kaliningradskiy Zatier) cutting off the city of Königsberg, the capital of East Prussia. As Albert Speer, Hitler's armament minister, confessed in his book *Inside the Third Reich*: 'When on 12 January 1945 the great Soviet offensive in the East, which Guderian had predicted, finally began, our defensive line collapsed along a broad front.'

As the Red Army relentlessly advanced westwards, it wreaked a terrible retribution for the atrocities that had been perpetrated on its own soil by the forces of Nazi Germany against the *unter-menschen* (sub-human) Slavs, as they had been discriminately categorised. Stories filtered through to German forward bases of unspeakable brutality, of arson, rape, plunder, mutilation and summary execution. It acted as the catalyst for a mass human exodus that was one of the greatest in all history.

Despite the ranting refusal of Hitler to allow an organised retreat to new defensive positions or to permit the evacuation of threatened civilians, Grand Admiral Dönitz was concerned that troops should not be allowed to fall captives of the Russians. He recognised, too, that in the post-war reconstruction period Germany would need all the manpower it could muster. Consequently, he organised for Operation Hannibal to be launched to rescue as many as possible across the Baltic Sea. Whether this was done surreptitiously or despite Hitler's opposition is not known. For the *Kriegsmarine* and the many commercial auxiliaries pressed into the operation, it was to be their finest hour.

Responsibility for the organisation and execution of Operation Hannibal was entrusted to General Admiral Oskar Kummetz, Naval High Command, Baltic, and Rear Admiral Konrad Engelhardt, head of the *Kriegsmarine*'s shipping department. It was no mean feat planning the shipping movements to ensure fuel was available where required and that the refugees flooding into Gotenhafen (Gdynia) and Pillau had food and shelter in the harsh conditions of the Baltic winter as they waited their turn to embark. Some had trekked huge distances in their bid to reach safety, leaving many suffering from fatigue and illness, and requiring medical attention. Countless injured soldiers also needed caring for. There was a great deal of chaos and confusion and, at times, outright panic.

There was also the ever-present threat from Soviet warplanes and submarines. Throughout the war in the East, up to this point, the German forces had dominated the Baltic Sea (or Ostsee), but the diversion of naval units to the relief operation allowed Soviet submarines to break out of the blockaded Gulf of Finland. They had been bottled up at Kronstadt but in increasing numbers they were released to cruise freely without the fear of intervention. At the same time, as both the Allied and Soviet air forces were able to move their bases closer to Germany, they had gradually assumed command of the air. Over the Baltic, Russian warplanes became as potent a threat as were the Russian submarines patrolling beneath the sea.

The Hannibal evacuation fleet comprised every type of vessel imaginable. Naval ships escorting the transports, besides performing protection duties for non-combatant ships, also carried their own contingents of evacuees. This was true even of the U-boats stationed in the area. Among the merchant ships of the evacuation fleet there was everything from ocean liners, cargo ships, short sea passenger ships, train ferries and many other types – in effect everything that was readily available.

The cost in shipping losses was inevitably heavy, both military and civilian. Naval losses added up to more than 220 ships of all sizes – one old battleship, thirteen destroyers, seven U-boats and around 200 smaller warships (minelayers, minesweepers, coastal escorts, landing craft etc.). The losses of the vessels that had been pressed into service as auxiliaries or were taken up from commercial trade for the operation were equally considerable. Between 23 January and 8 May 1945, 158 merchant vessels were sunk – but the cost in human terms was greater. It has been estimated that some 20,000 civilians alone were killed in the sea evacuation; military casualties amounted to well over 5,000, but these are conservative figures. The losses of fifteen Hannibal transports alone accounted for nearly 25,000 deaths. Among them were three that were sunk with casualties significantly greater in number than the victims suffered when the *Titanic* was lost.

WILHELM GUSTLOFF (3/1938)

Deutsche Arbeitsfront GmbH, Hamburg, Germany

The *Wilhelm Gustloff*, like the *Lancastria*, *Laconia* and *Cap Arcona*, is probably one of the better known ships described in these pages. Nevertheless, hers is a story that will be fully recounted here because, despite being acknowledged as the worst ever maritime disaster, it has received scant attention compared with that of the *Titanic*. At least until the advent of the internet, which has provided a forum for a concerted effort to redress this deficiency by bringing the tragedy to the attention of a wider audience.

The *Wilhelm Gustloff* not only holds the dubious distinction of having been lost in the worst ever maritime disaster, she is also remembered as being the very first purpose-built dedicated cruise ship, long before the explosion in the popularity of cruising holidays. She and her consort, *Robert Ley*, were the first of a planned fleet of specially commissioned passenger ships to provide sea vacations for the Nazi Party's faithful under the *Kraft durch Freude* (Strength through Joy) banner. In reality, it may well have been a disguise for the Nazi's real intentions for these ships for, in May 1939, they were deployed as troop transports repatriating the 'Condor' Legion from Vigo, Spain, to Hamburg and, when the Second World War started, they were hastily

The cruise ship *Wilhelm Gustloff*, the first new vessel constructed for the Deutsche Arbeitsfront's *Kraft durch Freude* cruise service. (Ludolf Timm)

relocated to the Baltic where after a short period in employment as hospital ships, they became base accommodation ships for U-boat personnel. At the beginning of 1945 this all changed when the *Wilhelm Gustloff* and other large, converted passenger ships moored along the Baltic coastline were swiftly reactivated as the core of a huge sea-lift evacuation, the 'sea-bridge' as Dönitz named it.

As already stated, a certain amount of evacuation had been underway from late 1944, principally from the Courland Pocket, which had been cut off by the Soviet Baltic offensive and, being completely isolated, had proved difficult to relieve or resupply. The official relief operation was not invoked until 23 January when, confronting a massive humanitarian emergency, Grand Admiral Dönitz signalled all naval commanders at Gdynia, instructing them to commence evacuations to ports beyond the Soviet reach, giving the operation the codename Hannibal. Since 20 November 1940, the *Wilhelm Gustloff* had been the home of the 2nd Submarine Training Division at Gotenhafen, an elite force of U-boat personnel who were hastily removed when she was assigned to one of the first big Hannibal convoys out of the Bay of Danzig.

Prior to departure for Kiel and Flensburg on 30 January, a huge number of people, mainly civilian refugees but also military personnel including wounded servicemen, boarded the *Wilhelm Gustloff*. There is a great deal of dispute over the precise number who embarked for that fateful voyage and many different figures are quoted, some perhaps more credible than others. It is not possible here to offer definitive figures, only to reiterate the information that, by examination, would seem the most reliable. What is for certain, it should be stressed, is that the *Wilhelm Gustloff*, which had been designed to carry a maximum of 1,465 passengers and 400 crew, was heavily over-loaded when she sailed.

Among those who boarded her were 918 naval officers and crew, 373 female naval auxiliaries and 162 wounded soldiers, of whom 73 were stretcher cases. The rest were refugees, mainly women, children and elderly men – the precise number not recorded for there simply was not the time or the means in the pressing circumstances to do that accurately. When the *Wilhelm Gustloff* left the quayside, it was estimated that there were at least 4,658 people on board but while the departure was delayed, barges came alongside and, from them, even more clambered aboard, adding to her comple-ment. While some recent attempts to arrive at a conclusive number for the *Wilhelm Gustloff*'s occupants are questionable, it is felt that the calculations of Heinz Schön, a recognised authority on the disaster, who suggests there were 10,582 including her crew – some 4,482 more than his original calculation – are the most reliable.

The *Wilhelm Gustloff* was able, finally, to get underway at 12.30 hours in convoy with the *Hansa*, a former Hamburg Amerika Line transatlantic liner, which was equally full. With them was the whaling vessel *Walter Rau* and, as a makeshift escort, the destroyer *Löwe* and the torpedo boat *TF-1*. On her bridge there were two mas-ters responsible for the ship, the naval Captain Wilhelm Zahn, commander of the U-boat crews, and her mercantile master, Captain Friedrich Petersen. Between them they debated the best course for the convoy to take, opting for the northerly, deep-water Emergency Route 58, which, though swept of mines, was too narrow to permit zigzag manoeuvres. It had the benefit of avoiding the more intensive minefields in shallower coastal waters, but it exposed the ships rather more to the danger of the torpedo menace.

The fact was that the convoy's escort was barely adequate. Moreover, the arro-gant submarine command based in Gdynia, having a contemptuous disregard for the capabilities of its Soviet counterparts and underestimating the potential danger, had failed to notify the 9th Escort Division, also located in Gdynia, of the convoy's imminent departure.

The convoy had not proceeded far when the *Hansa* experienced mechanical dif-ficulties and was compelled to return to Gotenhafen while the *Wilhelm Gustloff* continued on her way. A lack of maintenance of her diesel-electric engines that had been idle for four years then prevented her from making the sort of speed she had been capable of in her cruiseship days, but at least the weather was on her side. It was freezing cold with frequent snow squalls and low visibility. A number of fac-tors that occurred almost simultaneously conspired to suddenly worsen the *Wilhelm Gustloff*'s predicament, however. As the convoy was rounding the Stolpe Bank, north-west of Gotenhafen, the *TF-1* developed a leak and advised that she too would have to return to port. As night began to fall, Captain Petersen gave orders for the ship to be fully illuminated rather than run on standard blue, low-intensity lights, as he was more concerned about the risk of collision with another ship in the dark. Like the U-boat commanders back in Gotenhafen, he had unwisely underrated the Soviet submarine threat. Finally, just as the *Wilhelm Gustloff* had been made more conspicu-ous in the falling light, the weather also cleared.

After the outbreak of war, the *Wilhelm Gustloff* was moved to Gotenhafen where she was converted into a static hospital ship. (Arnold Kludas)

Aboard the Russian submarine *S-13*, Commander Captain Alexander U. Marinesko concluded from radio messages he had received announcing Soviet land successes, that an evacuation of German troops may have begun. The submarine had left Hangö, Finland, nineteen days earlier but thus far had encountered little in the way of enemy shipping while patrolling the area off the Pomeranian coast. Thus, when a glow was sighted on the horizon it instantly raised expectations. Although dismissed at first as the lighthouse on the Hela peninsula, it was subsequently deduced that the light was definitely coming from a ship when it was calculated that the seamark was too far distant to the south. The fortunes of *S-13*'s patrol were about to change – and with the help of the Germans themselves!

Marinesko manoeuvred his submarine into a position between the target and the coast, figuring that escorting ships would at least expect an attack to be made from that side because of the mines and shallow depth. Closing to a range of around 1,000m, three torpedoes were fired shortly after 21.00 hours, striking the hapless *Wilhelm Gustloff* along her portside. These caused massive detonations, which brought about an immediate list as forward and portside compartments flooded.

As built, the *Wilhelm Gustloff* carried twenty-two lifeboats, each with a capacity of sixty people, along with eighteen smaller boats and 380 life rafts: more than adequate for 1,400 peacetime passengers but a fraction of what was needed for the thousands she was carrying at the time of the attack. Besides which, the severe list had made it impossible to launch the starboard-side boats. Scenes of chaos and mayhem unfolded aboard the *Wilhelm Gustloff* as terror-struck passengers, many completely unfamiliar with anything to do with ships or the sea, completely disorientated in these strange surroundings, shoved and forced their way along companionways like a human tide, trampling dead bodies and each other as they tried to reach the open decks. Few had donned life jackets and, having turned in early, utterly fatigued by their desperate flight from the advancing Russians, many had totally inadequate clothing for the freezing conditions.

On the master's instructions, the *Wilhelm Gustloff*'s first officer, Louis Reese, had ordered the transmission of a Mayday call within minutes of the torpedoes striking the ship and Naval Command in Gotenhafen had, in turn, radioed to all ships in the vicinity to proceed with haste to the scene where the *Wilhelm Gustloff* was sinking off Stolpmünde, on the Pomeranian coast. The escort *Löwe* immediately responded to the emergency and was alongside within fifteen minutes, taking aboard survivors. Barely half an hour after the attack, the icy seas had already claimed hundreds of lives, but *Löwe* rescued as many as she could carry, huddling them into every corner of available deck space.

The *Wilhelm Gustloff* capsized at 22.18 hours with many of her occupants trapped inside her. Forty minutes later, she disappeared beneath the inky black sea completely.

Just as the *Löwe*'s commander was confronting the dilemma of whether to carry on with the rescue, despite the possibility that his ship could become dangerously overloaded, or to break off leaving thousands to their doom, the heavy cruiser *Admiral Hipper* hove into view, allowing her to leave. But the *Hipper*, commanded by Captain Hans Henigst, was ill-suited to continue with the recovery of survivors from the sea. Her high freeboard presented an insurmountable obstacle even with ladders thrown over her sides. It required a strength to climb up to her main deck that few of the weakened, barely alive survivors had left. Members of the *Hipper*'s crew bravely jumped into the freezing sea to assist as best they could, but it was obvious that it would take a long time to complete a rescue in these circumstances, time that neither the survivors nor the ship had. When the wakes of torpedoes were spotted by lookouts, Captain Henigst was left with no choice but to terminate the recovery effort to the utter horror of those still waiting to be dragged from the sea. It was later presented as a betrayal, but the fact was that the *Hipper* was unable to do more without risking being sunk herself at the cost of the lives of the 1,500 refugees she had already been carrying.

Other naval vessels that arrived on the scene, among them the *T-36*, *TF-19*, *TS-2*, *M-341*, *V-1703* and the Norddeutscher Lloyd coastal steamer *Gottingen*, were able to pick up only a few of the survivors who still were stranded in the corpse-strewn sea. In total, 964 people are believed to have survived the sinking of the *Wilhelm Gustloff*, although that number was depleted as others who succumbed to injuries and the effects of exposure were added to the fatalities.

Reports from a Polish diving expedition carried out in August 1955 describe the wreck of the *Wilhelm Gustloff* as being broken into three parts lying at various angles on their portside at a depth of 140ft (approximately 42m).

Apparently, it had been the intention originally to give the *Wilhelm Gustloff* the name *Adolf Hitler*, a plan scuppered when it was decided to make a martyr of the otherwise insignificant head of the Swiss Nazi Party who was assassinated in February

A newspaper feature from the *Soviet Weekly* of 10 May 1986 about the sinking of the *Steuben* and the *Wilhelm Gustloff*, showing the *S-13* and her commander, Captain Alexander Marinesko. Note that the Russians have spelt the ship's name as '*Gustlow*'. (Author's collection)

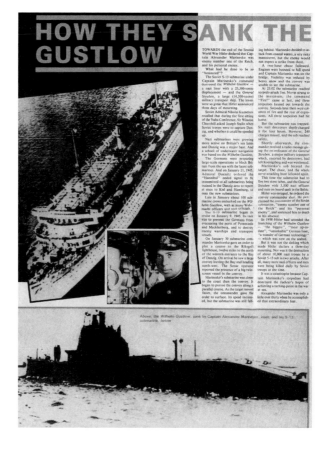

1936. Had she been named as first intended, her loss would have been the most appropriate metaphor for both the doomed Führer and the sinking German Reich, the latter occurring, as with the ill-fated refugee ship, with massive and needless loss of life. As it turned out, by May 1945 all three were history.

STEUBEN ex-*General von Steuben* ex-*Munchen* (6/1923)

Norddeutscher Lloyd, Bremen, Germany

The refugee ship *Steuben* had started life as one of a pair of intermediate liners constructed for Norddeutscher Lloyd's North Atlantic passenger services from Bremen and Southampton to New York. She was in fact the very first German-flag passenger ship to enter New York after the First World War when she arrived at the end of her maiden voyage in July 1923. After a devastating fire at New York on 11 July 1930, she was rebuilt as the cruise ship *General von Steuben*, her name shortened to *Steuben* in 1938, around the time when she was chartered to the Deutsche Arbeitsfront (German Labour Organisation) for KdF cruises. On the outbreak of war, she was moved to the Baltic to provide accommodation for U-boat crews based at Kiel.

In August 1944, the *Steuben* was reactivated for the transportation of wounded German soldiers from the increasingly overwhelmed field hospitals near the Eastern Front to full-scale medical facilities further west, safe from the threat of enemy bombardment. As such, she was not designated as a hospital ship but operated as an armed transport; she was certainly not painted in hospital ship colours. But it would have been to no avail for, in the wake of Germany's failure to respect the protected status of hospital ships, the Soviet Union served notice that it intended to do likewise. An official communiqué delivered to the German government in July 1942 stated: 'The Soviet Government gives notice that it will not recognise and respect German hospital ships according to the Hague Convention.'

As the German position in the east deteriorated and the human stream of wounded military and civilian refugees turned into a flood, the *Steuben* made an increasing number of relief voyages until, on 23 January 1945, she became part of Dönitz's official Operation Hannibal evacuation fleet.

Her end came overnight on 9/10 February 1945. During 9 February, while the *Steuben* was in Pillau (Baltiysk), she embarked a recorded 4,267 people before sailing late that afternoon. The majority of those taken aboard were wounded soldiers, around 2,800 in number, tended by 270 *Kriegsmarine* doctors, nurses and auxiliary medical staff, assisted by twelve nurses from Pillau. There were also 800 refugees. The *Steuben*'s crew was a mixture of naval and mercantile personnel, as had been the case

Originally the Norddeutscher Lloyd transatlantic liner *Munchen*, the *Steuben* was one of two evacuation ships sunk by the Russian submarine *S-13*. She is seen here as the *General von Steuben*, prior to the name being shortened in 1938. (Deutsches Schiffahrtsmuseum)

aboard the *Wilhelm Gustloff*. There were sixty-four gunner ratings to man the ship's anti-aircraft guns, and a further sixty-one naval ratings to perform other shipboard duties such as signalmen, radio operators and administrative staff. They were augmented by 160 mercantile seamen: engine room personnel, deck crew and catering staff. Finally, and perhaps controversially, 100 able-bodied soldiers returning home boarded the ship prior to departure.

Some accounts state that the *Steuben* was carrying as many as 2,000 refugees besides the wounded troops. The figures quoted here were sourced from the book *Steel Ships, Iron Crosses and Refugees*, although author Charles W. Koburger does caution that other sources claim different numbers for the total embarked. The respected German shipping author Arnold Kludas in *Great Passenger Ships of the World* concurs with Koburger, although he suggests alternatively that there were 4,950 in total aboard the *Steuben* when she sailed, 450 of whom were crew.

Bound for Kiel, but with a call at Swinemünde (Swinoujscie) apparently planned, the *Steuben* had not progressed far when she was attacked just after midnight by the Russian submarine *S-13*, the very warship that had sunk the *Wilhelm Gustloff* some ten days earlier. Two of the *S-13*'s torpedoes slammed into the *Steuben*, which, according to survivors' accounts, sank within twenty minutes. The prevailing conditions were much as they had been when the *Wilhelm Gustloff* was attacked and many of those who made it off the sinking ship perished in the freezing sea. Most of the

The Soviet submarine *S-13*, which sank the *Steuben* and the *Wilhelm Gustloff*. The *S-13*'s double 'success' accounted for the greatest loss of life ever in two sinkings, at more than 11,300 persons. (Voyenno Sovyetsky Morskoj Flota)

wounded, especially the stretcher cases, never made it that far and, trapped inside the *Steuben*, they drowned as she foundered.

With limited resources available to escort the evacuation convoys, there were few ships nearby to effect a rescue but the torpedo boat *T-196* managed to pick up around 300 survivors who were landed at Kolberg (Kołobrzeg). With those picked up by other craft, some 659 were saved. The dead, therefore, numbered 3,608 but Joachim Wedekind, a merchant marine officer who was aboard the *Steuben* at the time, insists that as many as 4,500 people were killed when she sank. Despite the uncertainty about the actual number of casualties, with the 9,343 estimated casualties from the *Wilhelm Gustloff*, Captain Alexander Marinesko of the *S-13* had gained the dubious, even shocking distinction of having caused the greatest loss of life ever in the sinking of two ships.

Like that of the *Wilhelm Gustloff*, the wreck of the *Steuben* was later located, in May 2004, by a Polish Navy diving team from the hydrographic survey vessel ORP *Arctowski*. The findings of the expedition were published in *National Geographic* magazine (February 2005). They reveal that the wreck is still largely intact, raising questions as to why it sank so quickly. It lies on its port side at a depth of about 70m. With no intentions of removing the *Steuben*'s remains, they have been designated, like those of the *Wilhelm Gustloff*, as a protected site – as much as anything to prevent pilfering by divers.

GOYA (1 / 1942)

A/S J. Ludwig Mowinckells Rederi, Bergen, Norway

The Germans seized the new Norwegian cargo ship *Goya*, then completing at the Akers MV Shipyard in Oslo, five days after her launch on 9 April 1940, at the time of the occupation of Norway. She was completed for the Germans, a process deliberately slowed by Resistance-inclined shipyard workers, on 6 January 1942, and entered service as a *Kriegsmarine* army transport. From 1 August 1943 she was attached to the 27th U-boat flotilla at Memel (Klaipéda) where she was used as a target ship for training submariners and testing torpedoes.

When fighting with the Red Army became critical, she was requisitioned in January 1945 to assist in the evacuation of the Courland Pocket. This work continued successfully through to mid-April.

On 16 April 1945 the *Goya* was at Hela, north of Gotenhafen where she had been directed to collect more than 6,000 refugees. As the war was entering its final phase and the Russians were breaking through German positions all along the withering front line, the situation was becoming increasingly desperate and evacuation ships, regardless of their size or capacity, were being encouraged to take aboard ever greater complements of passengers. A manifest of sorts compiled at the time documented some 6,100 people embarking, among them 200 men, the remnants of the 35th Panzer Regiment. As with the *Wilhelm Gustloff*, appeals to take more refugees from barges and small craft that surrounded the ship did not go unheeded. Only seven days

Some three to four years after her completion, the *Goya* was photographed in the Baltic under German control and heavily camouflaged in a splinter disruptive pattern. (Arnold Kludas)

earlier, General Otto Lasch had surrendered the city of Königsberg to Soviet forces, an act that had set off mass panic among the civilian population, contributing to the flood of refugees crowding the roads leading to Pillau, all anxious to escape across the bay to Hela.

There are claims that the *Goya* had well in excess of 7,000 souls aboard her when she finally weighed anchor, but the most reliable figures suggest that there were 6,385 in total, including her crew.

When she sailed, in convoy with five other ships bound for Copenhagen, their route took them along the Stolpe Bank, a treacherous course that led them straight into a channel swarming with Soviet submarines. It was less than twenty-five days from the end of the war and everywhere, on land and at sea, the Russians were pressing home their massive advantage.

Just before midnight, when 60 miles off Stolpe, near Cape Rozewic, the *Goya* was hit, amidships and astern, by two torpedoes. The submarine responsible was the *L-3*, commanded by Captain Vladimir Konovalov. Although the *Goya* had the speed to outpace most submarines, the convoy had been slowed when one of the other ships, the *Kronenfels*, had experienced mechanical problems and then come to a complete stop while repairs on her engines were carried out. The twenty-minute delay and the reduced speed proved to be critical and the *L-3* took full advantage of the brief window of opportunity.

The impact of the two torpedo explosions must have catastrophically weakened the *Goya*'s structure, for she broke in two with topside gear crashing down on the splintering decks and sank within seven minutes. Many were trapped in the holds with no means of escape, others drowned or rapidly succumbed to hypothermia in the icy sea. Just 183 survivors were rescued by the *M-256* and *M-328*, placing the sinking of the *Goya* among the very worst maritime disasters.

While there is uncertainty as to the exact number of people who had boarded the *Goya*, so too is there speculation about the extent of her casualties. The most reliable figure, and the one quoted by most sources, puts the number of dead at 6,202, although when added to the 183 survivors, the total falls well short of the 7,000-plus speculated to have been aboard the *Goya*. Norwegian sources state that there were from 6,203 to 7,028 dead and from 165 to 334 survivors. The precise numbers will never be known.

In the Führer Naval Conference of 18 April 1945, the loss was played down by the naval high command; the emphasis being placed on the numbers of wounded and refugees who *had* been safely transported westwards. The claim was that, compared with the success rate, barely 0.5 per cent had lost their lives.

Polish divers located the *Goya's* wreck on 26 August 2002, removing the ship's compass to confirm her identity. The wreck lies in the position 55.13N, 18.20E at a depth of 76m. The wreck was revisited on 16 April 2003, fifty-eight years to the day after the *Goya* was sunk. Since then, the Polish Maritime Office in Gdynia has designated it a war grave and placed a 500m-radius exclusion zone around it to deter looters.

As for Operation Hannibal, it continued right up to the end of hostilities with another huge convoy of sixty-five ships carrying 15,000 people departing Libau, Latvia, on the very day of Germany's unconditional surrender, 8 May. Although Hannibal officially ended on that day, evacuation voyages continued for another week even though such movements contravened and were prohibited under the surrender terms.

The words of Cajus Bekker in his book *Hitler's Navy War* serve to summarise the overriding humanitarian dimension of Operation Hannibal:

> The final operation – the rescue of two million Germans over the Baltic by merchant ships and what was left of the [German] Navy – was an accomplishment in the highest maritime tradition. Amongst all the confusion and uncertainty brought about by the German collapse, the crews uncomplainingly and successfully carried through the job out of sheer moral duty to protect their fellow-countrymen from enemy attack and save lives from looming danger.

For those who did not make it in this grand effort, the words of the German song said it all:

> On a seaman's grave there bloom no roses
> *Auf einem Seemansgrab, da blühen Keine Rosen*

Yet, even as this magnificent Hannibal rescue operation was coming to a close, reflecting the highest values of the human spirit in the worst of circumstances, more callous behaviour was being exhibited in the very same vicinity as sinister events unfolded.

1. Seen in an artist's impression, the *Queen Mary* bears down on the cruiser HMS *Curacoa*, which she cut clean through in the mid-Atlantic collision on 2 October 1942. It could have spelt tragedy for the great liner and the approximately 11,250 troops she was carrying. As it was, 338 of the cruiser's officers and crew lost their lives. (Mervyn Pearson)

2. Artist's impression of the *Principe Umberto* during the embarkation of Serbian troops at Valona in early 1916. (Istoreco)

3. Artist's impression of the torpedo attack on the *Principe Umberto* from a card published by the Austro-Hungarian authorities. (Mario Cicogna)

4. An impression of the *Lancastria* in her Cunard White Star Line colours by Charles Eddowes Turner, from a publicity image published by her owners. (Cunard Line)

5. The bottom-left section of the stained-glass window in the St Katherine Cree church, dedicated to the *Lancastria* and depicting the scene of the disaster. (David L. Williams)

6. The *Arisan Maru* and *Edogawa Maru* were built to the Class 2A standard design, two of about 130 ships of this type. This impression shows one of their sister vessels, the *Enoura Maru*. (Kihachiro Ueda)

7. The *Teia Maru* in an impression showing her in wartime colours. She was the former Messageries Maritimes liner *Aramis*. Note her unusual square funnels. (Kihachiro Ueda)

8. The *Akitsu Maru* was sunk while transporting Japanese troops, even though she had been adapted as an amphibious assault ship with a flying deck to operate army aircraft. (Kihachiro Ueda)

9. A model of the *Tsushima Maru* on display in the Memorial Museum, Naha, Okinawa. (Michael Lynch)

10. The cover of Rei Kimura's book about the sinking of the *Awa Maru* provides a good impression of the ship's appearance after she had been disarmed and repainted for her special, safe-passage mercy voyage. Besides her distinctive colour scheme, she was prominently illuminated overall. However, as the torpedo attack took place at night, the sinking ship would not have been visible. (Global Books)

11. An impression of the *Wilhelm Gustloff* sinking after she had been torpedoed by the *S-13* off the Stolpe Bank. In fact she would not have been visible in the pitch black of the Baltic night. (Michael Trim)

12. The Norwegian cargo ship *Goya*, seen while under completion in 1941 at the Akers MV shipyard in Oslo. Alongside her is the *Hoegh Carrier*, also under construction. (Erling Skjold)

13. The *Dona Paz* alongside at Tacloban, Leyte. (Lindsay Bridge)

14. The ferry *Le Joola* photographed at Brest on 22 November 1990 during her delivery voyage to Senegal. (World Ship Society)

15. The upturned hull of the *Le Joola* remained on the surface for sixteen hours after she capsized off West Africa on 26 September 2002. (Press Association)

16. The stranded *Costa Concordia* after she shuddered onto the rocks off Isla del Giglio on 14 January 2012. One of the largest vessels of her type to keel over onto her side, she presents major challenges if she is to be salvaged. The question that will remain to be answered, even if she is refloated, is will she ever sail again? There would be immense cost and psychological issues to overcome, which could ultimately mean she will be demolished for scrap. (Press Association)

11

COFFIN SHIPS

Where Hannibal had demonstrated powerful humanitarian instincts at work, events that followed in its wake revealed a darker side of human behaviour. One can only speculate now as to the full background and motives that led to the appalling disaster that engulfed the liner *Cap Arcona* and the cargo ship *Thielbek* on 3 May 1945 – only days before the ceasefire that would bring an end to war in Europe – but it is impossible to conclude that it was anything other than unsavoury in the extreme; an attempted act of deliberate extermination, of mass murder on a vast scale. As such, it should not, perhaps, be described as a disaster in the sense of an incident that had unintentional consequences but it is included here because it involved ships and occurred at sea.

There can be no doubt from looking at the wartime records that this grotesque plan was also in part a crude attempt to eliminate incriminating evidence. As the war was rapidly approaching its conclusion and those guilty of hideous war crimes sensed an imminent exposure to the full weight of Allied justice, it was their intention to conceal as much as possible of the evidence of Nazi atrocities for which they could be held accountable. Triggered by reverses on all fronts, as the Allies closed in on Berlin, prisoners from concentration camps all over Germany were forced on death marches for which there seemed to be no purpose other than to prevent them from being found, with, in all probability, the prospect of their execution en route.

It has been suggested that the prisoners gathered aboard these ships from KZ Neuengamme and its sub-camps, as well as from Stütthof and Mittelbrau-Dora, were, in fact, to be taken to neutral Sweden. These claims are based on the reported attempts made by Reichsführer Heinrich Himmler, head of the SS and Gestapo, to negotiate a peace deal via the Swedish Count Falke Bernardotte, in which it was proposed that some 15,000 prisoners of Scandinavian extraction could be repatriated. While the release of those particular camp inmates was in the event secured, in the so-called White Buses operation, there is no evidence to suggest that the intention was to treat any of the other, non-Scandinavian prisoners in a similar fashion. Besides, those prisoners who *were* repatriated to Sweden in the White Buses operation travelled between Copenhagen and Malmo aboard the small cargo ships *Magdalena* and *Lillie Matthiessen* and a Baltic ferry, none of them ships of ocean-liner size.

It should be borne in mind that the plan being hatched for the majority of the concentration camp prisoners involved the sequestration of four valuable transports, the *Cap Arcona*, *Thielbek* and *Athen*, plus the *Deutschland*, at the very time when they were desperately needed for the closing phase of the under-resourced Hannibal evacuation. In the circumstances, the diversion of ships of this calibre could only have been arranged by an authority senior to that of the local German naval authority, with a more sinister reason in mind.

Sadly, this episode was nothing other than an example, one of many, of the most extreme bestiality symptomatic of Master Race ideology, being meted out to the very last; a cruel and perverted terminal bid to eradicate Slavic, Polish and Jewish prisoners as part of the 'Final Solution'. All the evidence suggests as much for, with the war entering its final days, there were still those of such extreme racist and political persuasion within the Nazi hierarchy who were prepared to pursue their distorted beliefs to the bitter end. Indeed, the subsequent brief of the Allied investigating team charged with finding the full facts behind this incident was summarised in the words:

> This unit [HQ BAOR, War Crimes Investigation Team] is investigating the allegation that a large number of persons from concentration camps were placed on board various ships in Lübeck Bay immediately prior to the German surrender, with the deliberate intention that they should be drowned.

Local Gestapo chief, George Henning Graf von Bassewitz-Behr, who had collaborated with Karl Kaufmann, the Gauleiter of Hamburg, in the execution of the plan for the disposal of Neuengamme camp's prisoners, also testified as much. He stated that, incarcerated below the ships' decks, they were to be killed by deliberately scuttling the ships in deep water. Kaufmann stated that in so doing they were acting on orders issued direct from Heinrich Himmler.

There is no question that Adolf Hitler himself had declared that no live prisoners should be allowed to fall into enemy hands, and Himmler had issued directives along those lines that were disseminated throughout the Reich. Cloaked in ambiguity (and so suggesting there was latitude in how they should be interpreted; that concentration camp commandants could exercise discretion and do what they thought right in the circumstances), the directives were essentially ordering those to whom they were sent to liquidate everyone they held. Thousands were murdered in the genocide precipitated by these commands, and the countless deaths in the columns of the forced marches attest to the wilful disregard for the sanctity of life. As one Nazi put it, 'they were sub-human creatures with no right to live.' The utter eradication of the camp at Treblinka along with all the inmates there serves as a clear indication of how Himmler expected his orders to be implemented.

Nevertheless, there are those who would protest that nothing at all sinister was planned for the concentration camp prisoners. While the testimonies of Kaufmann and Bassewitz-Behr certainly compound all the suspicions, they may simply have been trying to deflect attention away from their own complicity or exercising the expedient of laying the blame for their actions on more senior decision makers. In the event, it proved to be impossible to extract any further elaboration from Himmler concerning the intended fate for the Neuengamme and other camp inmates. The day after his capture by British forces on 22 May, he committed suicide before he could be interrogated.

Fundamental questions challenge the notion that it was not the intention to murder prisoners in cold blood. For what other possible reason would so many have been placed on these ships which, it is understood, had insufficient fuel to make a voyage of even the shortest duration? (One testimony stated that the *Cap Arcona*'s oil tanks had been emptied and filled with gas and that explosive charges had been attached to the tank tops.) If the exercise was genuinely well-intentioned, why were not just a reasonable number embarked in an orderly fashion rather than cramming them aboard to such an extent that not only was there barely room to move, but concern arose among the officers about the effect it was having on their ships' stability? Why, too, did those very same officers attempt to refuse orders unless they had clear knowledge of what was intended for the ships and their occupants, and why, at such a late stage of the war, would a vessel be converted into and registered as a hospital ship for a single short voyage across the Baltic? Last but not least, for what reason were all the documents relating to the Neuengamme concentration camp also put aboard the *Cap Arcona*?

The one thing we know for certain pertaining to the losses of the *Cap Arcona* and *Thielbek* is that the Allies, in pressing home their attacks on the remaining, disintegrating elements of the Nazi war machine, regrettably turned this unfolding evil deed into a tragedy.

CAP ARCONA (9/1927)

Hamburg South America Line, Hamburg, Germany

THIELBEK (1/1940)

Knohr & Burchard, Hamburg, Germany

The records at The National Archives in London reveal that in excess of 10,000 concentration camp prisoners from Neuengamme, Mittelbrau-Dora and Stütthof, near Danzig, were marched and trained in cattle wagons to the port of Lübeck guarded by SS troops, arriving there between 19 and 26 April 1945. Those from Stütthof camp were intercepted en route by Russian soldiers and freed, while some prisoners from Mittelbrau-Dora were also conveyed along the Baltic coast on barges towed by the tugs *Adler* and *Bussard*. The prisoners were a mixture, approximately half and half, of prisoners of war and Jewish civilians of many nationalities, all in some way the victims of Nazi ethnic-cleansing policies. The prisoners of war mainly comprised Russians, including many of those transported earlier from Norway (like those who had been aboard the *Rigel*) and Polish servicemen, among them some who had been captured back in 1939 when Germany had stormed Poland to precipitate the war. Of course, had they not been forcibly moved, all would certainly

The Hamburg Amerika Line luxury liner *Cap Arcona*, second only to the Navigazione Generale Italiana-owned *Augustus* as the largest ship on the South American run from Europe in the late 1920s. The advent of the Italian ship occurred just nine days before that of the *Cap Arcona* as both ships commenced their inaugural voyages to the La Plata ports. (Hamburg Sud-Amerika Linie)

have been liberated by the advancing British troops who were about to secure that region of north-east Germany.

Waiting for them, anchored offshore from Neustadt in landlocked Lübeck Bay, were two large ships: the three-funnelled *Cap Arcona*, the pre-war flagship of Hamburg South America Line on the passenger run from Hamburg to Rio de Janeiro, Montevideo and Buenos Aires; and the *Deutschland*, one of a quartet of trans-atlantic liners that had been operated by Hamburg America Line. In port at Lübeck were the smaller but modern cargo ships *Thielbek* and *Athen*, the latter a 1936-built 4,451 gross ton vessel owned by Deutsche Levante Linie, Hamburg, commanded by Captain Fritz Nobmann, which had been laid on to act as the ferry taking prisoners from the shore out to the anchored ships. The *Deutschland* had apparently been desig-nated as a hospital ship but there is no satisfactory explanation for this, as it does not seem to have had any relevance to the murderous plan about to be executed and she was not painted as such. It is only speculation, but the prisoners may have been advised this was her role to allay their concerns about what was happening. All four vessels had been laid on by Karl Kaufmann who, besides being the Gauleiter of Hamburg was, conveniently, the Reich Minister for Shipping (*Reichskommissar für die Seeschiffahrt*).

Earlier, on 17 April, the masters of the *Cap Arcona* and *Thielbek*, Captain Heinrich Bertram and Captain John Jacobsen, had been informed that they should prepare for

The cargo ship *Thielbek*, seen post-war as the *Reinbek*, the new name she received after she had been salvaged and repaired. She remained with the Knohr & Burchard company until 1961 when she was renamed *Magdalena*, ending her life under the fitting name *Old Warrior* when she was broken up at Split in 1974. (Rolf Meinecke)

a special operation. Though both vessels had been chartered by the *Kriegsmarine* for Operation Hannibal, they received orders that they were to be laid up temporarily at Lübeck. The *Cap Arcona*'s crew was reduced to a skeleton of just seventy-two men. She was not refuelled and, apart from a sufficient quantity for crew use alone, all lifebelts and lifejackets were removed and taken shore. It was said that other buoyant deck objects were also removed and the lifeboats were deliberately holed to render them unserviceable.

Later, the two captains were notified of the plan to load prisoners onto their ships. When they returned to the *Cap Arcona* and *Thielbek* to inform their crews of this, they made it known that they had both declined to co-operate.

As soon as the prisoners started to arrive at Lübeck, efforts to load the ships began. The *Thielbek*, still berthed in the port, had some temporary latrines installed and quantities of straw were dumped into her holds for the prisoners to sleep on. What followed over the next few days serves to show the conflict that arose between those involved in this inhumane operation: on the one hand the ships' officers and senior naval personnel who openly resisted the plans, and top-ranking SS officers who used intimidation and threats in order to achieve their aims on the other.

The precise dates are uncertain, different accounts placing events between 20 and 23 April, others between 23 and 26 April. Either way, the prisoners, still confined within the rail wagons, awaited the outcome of the manoeuvring between the parties, their plight worsening with every hour that passed. Strange as it may seem, representatives of the Swedish Red Cross were present as the scenes in Lübeck and Neustadt unfolded and they saw to it that all the prisoners, with the exception of the Russians, at least received a food parcel.

SS officers, headed by Sturmbannführer Christoph-Heinz Gehrig, arrived in Lübeck from Neuengamme and ordered Captain Nobmann to embark 2,352 prisoners along with some 280 guards aboard the *Athen* and take them out to the *Cap Arcona*. Nobmann initially refused but, threatened with execution by firing squad, he reluctantly complied with the order. When the *Athen* arrived alongside the *Cap Arcona*, Captain Bertram refused to accept the prisoners. After some negotiation, the *Athen* was ordered to be taken further out to sea where the bodies of already dead prisoners were thrown overboard before she was allowed to return to Lübeck.

Infuriated by Bertram's resistance, Karl Kaufmann had Hauptsturmführer Horn contact John Eggert, the chairman of the Hamburg South America Line, to get him to impress upon the *Cap Arcona*'s captain the need to accept the orders he had been given if he did not want to suffer the consequences. This he promptly did but Captain Bertram was not to be so easily coerced. He was deeply unhappy with what he either knew or had deduced was to be the planned destruction of his ship, let alone the slaughter of thousands of innocent lives, and he immediately contacted Admiral Engelhardt, the head of naval transport.

A stern quarter view of the *Cap Arcona* making a departure while engaged in commercial passenger service to South America. Ironically, in 1943 the *Cap Arcona* was used in the production of a feature-length propaganda epic inspired by Joseph Goebbels, entitled *Titanic*. (World Ship Society)

Engelhardt protested vehemently about the impounding of the *Cap Arcona*, *Deutschland* and the other ships all vital to the continuing Hannibal effort, and he delegated Captain Rössing from his staff to convey his objections to Kaufmann. However, Rössing was thwarted and never did get to see the Gauleiter. In a pre-emptive move, Kaufmann sent Gehrig and other SS officers back to Lübeck to take possession of the *Cap Arcona*, by force of arms if necessary.

For a second time, the *Athen* drew alongside the big former liner but once more Bertram refused to allow the cargo ship to secure her lines. While the *Athen* anchored nearby, SS officers Gehrig, Lewinski, Klebeck and others boarded a U-boat school launch to reach the *Cap Arcona* where they issued a written order to Captain Bertram to accept the *Athen's* prisoners or he would be arrested and summarily shot. Efforts to negotiate were in vain and, against his better judgement, Bertram was compelled to accede. The *Athen* was finally able to discharge. Embarkation continued over the days that followed aboard both the *Cap Arcona* and the *Thielbek*, still in port.

The conditions on board the ships were grim. There was little provision of food or water and the toilet facilities were hopelessly inadequate. Buckets were lowered into the holds but gastroenteritis was prevalent and the stench was overwhelming. Even while the ships were being loaded there were numerous fatalities from among the already sick and impoverished prisoners, the bodies of the victims callously discarded into the sea.

As the numbers boarding the *Cap Arcona* and *Thielbek* mounted, further objections were expressed, warning that neither ship had sufficient capacity to accommodate so many. Captain Bertram continued to protest vociferously, insisting that his ship was

The Deutsche Levante Linie's *Athen* of 1936 was used to convey concentration camp inmates from Lübeck and Neustadt to the *Cap Arcona* anchored in Lübeck Bay. Set afire and severely damaged, she was recovered after the war, restored and returned to service, surviving as the Polish-flag *Warynski* until 1970. (Author's collection)

being dangerously overloaded, but he was warned not to resist the orders of the SS and allow embarkation to continue. He was given reassurances at a conference he was asked to attend in Hamburg on 29 April that Count Bernadotte was arranging to have the prisoners taken to Sweden. In fact, apart from the White Buses internees, the release of only around 300 of the prisoners was secured through the intervention of International Red Cross representative Paul de Blonay. A day later, these few were placed aboard the small cargo ship *Hili Mathieson* at Neustadt bound for Sweden. To the evident irritation of SS officers, de Blonay was also able to secure the freedom of another, quite separate group of 1,450 prisoners waiting in Flensburg aboard the ship *Rheinfels*, having them transferred to the Red Cross ship *Homberg*. They, too, were taken to neutral Sweden.

It is estimated that in excess of 6,500 were herded into the *Cap Arcona*'s holds and deck spaces all over the ship under the guard of up to 600 SS troops. Nevertheless, some 1,998 were finally put back on the *Athen* and returned ashore, leaving from 4,000 to 4,500 still on the ship. In his testimony given later, a Julius Schaetzle stated the number of prisoners remaining on the *Cap Arcona* had been 3,985, but Paul Staszek, one of the ship's clerks, said the number could still have been as high as 5,500.

Meanwhile, the prisoners boarding the *Thielbek* had swollen to around 2,800 even though she was a fraction of the size of the *Cap Arcona*. On 2 May, at 14.00 hours, the *Thielbek*, having no power of her own, was towed into the bay off Neustadt where she was anchored near the two larger ships. The same day, British troops entered Lübeck supported by RAF aircraft as they continued their advance into the city.

The following day, RAF Hawker Mk 1B Typhoon fighter bombers from 83 Group of the 2nd Tactical Air Force, whose pilots had been alerted to the possibility of Nazi criminals attempting to escape by ship, came across the *Cap Arcona*, *Thielbek* and *Deutschland* anchored near Neustadt. The movements between shore and ship, as well as the massed crowds ashore, were quite discernible. Concluding that this was an instance of what they had been warned to look out for, they prepared to attack.

Led by Squadron Leader Derek L. Stevenson, the assault began in mid-afternoon, at approximately 14.45 hours, with aircraft of 184 Squadron based at RAF Hustedt initially targeting the hopelessly exposed *Cap Arcona*. Hit repeatedly by 60lb rockets and 500lb bombs, the stricken ship was soon ablaze from end to end. With the fire hoses destroyed by the flames and the lifeboat davits damaged, whether or not the lifeboats would ever have floated, the order was given to abandon ship. Meanwhile, the second wave of Typhoons of 198 Squadron from Plantlünne under Group Captain Johnny R. Baldwin turned their attention to the *Deutschland* and *Thielbek*.

The *Deutschland*, hit repeatedly and burning furiously, began to list. Nearby, the smaller *Thielbek* was swiftly reduced to a blazing wreck and she too sank in a matter of only minutes after the attack had begun. Of her 2,800 prisoners, only some 100 to 125 were rescued. In short order a third and fourth wave of aircraft from 193 and 263 Squadrons based at Ahlhorn continued to pound the ships, led respectively by Squadron Leaders Donald M. Taylor and Martin T.S. Rumbold, followed by a fourth wave of yet more aircraft from Ahlhorn, 197 Squadron under Squadron Leader Kenneth J. Harding.

Hamburg Amerika Line's *Deutschland* was also sunk during the RAF raids on Lübeck Bay on
3 May 1945. Although the exact numbers of her occupants or casualties are not known for certain,
some say she was virtually empty compared with the *Cap Arcona* and *Thielbek*; others that she had
2,000 women prisoners aboard. (Hapag-Lloyd)

The *Athen*, which had returned to Neustadt and was alongside the quay in the
course of loading the next contingent of prisoners to be taken out to the bay, possibly to the *Deutschland*, was not hit during the attacks. While the assault on the
anchored ships was in progress, British troops were in the process of taking the port
and, to avoid capture, the *Athen*'s officers, crew and the military guard had abandoned
the ship and disappeared ashore amid the confusion.

Meanwhile, back on the *Cap Arcona*, there were scenes of the utmost terror and
carnage. While aircraft continued to bomb and strafe the three ships, thousands were
trapped below deck in the burning liner, prevented from escape by SS guards and
suffocating in the flames and smoke. With little warning, at around 15.45 hours, the
Cap Arcona rolled over onto her port side coming to rest partially submerged in
shallow water and sealing the fate of most of those still within her. Some managed
to break free, clambering out onto her exposed hull. Other escapees jumped into
the sea, still extremely cold from the Baltic winter, only to perish from drowning or
hypothermia. But there were other hazards waiting for those who made it into the
water, for, still unaware of who it was they were shooting at, the Typhoons turned
their cannons on the prisoners struggling to reach the shore. Waiting there for the
few that managed to make it to dry land were SS troops who mowed them down
mercilessly by machine gun. Among those troops were 490 guards from the ship

The wreck of the *Cap Arcona* seen in the process of being cleared from Lübeck Bay in the late 1940s. (Crown Copyright)

who had been picked up by rescue boats in preference to prisoners in the water. Almost 4,200 people from the *Cap Arcona* died, for only 314 prisoners and a small number of crew members, among them Captain Bertram and Second Officer Thure Dommenget, survived the ordeal to inform the Allies of what had happened.

During the attack, a flight of F-6 Mustang aircraft from the US Army Air Force's 161st Tactical Reconnaissance Squadron arrived on the scene to photograph the burning and capsized wrecks and survivors in the sea, a grisly record of an appalling event, even for wartime.

Having captured Neustadt, the naval liaison officer to No.8 Corps, completely unaware that prisoners were aboard the ships being attacked in the bay, ordered that no craft whatsoever were to leave the harbour or from nearby Pelzerhachen, unwittingly preventing the continuation of any rescue.

Around 17.00 hours the attacks ended. An hour later, when the naval liaison officer was finally notified of the true situation, immediate arrangements were made to get rescue vessels to the scene. The *Deutschland* sank some hours later. Later still, the *Cap Arcona*'s burned-out hulk drifted ashore. (Both wrecks were removed and broken up in 1949.) After the prisoners aboard the *Athen* had been disembarked by the British military and taken into care, some of them, seeking vengeance, returned in the night to set the ship on fire. To prevent her from setting the jetty alight, she was towed out of the harbour and left to burn out. The *Athen* and the *Thielbek* were later salvaged and, after repairs, returned to service in the post-war years, the latter under the name *Reinbek*.

Besides the casualties on the *Cap Arcona* and *Thielbek*, an unknown number had probably perished on the *Deutschland*. It was said that all her crew escaped and, according to a sworn statement from her captain, that there had been no passengers aboard, but de Blonay, the Red Cross representative, received reports rumouring that up to 2,000 women prisoners had, in fact, been embarked. In the official Allied report, published later, it was speculated that, if she was not already occupied, it had been the intention to load her in like fashion to the *Cap Arcona* and *Thielbek*, an intention frustrated by the attack of the RAF planes. Arrangements were made for Royal Navy divers to search the wreck of the *Deutschland* but, if it exists, any report into what was discovered cannot now be found.

Among the senior German mercantile personnel killed on their ships were Captain Jacobsen, First Officer Andresen and First Engineer Lau of the *Thielbek*.

The RAF attack on the ships in Lübeck Bay on 3 May 1945 had collectively resulted in the deaths of almost 7,000 people, few of them enemy personnel, in what was probably the worst friendly fire incident of the Second World War. Since then, questions have been repeatedly raised as to whether the tragedy had been avoidable. They arise from the many claims that the British authorities had been warned in advance of the presence of ships carrying prisoners.

A testimonial, purported to have come from an unnamed British pilot who had flown in the reconnaissance flight that found the *Cap Arcona*, *Deutschland* and *Thielbek* (which cannot be verified), asserted that he had suggested to Allied Intelligence that the ships should be left alone as they would be valuable after the war's end and that he expressed surprise when he subsequently discovered they had been attacked. As no reference to a document containing such a claim can be found, it may be no more than hearsay. Yet another claim in documents held by the Dutch Institute of War Documentation (NIOD) notes that the British government had been warned by the government of Sweden that prisoners were aboard ships in the region of Lübeck and southern Denmark. However, it is not known whether this was referring to their own citizens being repatriated under the White Buses operation.

A more specific charge against the British is contained in the once-secret official report on the investigations carried out by Major Noel O. Till in June 1945, which is now among the government documents in The National Archives at Kew, London. It reveals that British ground forces already in the Lübeck area had been informed about the existence of prison ships in the bay off Neustadt on 2 May, the day before the attack was launched, by Paul de Blonay of the International Red Cross. He had informed Major General Roberts, commanding the 11th Armoured Division, of this and he was assured that a message to this effect had been transmitted to higher authority. An RAF intelligence officer attached to 83 Group RAF is reported as admitting under questioning that messages had been received on 2 May, alerting them to the presence of ships loaded with concentration camp prisoners and, although there had been adequate time to convey this information on to the operational squadrons, through some oversight it had not been. The headquarters of the 2nd Tactical Air Arm at Süchteln certainly had no knowledge of the transportation or boarding of concentration camp prisoners.

While this would, on the face of it, place much of the responsibility for the tragedy on the shoulders of the RAF personnel who had failed to pass this vital information on to the squadron commanders and pilots, it has to be balanced against other intelligence that had been forwarded simultaneously. Allied Intelligence had also received signals informing them that a large number of high-ranking Nazi officers and SS troops were boarding ships in ports along Germany's Baltic coastline with the intention of escaping to Norway where they were to make a last stand that could have extended the war and cost countless additional casualties.

A worrying dimension of the *Cap Arcona–Thielbek* disaster that has recently emerged is the increasingly outspoken claim that it should be regarded as a British war crime. Describing it as a particularly barbaric attack, one such source calls it a violation of international law and suggests that had Germany rather than Britain ended the war as the victor, the British pilots and their commanders could have been tried and executed as war criminals. There is no question that the British military did receive advice from several quarters alerting them to Nazi plans to apparently ship concentration camp prisoners out of the collapsing Reich without knowing where to or for what purpose. The failure, for which criticism of the British would be justified, was that this intelligence was not subsequently passed on to forward bases, although it is not known how explicit or specific the warnings that had been transmitted were, and that orders were not issued for aircrews to exercise caution when attacking German shipping. Of course, if there had been doubts about the reliability of the alerts received or the information they contained, coupled with conflicting advice in other intelligence reports, it is difficult to see how, in the muddled circumstances as the war was ending, unequivocal orders for restraint or intervention could have been appropriately worded.

What is beyond question is that the crews of the RAF bombers that attacked the ships anchored in Lübeck Bay had no idea that they had prisoners aboard them. They were following their commands in accordance with Operation Order No.73, which called for the 'Destruction of the concentration of enemy shipping in Lübeck Bay west of Poel Island and northwards to the border of the security zone'. The outcome of the bombardment, while appallingly tragic, was completely unforeseen and unintentional. The first time any of these flying officers became aware that by their actions they had slaughtered Allies and friends was as late as 1975.

When it comes to attributing blame, those who would level accusations of war crimes at the British should remember that if the Nazis had not unecessarily placed those prisoners aboard the *Cap Arcona* and *Thielbek* in the first place, then there could not have been a tragedy. They should remind themselves, too, of what had been intended for those prisoners by the Nazis; that had the Allies not intervened when they did they would all have been killed when the ships were scuttled; and they should reflect on the fact that many of those who struggled ashore having escaped those floating coffins were callously murdered by SS troops waiting for them.

Much is made of the passage in Major Till's report that criticises the dissemination of the RAF's intelligence, which, had it been handled better, may have prevented the tragedy. Conveniently, though, little attention is given to the following words that also form part of the summary:

Memorials to the *Cap Arcona* and *Thielbek* disasters are at Neustadt … (Rolf Meinecke)

… and elsewhere along the Baltic coastline, as reminders of this appalling double tragedy. (Genet/VW Polonia)

The conclusions [reached elsewhere in the report] do not in any way affect the responsibility of the German authorities for placing these prisoners on board these ships.

Whatever the ultimate intention, these prisoners were in fact placed on large undefended ships in the middle of a bay, with no adequate life-saving appliances, at a time when all shipping around the coast of Germany was constantly being attacked by the British RAF.

It is submitted that this was done either (a) with the deliberate hope that they would be exterminated by the RAF, or at any rate (b) with such total disregard for their safety that the act becomes an act of manslaughter, akin to murder.

In wartime, good men are obliged to do things that in any other circumstances they would find repugnant, but guilt for the consequences of their actions should unquestionably rest with those who would knowingly place the innocent in the line of fire, either as human shields or in circumstances where the likelihood of being killed was virtually certain. Among those good men was Captain Heinrich Bertram of the *Cap Arcona*, who was completely exonerated of any wrongdoing. Major Till said of him: 'He did his best to prevent the prisoners from being placed on his ship and he appears to have done all that was possible when the ship was attacked.'

Mass graves were dug to bury the huge number of bodies of the victims of the *Cap Arcona* and *Thielbek* disaster, many of which continued to wash ashore for days and weeks afterwards. There are now memorials to the victims at Neustadt in Holstein and other places in the Lübeck area, in the cemetery at Grömitz and at Klütz, Scharbeutz and on Poel Island, all of which commemorate those terrible events and keep alive the memory of so many people needlessly killed within days of their salvation.

⊷⊶⊷

Another major shipping disaster along the lines of that of the *Cap Arcona* and *Thielbek* occurred later that year on the far side of the world from Europe, near Japan. Unlike the disaster in Lübeck Bay, which took place just days before the end of hostilities, the loss of the *Ukishima Maru* happened nine days *after* the end of the war in the Far East.

Mention has already been made of 'comfort women' being ferried to the Japanese Empire's outposts for the bodily pleasures of the men stationed far from home on distant bases; principally, no doubt, the officer ranks. Contrary to the impression that term may imply, though, these were not all government-funded Japanese prostitutes. Many were sex slaves, women forcibly removed from Korea but also China, not only for the benefit of soldiers overseas but also for those military personnel running work camps and forced-labour industries in Japan itself.

Korea had been annexed by Japan in 1910 for its rich mineral resources and it was subsequently colonised. Every effort was made to suppress Korean national identity: the language was banned, important historical artefacts were plundered and in all respects, the Japanese way of life, law and custom was imposed upon the Korean people. The Japanese, who were reviled by the ordinary Korean people as an unwelcome and brutal colonial presence, themselves regarded and treated the occupied population as inferior, worthy only of menial and degrading employment as a slave workforce. During the Second World War, this source of labour was exploited to the maximum and, besides 'comfort women' of Korean origin, tens of thousands of Korean workmen with their families were shipped to Japan. Many were sent to Aomori prefecture in the north of Honshu where, on a remote island, they were employed digging a network of underground tunnels and storage facilities in a secret military base.

With the end of the war on 15 August 1945, the complex largely complete, the Koreans – forced labourers and sex slaves alike – were organised into parties for return to their homeland.

UKISHIMA MARU (3/1937)

Osaka Shosen Kaisha, Osaka, Japan

The eight-year-old passenger-cargo ship *Ukishima Maru* was requisitioned for the task of transporting home the Korean nationals. As such, on 22 August at Ominato in Mutsu Bay, where she had been directed prior to the capitulation, she boarded a total of 3,725 Koreans, ostensibly for the voyage to Busan. At this point, two versions of events emerge: the Japanese perspective of what followed and the Korean view. What is not disputed is that from the port of embarkation the *Ukishima Maru*, after departing at 22.00 hours, headed south along Japan's west coast for the naval base of Maizuru, near Kyoto, rather than directly across the Sea of Japan to Korea. She arrived in Maizuru Bay, off Jajima Island, two days later, on 24 August. There, at 17.20 hours, she was blown apart in a massive explosion, broke in two and sank, killing most of her occupants.

The Japanese claimed, without offering an explanation for the ship's deviation of course, that the *Ukishima Maru* had struck an American naval mine. It seems that the American occupying officials concurred with this claim, though how they reached that conclusion without having apparently witnessed the incident is difficult to comprehend. Furthermore, the Japanese government's official figure for the number of casualties gave those killed as 524 Koreans and twenty-five Japanese, without offering any satisfactory account for the whereabouts of the very large number of individuals who they claimed had survived the sinking.

The Korean standpoint could not be more different. Both the North and South Korean governments hold the view that the *Ukishima Maru* had been deliberately scuttled in a war crime perpetrated under the culpable influence of the vanquished Japanese government, in order to conceal evidence of the hidden Japanese military facility from the occupying Americans. To that end, after the *Ukishima Maru* had arrived at Maizuru, it is claimed that the hatches were sealed, trapping the passengers in the holds and, following that, explosives were taken deep inside the hull and placed precisely where they would break the ship's back. On detonation, the *Ukishima Maru* sank within minutes. The Koreans also protest that the number killed was much greater than the official Japanese figure; that there were only around eighty survivors, meaning that about 3,650 had perished.

An impression of the *Ukishima Maru* on auxiliary service during the Pacific War and prior to her deliberate sinking while packed with Korean nationals after hostilities had ended. (Kihachiro Ueda)

One of the survivors testified in 2005 that prior to the explosion, the majority of the Japanese officers and crew had hastily abandoned the ship. The Japanese records show that 230 of their 255 naval personnel made it safely ashore. It has also been argued that there is no plausible explanation for the disappearance of 3,200 Koreans, who were certainly not rescued.

The Japanese suggest that the Korean claims of wholesale slaughter are exaggerated, based on Leftist propaganda emanating from radical members of the Korean League. In response, the North Korean government points to the deliberate suppression by the Japanese government of the report of an official investigation compiled in 1950, which supposedly contains a 'verified' passenger list. Apart from denying the existence of the report, since disproven, other false assertions made by the Japanese have since come to light.

Arising from this, the surviving victims and their families have pursued claims against the Japanese government, filing a lawsuit that sought compensation in the sum of 8 billion yen (approximately £65 million/$100 million in 2012 terms), an official apology and the return of the remains of victims, which are currently kept in a shrine in the Yutenji Temple, Tokyo.

Matters were complicated by the fact that the San Francisco Peace Treaty of 1952, between the USA and Japan, unilaterally stripped Koreans of Japanese nationality, which, as the citizens of a colony, they had previously held. This rendered them ineligible for compensation as Japanese war victims or bereaved families. Effectively, from that point the *Ukishima Maru* incident became a diplomatic issue at State level, although the Korean governments (both North and South) nevertheless left it to individuals to pursue a case for damages and the acknowledgement of the offence.

On 27 August 2001, in the Kyoto District Court, a settlement of sorts was reached whereby the Japanese government agreed to pay the paltry sum of 45 million yen (approximately £265,000/$375,000) to just fifteen South Korean claimants who were either surviving victims or the relatives of survivors. The claims of a further sixty-five plaintiffs were rejected, on the grounds that their relationships to Korean casualties or survivors of the *Ukishima Maru* were in doubt. The court also denied the request for the return of the victims' remains and ruled against the demand for an official apology.

Notably, though, in a rare castigation of Japan's wartime conduct, the Kyoto Court held the Japanese government of the time to be culpable of failing in its duty to transport the Korean passengers in safety, despite a confused situation and the ambiguous status of the Koreans and their employers. Of particular interest, too, was the judge's speculation on the cause. While the theory that the explosion had been caused by a mine was upheld, he conceded that it was quite possible that the mine had not been American but had been deliberately planted by the Japanese military to cause the explosion.

As one commentator has said, the full and undisputed facts of the *Ukishima Maru* case will never be known, but Japanese contempt for the native Korean was without doubt at its root. A South Korean activist, Chou Jae Jui, commented: 'Putting together all the various pieces of evidence, it's likely that the Japanese soldiers committed mass murder by bombing the ship.' He added that, whereas the ship's passengers had been transformed from enslaved colonials to free citizens of a newly independent Korea, the disgruntled Japanese had been reduced from proud warriors to humiliated servants of a defeated regime, and it was that which may have motivated their appalling deed. The controversy surrounding both the cause of the sinking and the actual numbers of passengers and dead will remain unresolved, the precise facts shrouded forever in mystery.

The wreck, lying close to the shore near Maizuru, was later cleared. A film of the *Ukishima Maru* incident, made in North Korea in 2001 and screened on the fifty-sixth anniversary of the disaster, came under criticism when comparisons were drawn between it and the movie *Titanic*, referencing James Cameron's recent crowd-pulling blockbuster about the loss of White Star's flagship. Survivor Chung Ki-Young disparagingly challenged such a parallel. 'There was no time for such romance [aboard the *Ukishima Maru*],' he said. 'It was hell!'

12

NOT ALWAYS AT SEA

On 21 April 1865, the Mississippi paddle steamer *Sultana* suffered a boiler explosion so severe that she sank, a raging inferno, off Tagelman's Landing, 8 miles north of Memphis. Despite the fact that she was operating on an inland river, the *Sultana* was not a small ship. At 1,719 gross tons, she was as big as some of the smaller short-sea ferries that operated across the English Channel and Irish Sea until as recently as the 1950s.

Although licensed for just 276 passengers, she was carrying 2,309 people besides her crew of eighty-five. All but seventy of them were Northern prisoners, many invalided, being returned home at the end of the American Civil War. As a result of the sinking, all but 741 of those aboard the *Sultana* lost their lives, either killed in the explosion, in the fire that the explosion started, or by drowning. It remains, to this day, the worst ever American maritime disaster.

Despite having occurred almost fifty years prior to the loss of the RMS *Titanic* in April 1912, the loss of the *Sultana* has a particular relevance to this publication. With a death toll of 1,653, the loss of the *Sultana* was more grievous than that of the *Titanic* and, as such, it demonstrates that the sinking of the *Titanic* never was the world's worst maritime disaster.

The *Sultana* incident also reveals that close proximity to land, and so within the easy reach of would-be rescuers, may be of little consequence and have little influence on the potentially calamitous outcome of a shipping accident. Estuarine and coastal vessels that fall victim of collisions, severe weather, strandings or other hazards, given an unfavourable mixture of circumstances, are just as much at risk of sinking before help can arrive and, if heavily loaded, they can suffer equally extreme numbers of casualties. A string of conspicuous passenger ship misadventures from over the past twenty or so years bears witness to this, including the *Herald of Free Enterprise*, *Dona Marylin*, *Salem Express*, *Moby Prince* and *Dashun*, as well as the *Dona Paz* and *Le Joola*, described in the next chapter.

⊷⟺⟺⊶

Another country which, like the United States, has long and wide navigable waterways is China, notably the Yangtse and Zhu rivers. Some of the steamships that operated on these rivers and their tributaries, though necessarily of a shallow

The scene at Tagelman's Landing, Memphis, on 23 April 1865, after the explosion of her boilers caused the *Sultana* to catch fire and founder. (Library of Congress)

draught, were large in size; in some cases of sea-going proportions. Three incidents that involved vessels of this type, which occurred in this arena, are among those that rival the *Titanic* for gravity.

Each of the incidents described on the following pages was associated with the Chinese Civil War that erupted, initially in skirmishes and localised acts of violence, after the end of the Second World War, following defeat of the Japanese on the Chinese mainland. They encompass losses involving regular troops and refugees.

The uneasy alliance agreed between the Nationalists under Chiang Kai-shek and the Communists under Mao Tse-tung, to combat a common foe, broke down once the struggle for domestic domination resumed. Hostilities between the parties had preceded the war with Japan for there had been a state of open conflict between Communist guerrillas and the Kuomintang since as far back as 1927.

In its early phases, following resumption of open hostilities in April 1946, the Civil War proper was centred on north-west China and the Communist stronghold of Yan'an, which the numerically superior and better-equipped Nationalists took in early 1947. It proved to be a limited and catalytic success. The setback stimulated a massive Communist counter-offensive, which proved, ultimately, to be unstoppable.

HAI CHU ex-*Kaishu Maru* ex-*Hang Cheong* (1923)

China Merchants S.N. Co., China

The dust of the Second World War had barely settled when the dormant antipathy between the Chinese Nationalists and Communists resurfaced, compelling the movement of forces to those areas where pitched engagements were already taking place, or to locations where strategic offensives were planned.

The Nationalists' objective was to take the battle to the Communists and attack their strongholds in the mountains of Shaanxi province in north-west China, targeting in particular their main headquarters at Yan'an. This required the movement of armies stationed in southern China, which earlier had been engaged in fighting Japanese forces along the borders with Vietnam and Burma. The National Revolutionary Army's 8th Army was moved to Guangzhou (Canton) in readiness for transportation up the coast to Shanghai, from where military trains would take them into the hinterland to prepare for combat.

Among the ships requisitioned for the conveyance of these soldiers to Hong Kong, where they were to board bigger ships, was the small river steamer *Hai Chu*, which had originally carried the name *Hang Cheong* under British registry after her completion at the Taikoo Dockyard in Hong Kong. Though propelled by twin screws, she had only small six-cylinder engines capable of a maximum of 57hp, and she had only two decks. Although the 90-mile voyage down the Zhu River was only of short duration and in sheltered waters, the number of people the *Hai Chu* carried on that final, fateful passage was truly bewildering. Exact figures do not appear to exist but at the time, Lloyd's List reported that the vessel was carrying about 2,000 soldiers, 100 civilian passengers and a crew of 90 under her Norwegian master, Captain Thorbjornsen.

The ship sailed on 9 November 1945 and had completed half the journey when, as she was passing Boca Tigris at the point where the Zhu River enters the broader expanse of water north of Macau (Macao), she ran onto a mine. It was almost certainly an uncleared Japanese or American mine from the recent world war that had broken free to enter the main shipping channel.

Typical of Chinese river steamers, the *Hai Chu* had a shallow draught and a flat bottom. The detonation ripped out the vessel's bottom and she sank within a few minutes. The heavily equipped Chinese troops did not stand a chance once pitched into the sea and dragged under by the weight of their uniforms and weapons. Just as it is today, the waterway was bustling with small craft and three motor junks that witnessed the incident swiftly proceeded to the scene to render assistance. Despite their efforts, they were unable to rescue more than an eighth of the *Hai Chu's* occupants. The stricken ship had sunk before they reached her so that their emergency effort mainly entailed dragging survivors out of the sea.

More than 1,700 men of the Chinese 8th Army lost their lives; only 240 were saved. Of the civilians aboard the *Hai Chu*, seventy-eight died, alongside sixty-nine crew casualties. Captain Thorbjornsen was one of the survivors.

The setback the *Hai Chu* tragedy caused the Chinese Nationalists paled into insignificance, despite its magnitude, when compared with the huge casualties that were to be sustained during the next four years of fighting in the Civil War.

⁘⇒◦⇐⁘

The assault on the Communist base at Yan'an, launched in July 1946, proved to be successful and was accomplished during March 1947 with the taking of the city. But as the catalyst for a tenacious counter-offensive, these successes were followed by a sequence of major reverses. First, the Communist Chinese People's Liberation Army (PLA) opened an offensive to push their Nationalist opponents out of Shaanxi. Simultaneously, marching across country to the north-east, they sought to take control of Manchuria, filling the vacuum left there after Soviet forces had begun to withdraw in March 1946.

By late 1948, the city of Xi'an was taken as the Nationalists lost control of Shaanxi in central China, and when Shenyang in Liaoning was captured it left the Nationalists with only a tenuous grip on China's north-eastern provinces. Despite calls from General Chiang Kai-shek to resist the Communist advance, it was obvious to his subordinates that the dwindling Nationalist units had to be withdrawn to avoid a complete rout and to permit the strengthening of a new defensive line across on the far side of the Gulf of Chihli (Bo Hai) in Shandong province. To achieve this, the port of Yingkou had to be secured and kept open to permit ships to evacuate as many Nationalist soldiers as possible.

HSUAN HUAI ex-*Teng 1402* ex-*Northern Master* ex-*Samuel R. Curwen* (2/1945)

Ministry of Transportation, Republic of China

In the decisive Liao-Shen campaign from 12 September to 2 November 1948, the Nationalist Revolutionary Army's (NRA) 52nd Army was initially deployed in defensive positions south of Shenyang, in the Anshan-Liaoyang region. A force some 250,000 soldiers strong, it was the only surviving, virtually intact unit remaining to the Nationalists in Manchuria. However, when, soon after the campaign began, the Communists first besieged and later captured Jinzhou, it cut off the sole overland supply route to the 52nd Army and other NRA units. Attempts were made to relieve Jinzhou but they resulted in the defeat of the NRA Eastern Advance Army at Tashan, west of Dalian, between 10 and 16 October; and the NRA Western Advance Army at Liao'xi between 8 and 28 October 1948, securing for the Communists the area south of Yingkou.

Accepting that provision had to be made for a withdrawal of surviving units, the NRA 52nd Army was finally ordered to fall back and secure the port of Yingkou on Liadong Bay, then held by the Communist PLA. This objective was accomplished on 24 October 1948 and, following the loss of Shenyang and Anshan on 27 October,

An N3-S-A2 type standard cargo ship, of which the ill-fated *Hsuan Huai* (ex-*Northern Master*, ex-*Samuel R. Curwen*) was another example; this is the *Rondane*, completed originally as the *Kimball Harlow*. These vessels were commonly referred to as 'jeeps'. (Kenneth Wightman collection)

arrangements were immediately started to evacuate the remnants of the Advanced Army's forces using naval vessels based at Huludao.

Within three days, the PLA had again encircled Yingkou, increasing the urgency of the troop evacuation. Early in the morning of 31 October, two ships left for Huludao carrying the NRA HQ staff and the 52nd Army's 25th Division. Meanwhile, men of the 52nd Army's 2nd Division, some 6,000 men of the 4th, 5th and 6th Regiments, were boarding the steamer *Hsuan Huai*.

The *Hsuan Huai* was a small American-built cargo ship (not a river steamer like other vessels described in this chapter), which had been sold after a two-year spell under British ownership as the China Merchants Steam Navigation Co.'s *Northern Master* to the Republic of China's Ministry of Transportation, along with seventeen more ships of the same class. Built to a standard design, they were classified as N3-S-A2 type under the categorisation system of the United States Maritime Commission.

Space aboard the *Hsuan Huai* was severely restricted. Soldiers of the 5th Regiment and part of the 6th were ordered to occupy the lower holds. The remainder of the 6th Regiment, along with all the men of the 4th Regiment, were accommodated in the upper holds and on the main deck. According to the accounts of survivors, drums of petroleum had also been stowed in the holds along with a quantity of ammunition. Lloyd's List confirmed this, indicating that the volume of petrol aboard the *Hsuan Huai* was of the order of 3,000 barrels.

On 2 November 1948, fire broke out aboard the *Hsuan Huai*, attributed to the soldiers smoking below deck. It is not known whether they had been ordered to refrain

The smouldering and listing *Hsuan Huai* as she was found at Yingkou on 2 November 1948. Looking on, with his rifle slung over his shoulder, is a Communist soldier from the People's Liberation Army. (People's Liberation Army, PRC)

from this activity because of the volatility of the ship's cargo. Either way, the fire had soon taken a grip in the ship, still moored alongside the quay, and efforts to extinguish it by soldiers and sailors were unsuccessful. It can be concluded that the sequence of events was rapid in the extreme and worsened dramatically before any kind of disembarkation was commenced. When the ammunition and petrol exploded it triggered panic as the *Hsuan Huai* was engulfed in flames. Troops on the main deck and upper areas jumped overboard to escape, although many drowned. As for those who were located deeper inside the ship, they were trapped below as men rushed the ladders and stairways, blocking them in the panic and preventing an orderly abandonment.

According to the NRA 52nd Army's official history, the disaster claimed the lives of 3,000 officers and men. Those who survived were placed aboard smaller vessels, which were hastened out of Yingkou to avoid capture by the PLA, which by then was close to retaking the port. From Huludao, they were taken on to Shanghai where they fought a valiant defensive action north of the city, along a line from Yuepu to Liuhang between 10 and 27 May 1949. Thereafter, the 52nd Army was disbanded.

When the PLA entered Yingkou that same day, 2 November, they found the smouldering wreck of the *Hsuan Huai* in the harbour and filmed it for a documentary, which has since been compiled with other footage under the title *Iron Horses and Frozen Rivers – The War of Liberation in Manchuria*.

The *Hsuan Huai* disaster was for many years (and, for that matter, still is in some sources) referred to as the loss of an un-named Chinese troopship with 6,000 lives – the figure incorrectly referring to the total number of people who had embarked on the ship. *The Times* of Monday 6 December 1948, quoting an Associated Press correspondent, reported the incident in much this fashion in a story under the heading 'Chinese Shipping Disasters – Two Steamers Sunk by Explosions', the second ship referred to being the *Kiang Ya* (see overleaf). The report was as follows:

A Chinese merchant ship exploded, killing 6,000 Chinese, mostly troops, during the Chinese Government's evacuation of Yingkow, Manchuria, a month ago. Most of the 6,000 victims were part of the Chinese Government's 52nd Army whose remnants are now manning the Nanking–Shanghai defence line.

The disaster was disclosed by official Nanking sources to reporters asking for comment on the Yangtse disaster which had been described as 'the greatest maritime disaster'. 'It wasn't' the officials said, then told of last month's Yingkow disaster.

In the confusion of the evacuation and the Nationalist government's rapidly unravelling grip on power, Lloyd's of London and other agencies never obtained the ship's identity. The *Hsuan Huai* remained anonymous until recent research in official Chinese documents, notably the volumes of 'Guo Gong Sheng Si Da Jue Zhou' ('Decisive Battles of the Chinese Civil War'), revealed her identity. Photographs of the burning ship taken by Communist photographers clearly show her name in Chinese characters on the side of her hull and in the letters of the English phonetic alphabet at her bow.

⊷══◎══⊷

With the loss of Manchuria, followed soon after by defeat near Xuzhou in the Huai-Hai campaign, the Communist forces further extended their area of control, and by the end of January 1949 they occupied much of the Jiangsu, Anhui and Henan provinces along with Beijing, which was established as the new capital of China.

Thanks to the stubborn resistance of units, such as the surviving members of the 52nd Army, the area south of the Yangtse remained in Nationalist hands through to April 1949. It was not until then that the cities of Nanking and, two months later, Shanghai fell to the Communists. Well before that date, as if defeat was expected and it would only be a matter of time before the Nationalist rule would collapse altogether, refugees were already scrambling aboard ships all along the eastern coastline to get to Taiwan across the Strait of Formosa, before it was too late.

KIANG YA ex-*Hsing Ya Maru* (12/1939)

China Merchants S.N. Co., China

One such vessel pressed into service for this desperate human flight was the *Kiang Ya*, a Japanese-built coastal steamer that had been acquired in 1947 for operation on Yangtse routes. Just nine years old, she was certificated to take a maximum of 2,200 passengers, many on deck. Overcrowding by refugees on departing ships was rife, and besides ticketed passengers, large numbers of stowaways managed to get aboard, mingling in the crowds who jostled up the gangways and onto deck. Officials who were charged with checking all who boarded were so overwhelmed by the human tide that beset them, they found it an impossible task to undertake reliably.

The embarkation of the *Kiang Ya* on 3 December 1948 very much fitted this description. She had set out earlier from Nanking where she had taken aboard 2,250

The *Kiang Ya*, built originally for Japanese owners, sported a distinctive goalpost-style foremast just ahead of her bridge. (Press Association)

paying passengers, already in excess of her permitted complement. Contemporary accounts state that this number had been swollen by up to 1,200 stowaways. A call at Shanghai, prior to continuing to Ningbo in Zhejiang Province, south of Hangzhou Bay, had added to the difficulties and it was estimated that as many as 4,000 people were aboard her when she sailed out of the Huangpu River past Wusong at 18.30 hours in the early evening.

During the night, as the *Kiang Ya* was passing south of Tung-sha, some 30 miles from the Wusong breakwater beyond the island of Hengshxiang, her master was compelled to make an evasive manoeuvre to avoid a collision with two junks that lay in her path. The change of course took her beyond the main shipping channel and, before the helmsman could direct her back onto it, a huge explosion occurred at her aft end crippling her engines, throwing the ship into darkness and, of greatest importance, disabling her radio room so there was no means of calling for aid. The *Kiang Ya* began immediately to sink at the stern, and after only a very short interval had settled upright on the bottom in shallow water with just her upper works and funnel above sea level.

From this point, the *Kiang Ya* incident unfolded much as that of the *Titanic* thirty-six years earlier, with over-optimistic claims transmitted to press agencies regarding the fate of her occupants. For the *Titanic*, the headlines of at least one of the early American editions had claimed 'All Saved From Titanic After Collision', a grossly erroneous announcement that sadly raised the hopes of waiting relatives, only for them to be cruelly dashed as more accurate news emerged. It was much the same for the *Kiang Ya* as officials from the China Merchants Steam Navigation Co., her owners, sought to minimise the consequences of the incident.

Initially, it was stated that the ship had been carrying only 2,150 passengers and that it was not possible to confirm claims that from 300 to 700 people had lost their lives. Officials asserted that rescue craft were continuing to search for survivors and most of the *Kiang Ya*'s occupants had reached safety on small craft and that, as they were widely dispersed, precise numbers for either casualties or survivors could not be given.

It was true that launches and other small rescue vessels *had* gone to the *Kiang Ya*'s aid and that survivors had been helped ashore along the banks of the Yangtse, but those very survivors challenged the owners' statements, arguing that in excess of 4,000 people had been aboard the ship.

It seems that, in the wake of the explosion, the *Kiang Ya* had settled quickly and besides those killed by the blast many were drowned, trapped in the lower decks. Despite the owners' protestations, it transpired that the *Kiang Ya* had been so severely crowded that the gangways and staircases had been completely obstructed by sleeping passengers. Those who had been on the upper decks and open spaces were more fortunate but had to wait for hours standing in water up to their waists before rescue arrived. The effects of exposure, in the freezing weather of the Chinese winter, also took its toll.

First on the scene, around three hours after the mine discharged, was the steamship *Hwafoo*, which appears to have come across the wrecked *Kiang Ya* more by chance than design. Discovering the desperate situation of the victims, she immediately radioed for help, belatedly setting in motion the acutely needed rescue operation.

Over the hours and days that followed, as survivors, many of them seriously injured, were taken to hospitals in Shanghai, a more realistic picture of the outcome of the disaster was revealed. By the end of 5 December 1948, in an announcement in the independent daily newspaper *Takungpoo*, the China Merchants Co. declared that 1,000 had been rescued, including 122 crew members. Out of 1,600 still missing, (a surreptitious disclosure that, in fact, there had been at least 2,700 aboard the *Kiang Ya*), it was thought that most had been landed at points well beyond the city's limits, and knowledge of them and their whereabouts would become known as information filtered through.

The very next day, and over the three days following, the figures for casualties and those rescued were repeatedly readjusted, exposing the true extent of the tragedy. Even after the death toll had risen to 3,000, with 140 or so bodies recovered, it was conceded that as many as 2,000 more could still be unaccounted for. Later, the number of missing increased to 3,520 with 700 people, or thereabouts, known to have been picked up.

Today, the figure of 3,920 lost lives is attributed to the *Kiang Ya* disaster. However, this may be a considerable over-estimate even though the more accurate number remains extreme. Nevertheless, there is the suggestion of considerable exaggeration of the casualty figure. In November 1997, the results of a thorough investigation into the loss of the *Kiang Ya* were published by the People's Communication Press in a book entitled *A Brief History of Navigation on the Yangtse River*. Its author, Chen Jianguo, was the deputy chief editor of a commission created to compile the history.

Chen Jianguo and his team searched through countless documents – inquiry reports, survivors' accounts and newspaper articles. From these it was deduced that there had been 3,253 passengers aboard the *Kiang Ya*, among them some 400 disbanded Kuomintang soldiers plus 2,607 civilians who had paid for the privilege of taking passage on the ship. The remaining 246 passengers comprised, besides stowaways, many un-ticketed friends and relatives of the 191-strong crew.

Chen Jianguo adds that the records show that 2,353 victims were identified, which means that the number rescued was at least 1,091, although it had to be said that some of those survivors may have died subsequently from their injuries or from the effects of exposure.

If there was dispute about the numbers of occupants and victims of the *Kiang Ya* then there was also much speculation about the cause of the explosion; Lloyd's List reports, in issues from 4 to 9 December 1948, follow the debate. At first, the China Merchants Steam Navigation Co. blamed the Communists for the detonation. A spurious claim, attributed to an un-named survivor, said that when two Communist junks had approached the *Kiang Ya* explosives had been thrown from them onto the passenger vessel's deck. Later, it was admitted that the vessel might have struck a wartime mine.

The debate continued with several theories conjectured. Among the possibilities was an explosion of combustible cargo; a boiler explosion – discounted after divers surveyed the ship's interior; a time bomb planted by Communists or, as already suspected, a mine.

On 7 December, a special Chinese/American Technical Mission was sent to the scene to perform a thorough examination of the ship with the aid of a team of forty divers. The specialist group was drawn from Shanghai's foremost shipbuilding technicians aided by two Americans who were experts in explosives. Their conclusion was that a mine was the most likely cause of the blast, although the possibility that hidden explosives may have been responsible was never completely ruled out.

The wreck of the *Kiang Ya* was later salvaged with the aid of Japanese experts after the Civil War had ended. Fully repaired, she was restored to service in 1959 under the name *Dong Fang Hong 8* and operated by the China People's Steam Navigation Co., Shanghai. She was finally disposed of for scrap around 1992.

TAI PING ex-*Choluteca* (1921)

China Pacific Shipping and Trading Co., China

The exodus to Taiwan, as the Chinese Civil War proceeded towards its culmination, encompassed emergency sailings from ports all along the Chinese coastline as Communist forces pushed eastwards across central and southern China; each ship was packed with anguished passengers running the gauntlet of the weather, sea conditions and Communist patrols. Among them were other vessels that never reached their destinations, adding to the growing roster of losses.

Another major disaster involved a ship that sailed from Shanghai on 27 January 1949, barely ten months before General Chiang Kai-shek and his staff and ministers fled to Taiwan, signalling the end of the Civil War and the establishment of unchallenged Communist rule from that October.

At 23.45 hours, after leaving port with almost 1,600 people on board, the vast majority of them refugees, the *Tai Ping* was in collision in foggy conditions with the cargo steamer *Kien Yuan* bound from Keelung for Shanghai with coal. The point of impact was approximately 4.5 miles south of the lighthouse on Bonham Island (Bai-Chieh Shan) in the Bonham Strait (Bai Jiexia) that runs between the Zhoushan (Chusan) islands.

The *Kien Yuan*, owned by Kiensing Steamship Co., was the former *Oise* of Compagnie Générale Transatlantique (French Line). She sank within five minutes. The *Tai Ping* remained afloat for only twenty minutes, her vast complement unexpectedly finding themselves at the mercy of the sea with little help at hand. She sank off Qushandao, one of the islands of the Zhoushan archipelago.

At the time, the Australian Tribal-class destroyer HMAS *Warramunga*, under the command of Captain Wilfred Hastings Harrington, deployed on Far East occupation duties, was within close sailing distance of the stricken *Tai Ping* and, having intercepted her Mayday signals, advised that she was heading for the scene to assist. Subsequently, she reported that she had picked up just thirty-five survivors: thirty-one males and four females. No trace of either ship or of any lifeboats was found. The *Warramunga's* officers speculated that the boats, carrying other survivors, may have reached shore somewhere in the islands. In fact, all had gone down with both ships, no doubt still suspended from their davits. On arriving at Woosung (Wusong) with these few survivors, it soon became apparent that they were the sole inhabitants of either ship who had been recovered, a revelation that testified to the fact that there had been another lamentable calamity on a vast scale.

Five days later, Lloyd's List disclosed that, besides human lives, a valuable hoard had also been lost with the *Tai Ping*. Not only had there been countless Chinese people striving to escape the Communists, but there was also a considerable endeavour to remove Nationalist government stocks and hard cash. All told, there had been several hundreds of cases of securities aboard the *Tai Ping*, all carried down to the seabed with her. Escorted by six custodians, only one of whom lived to disclose his mission, the booty comprised government bonds, gold bars and thousands of dollar and yuan notes.

⊷═◉═⊷

Brief mention should be made here of another Chinese river steamship lost, so some reports suggest, with great loss of life; in excess of 2,000 souls. This was the former *Woosung* of the China Navigation Co. (John Swire & Co.), a large vessel of 3,426 gross tons, seized by the Japanese at Hankow on 8 December 1941. Condemned at the Sasebo Prize Court in January 1942, she was renamed *Reizan Maru* and returned to service as a Japanese auxiliary transport under the management of Koa Kaiun Kaisha.

The Swire river steamer *Woosung*, berthed at Shanghai in the early 1920s. Later, as the *Reizan Maru*, her loss by mine explosion on 18 January 1945 was the first to involve an estuarial craft whose casualties may have exceeded those of the *Sultana*. Or had she been confused with the *KiangYa*? A former China Navigation fleet-mate, the *Ryuzan Maru* (the ex-*Changsha*), was lost in similar circumstances in the same area nine days later, but with fewer casualties. (John Swire, University of Bristol)

Like the Chinese Nationalists only months later, the Japanese had been obliged to shift military units around in the closing phases of the Second World War as the threat confronting them moved from theatre to theatre. In January 1945, numerous river craft, among them the *Reizan Maru*, were requisitioned to convey soldiers along the Yangtse to the coast where they could board larger sea-going transports. In the course of this, on 18 January 1945, the *Reizan Maru* struck an American-laid mine and sank.

However, it has proved impossible to determine the exact number of casualties suffered in this incident and it is believed, in claiming that there were more than 2,000 casualties, the ex-*Woosung* may have been confused with one of the other losses described in this chapter, most probably the *KiangYa*.

13

FERRIES IN PERIL

So far, the disaster accounts described in this book have all occurred during wartime circumstances of one sort or another, but in recent times the prospect of severe loss of life at sea, more severe than that of the *Titanic*, affecting ships involved in commercial service has come back to haunt us. The SOLAS Conventions introduced in the wake of the *Titanic* tragedy, intended to prevent a recurrence, have barely kept pace with the developments of marine science, the changing trends of maritime travel or the evolving aspirations of passengers.

We live today in an age of mass passenger transportation by air, sea and on land. As far as maritime travel is concerned, it takes two distinct forms, each giving rise for concern for different reasons: intensive ferry services in certain parts of the world, especially those where national territory is spread over complex island archipelagos; and in the burgeoning pleasure cruise industry. The latter is reflected in the construction of ever-larger cruise ships with accommodation spaces now providing for multiples of thousands of passengers, rather than multiples of hundreds as in the past, in order to satisfy the increasing level of demand.

The issues of passenger safety that have grown in parallel with the expansion of these modern forms of maritime transport pose questions that are little different to those which confronted designers, builders and operators prior to April 1912 when the *Titanic* was lost. Now, just as then, an acceptable and appropriate balance needs to be reached between the regulatory demands on the one hand and the need for operational efficiency and commercial profitability on the other. A glance at the records and statistics compiled by such agencies as Lloyd's reveals that serious maritime accidents involving ferries have occurred with an unabating frequency over a twenty-to thirty-year timeframe, suggesting that the scales have been tipped unfavourably away from a minimum acceptable safety standard.

Drawing obvious conclusions for the causes for many of these incidents – overcrowding, lack of maintenance, disregard of safety procedures, poor crew discipline – has conspired to allow them in many cases to be dismissed as inevitable, given the widely held belief that such inadequacies are peculiar to certain undeveloped and emerging maritime nations. Such simplistic explanations have, though, been found wanting and even, to some extent, erroneous when it comes to making sense of certain losses. Take, for instance, the *Herald of Free Enterprise*, a British ship, which capsized at Zeebrugge in March 1987, or the Baltic ferry *Estonia*, operating between two

Scandinavian countries, which foundered in September 1994. The official inquiries into these disasters revealed that the former had set sail without being properly secured for sea in a failure to carry out essential, pre-departure procedures, while the latter had suffered a failure of the seals of her bow visor, causing them both to fall victim to the phenomenon known as the free surface effect.

That in itself was not the whole answer. There appeared to be a more deeply rooted cause in which the overall culture of shipboard practices and disciplines was heavily influenced by the relentless pressure to increase operational efficiency. Though it had not been the explicit intention, this had nevertheless elevated commercial profitability above passenger safety – if only because the one precluded or interfered with the other to the extent that they were no longer mutually compatible or attainable. Manifest in other forms of corner-cutting, it resulted in such things as reduced manning levels, neglected maintenance, inadequate crew training, lax attitudes concerning evacuation procedures and the failure to keep proper passenger manifests; all of which were consistently identified as contributory factors in the spate of shipping disasters at that time, and all indicators of regimes lacking a fundamental safety consciousness.

Trends in modern ferry design have also, to some extent, been influenced by commercial objectives, with consequences that have not helped the situation. The placement of broad, un-partitioned vehicle decks below the waterline has undermined buoyancy reserve in the event of flooding, while high-sided box-like superstructures, now conspicuously characteristic of vessels of this type, have made emergency disembarkation a lot more difficult. Simultaneously, the dramatic growth in size of passenger/vehicle ferries has exacerbated these problems. Discharging and loading inevitably take longer, increasing the pressure to achieve faster, and potentially unsafe, turnarounds, besides which, with greater passenger complements, the time to evacuate in an emergency would also be extended, a matter critically aggravated should use of the lifeboats on one side be lost.

Back in the 1980s, the nature of ferry operation and regulation, and not just in known maritime black spots like Indonesia, Bangladesh and the Philippines, along with hazardous aspects of ship design, appeared to be pointing at imminent disaster on a potentially epic scale. At the end of each year *Safety at Sea* magazine presents an 'Annual Review', a summary of the accidents and incidents of the preceding twelve months, along with observation and comment from a professional standpoint. In 1986, the review was written by Douglas Foy. In it, while reflecting on the disaster that had befallen the ferry *Dona Josefina* in Philippine waters in April of that year, he concluded with an uncannily prophetic observation: 'Unless there is tighter control of ferries in South East Asia we can expect to read about a further loss of life of about 1,000 in the year 1987.'

Little could he have realised that his prediction would come true in the most appalling circumstances barely twelve months later. But his estimate of 1,000 casualties fell short by a factor of more than four. What happened on 21 December 1987 was to be the worst ever peacetime maritime tragedy, dwarfing the loss of life when the *Titanic* sank. It was also the worst case of children killed at sea to that date.

DONA PAZ ex-*Don Sulpicio* ex-*Himeyuri Maru* (4/1963)

Sulpicio Lines, Philippines

The inter-island Philippines ferry *Dona Paz* collided with the oil tanker *Vector* in clear weather on Sunday, 21 December 1987. Bound from Batangas, Luzon, to Masbate, the 629 gross ton *Vector* was carrying 8,800 barrels of highly inflammable petroleum products, the equivalent of 1.4 million litres. The *Dona Paz*, licensed to carry a maximum of 1,518 passengers, which was en route from Tacloban City, Leyte, for Manila, was in fact overcrowded with passengers, mostly migrant workers and their families, heading home for the Christmas festivities. She was also carrying vehicles.

Like most Philippines ferries at the time, the *Dona Paz* was not operated in accordance with stringent safety regulations. Indeed, her operation was subject to few controls. Earlier in her career, on 6 June 1979 under the name *Don Sulpicio*, she had suffered a fire and been beached on the coast of Batangas. Though declared a constructive total loss, she was repurchased by her owners and, after repairs at Cebu, returned to service as the *Dona Paz* late in 1981. Like other ships of her type, she was not classified or inspected to the standards of any international classification society, despite her size and capacity. Thus, she had been allowed to deteriorate and was in a poor condition at the time of her second accident. The lax attitude to maintenance of the ship and its equipment was also reflected in the sloppy discipline and poor seamanship of her crew. This was despite the fact that, even before the December 1987 event, there was estimated to be an annual death toll of 20–30,000 on Filipino ferries, which carried some 11 million travellers on its network of ferry routes. In the fifteen years from 1972 to 1987, ferries operating on routes in the Philippines had been involved in eighty collisions, resulting in 117 vessels sinking. As Feliciana G. Salonga, the President of the Philippines Shipyard and Engineering Corporation, later put it: 'We all bewail these incidents but the fact is we have known about the problems for years.'

The collision between the *Dona Paz* and the *Vector* occurred in the Tablas Strait between the islands of Mindoro and Marinduque. The impact of the collision ruptured the petroleum containers on the *Vector*, igniting their contents and creating a massive fireball that rapidly spread and engulfed both vessels. Aboard the *Dona Paz*, confronted by this fiery menace, those passengers who were able rushed to the side of the blazing ship away from the inferno in sufficient numbers, given the vessel was overloaded, to cause her to list alarmingly and turn over onto her beam ends. It all happened within minutes.

Only 275 bodies were recovered from the sea or washed ashore on the nearby coastline, even though it was known that the *Dona Paz* had been carrying at the very least a full passenger complement. It led a United States Air Force spokesman, whose helicopters were deployed in the attempted rescue, to say concerning the absence of people either alive or dead: 'It was as if it never happened.' Coastguard officials stated that the *Dona Paz* had carried fifty-three life rafts and other life-saving appliances, although this could not be verified. In any event, there had not been time to launch even one of them.

This picture of a Sulpicio ferry was widely circulated as a view of the *Dona Paz*. In fact, it shows the very similar *Dona Ana*. (Sulpicio Lines)

The fact is that many had been asphyxiated as the fire enveloped them, the intense heat consuming the oxygen, only for them to be incinerated. Others had been trapped inside the hull and could not escape. As for those who managed to leap from the decks into the sea, the sharks that infest those waters accounted for the majority. There were just twenty-seven survivors from the *Dona Paz* and two from the *Vector's* crew of thirteen, all but one of whom were picked up by fleet-mate *Don Claudio*, which continued to scan the dark waters for three and a half hours before it returned to port. The last survivor to be found was a 5-year-old boy who had miraculously clung to a piece of floating wreckage for almost two days before he was pulled to safety by fishermen close to the coastline of Mindoro, late on 22 December 1987.

After the rescue effort was abandoned, attention turned to investigating the causes of the collision and to establishing the facts with regard to the number of people who had been aboard the *Dona Paz* and how many had lost their lives. Fearing both legal and governmental recriminations and facing a hostile media and public reaction in the wake of many preceding ferry incidents, Sulpicio Lines immediately pronounced that their ship had not been overloaded.

Progressively, through interviews and interrogations conducted by the National Bureau of Investigation (NBI), the truth of the situation emerged. On 23 February 1988, NBI spokesman Gordon Uy, speaking in Manila, conceded that at least 3,158 people had been aboard *Dona Paz*, of whom 3,099 were passengers. Simultaneously, though, officials in Tacloban challenged those figures, providing alternative numbers of 3,601 passengers and fifty-nine crew members. This contrasted with the ship's passenger manifest, which recorded only 1,480 full-fare adults, twenty-six half-fare juveniles and fifty-six non-paying minors.

This is a view of the *Dona Paz* taken earlier in her career when she was named *Don Sulpicio*. (James Shaw, courtesy of the World Ship Society)

Further complicating the picture were the ticketing arrangements typical of the Philippines, along with the practices for recording passengers boarding ferries. An official of Sulpicio Lines disclosed, surreptitiously, that extra tickets could be purchased aboard their vessels at a cheaper rate. Though illegal, the money no doubt pocketed by whoever was unscrupulously performing those transactions, it was a widespread practice. It meant the passengers concerned were not listed on the manifest. The conclusion that may be drawn, knowing this practice was customary, was that many never even bothered to buy a ticket at all. Two other categories that did not appear on the passenger manifest were holders of complementary tickets and children below the age of 4. It was estimated that as many as 1,000 children were travelling on the *Dona Paz* but not all would have been so young, of course.

Over the days and weeks following the disaster, the casualty list continued to grow as relatives reported missing persons to the authorities who it was known had been travelling from Tacloban to Manila at that time. It was impossible to arrive at a definitive number in such circumstances. Many different casualty figures have been quoted since, ranging from 4,045 to 4,370. The most astonishingly improbable number, though, was the official death toll of 1,565, declared despite all the clear evidence that the real figure was much higher! In itself worse than that of the *Titanic*, it disregarded all the NBI-gathered proof to the contrary.

The government inquiry that followed was perfunctory to put it mildly. It was certainly not conducted in a fashion becoming the scale of the tragedy. Relatives of the dead and the very few survivors had little faith in the integrity of the legal system. Aware of their government's track record in such matters, they were intensely cynical about its purpose, doubted the honesty of the proceedings and generally boycotted the affair altogether. They knew that the apportioning of blame would doubtless be swayed by covert dealings out of sight of the public and the media, and they were mainly concerned with seeking compensation from the *Dona Paz*'s owners.

When the court of inquiry did eventually publish its findings, they were both inexplicable and perplexing. They placed the blame totally on the *Vector*, on behalf of which there had been little if any first-hand testimony or defence, having lost all but two of the men manning her. In contrast, it completely exonerated the *Dona Paz* and Sulpicio Lines. This was despite the company's poor prior safety record – four ships lost between March 1977 and June 1979 – and much damning evidence:

- that the *Dona Paz* was overloaded, seriously, and to an extent that compromised her stability.
- that, from the survivors' testimonies, officers had been below decks drinking at the time of the collision and that the ship had been in the sole charge of the emergency or relief mate.
- that the *Dona Paz* did not carry a radio, whether or not there had been time and opportunity to use it, which meant that the Manila Rescue Co-ordination Centre was unaware of the collision until 07.00 hours local time on Monday 22 December, nine hours after it occurred.
- that the *Dona Paz* had a crew of only fifty-nine, a total that included waiters, stewards and engineers, for a passenger complement, according to the licensed allocation, of 1,518, a wholly inadequate ratio.

It has to be said that, had any other conclusion been reached, it would not only have reflected on the owners of the *Dona Paz* but it would also have pointed the finger at the government itself and, in particular, the failings of its Transport Ministry.

Arising from the inquiry ruling, and effectively freed from corporate responsibility, Sulpicio agreed to pay only the minimum compensation according to Philippines law and only to those who could offer proof that a ticket had been purchased or could demonstrate in some other irrefutable way that a relative had been on board.

As a token of its supposed authority, and a hollow one in the extreme, the Philippines government temporarily suspended Sulpicio Lines' operating licence and ordered safety checks to be carried out on all the company's ships.

Regrettably, the failure of the Philippines government to take wholly appropriate action in the wake of the world's worst ever peacetime maritime disaster, sent all the wrong signals. It was a green light for 'business as usual' to local ferry operators and, with the continuation of bad practices, the potential for more serious accidents remained. It came as no real surprise, therefore, when twenty years later, after a string of less extreme incidents, another Sulpicio ferry was lost in catastrophic circumstances. This was the *Princess of the Stars*, overwhelmed by a storm on 22 June 2008, which caused her to capsize at the cost of 814 lives.

An explanation has been given for the apparent inevitability of ferry disasters in the Philippines, which concludes that the absence of regulation is not the sole factor. In April 1988, Feliciana G. Salonga spoke fatalistically about the disaster and the prospects for a safer future in an article entitled 'Ferry Tragedy Prompts Safety Moves':

You cannot really blame the people or even the officials. There simply are not enough services, so the passengers are desperate to get aboard and the temptation for poorly-paid, so-called supervisors to co-operate is obvious. The same applies with owners who avoid ship inspections by buying licence extensions.

This complacent attitude seems to be borne out by the response of the victims' families and the wider Filipino public. Considering the *Dona Paz* loss accounted for the greatest ever number of civilian casualties, it is perhaps surprising that there has been no endeavour to erect a monument of any description as a lasting memorial to the dead. It seems the outrage at this extraordinary waste of life on an unprecedented scale in peacetime has all too swiftly abated and the memory of those hapless souls has been all too soon committed to oblivion. The people of the Philippines are strongly family orientated with profound religious values but as one commentator put it: 'Sadly, Filipinos have short memories. As for Philippines' ship operators, well they have total amnesia.'

For a while, in the wake of the disaster, it appeared that changes for the better would indeed be made. There were many declarations of good intent, such that it was honestly thought that, for the first time, something of substance would be done to really improve the safety record of ferries operating in the Philippines. There was talk of new regulations to require local vessels to be certificated and inspected by classifications bodies as a means of putting pressure on their owners to reverse the years of neglect and deterioration, of making radios and communication equipment mandatory, and of providing better training for seamen manning domestic vessels with more meaningful qualifications for officer grades. Given that, subsequent to the event, the situation remained largely unaltered, the comments expressed by one industry observer, in which both hope and a measure of cynicism were combined, were particularly pertinent: 'Indeed all the requirements for operating a good service at last have a real chance of being introduced to the statute books but seeing the miracle come to pass will, indeed, take time.'

⊷⊶⊙⊷⊶

There seems little doubt that while ferry accidents, and serious ones at that, have not always occurred in the world's poorer regions, there was and is a particular problem as far as ferry operations in the developing world are concerned. The facts speak for themselves, for there have been countless fatal accidents involving ferries around Africa, in India, Pakistan, Bangladesh and Indonesia as well as the Philippines. Among them was an occurrence that exhibited many of the deficiencies that had been present in the *Dona Paz* disaster, and which again highlighted the consequences of an absence of regulation.

Whether in the developed world where there has been a stubborn resistance to greater regulation, viewed as a frustration to profitable operation, or in the Third World where there is an almost complete lack of control of shipping, often compounded by corrupt and incompetent officialdom, the outcome has been much the same: increasing numbers of ferry incidents and fatalities. The following list reveals some of the worst cases:

SHIP	LOSS DATE	CAUSE	SEA AREA	DEATHS
Don Juan	22 April 1980	collision & foundered	Philippines	896
Herald of Free Enterprise	6 March 1987	capsized	North Sea	193
Dona Paz	20 December 1987	collision & fire	Philippines	4,354
Dona Marilyn	24 October 1988	foundered	Philippines	254
Salem Express	4 December 1991	stranded	Red Sea	464
Senopati Nusantara	29 December 1996	foundered	Indonesia	394+
Estonia	29 September 1994	capsized & foundered	Baltic Sea	852
Al Salam Bocaccio 98	3 February 2006	fire & foundered	Red Sea	1,198
Princess of the Stars	22 June 2008	capsized	Philippines	814

Such profound evidence should act as a brake on any thoughts about relaxation of the rules. It also highlights the need to urgently tighten up or introduce controls in those countries that currently lack the experience, means and money to enable them to improve matters over which they have sovereign responsibility.

A report by journalist Dag Pike, entitled 'Ferries in Peril' in the *New Scientist* of 8 August 1985, focused its concerns on collisions, fire and sabotage, questioning the merits of modern ferry design which, in that writer's view, could only adversely affect survivability should any of those events be experienced. The article reflected on how, as competition had increased and the need for economies had grown, expediency was replacing common sense where safety aspects were concerned. Strange as it may seem, the feature did not consider at all what is perhaps the most serious hazard facing modern roll-on roll-off (Ro-Ro) ferries: the inherent weakness of the single compartment standard of subdivision and the risk of capsizing caused by the free surface effect. And this despite the increasing evidence of the vulnerability of vessels with vast open vehicle decks, which had been accumulating over the years. Besides many minor incidents, a string of major ferry accidents – the *Princess Victoria* (January 1953), *Toya Maru* (September 1954), *Heraklion* (December 1966), *Wahine* (April 1968), *Herald of Free Enterprise* and *Estonia* – accounting collectively for 2,500 deaths, had all been attributed to this cause, all of them of the Ro-Ro type. Not surprisingly, Ro-Ros were dubbed 'roll-on, roll-over' vessels.

While the gathering data was overwhelming, little had been done in thirty-five years to address the fundamental problem of the single compartment design, other than the introduction of stricter rules on hull door closure and, latterly, the requirement to install electronic monitoring devices. Nothing had been considered in the form of fail-safe mechanisms to provide for human error. Moreover, there seemed to be a lack of urgency in the pursuit of a fully effective remedy for the design's inherent shortcoming; even though the brief of one study, specifically concerned with the crucial effects of water accumulating on lower decks in the event of hull breach, had stated: 'Simply put, roll-on roll-off ferries with more people, cars, trucks and buses

The loss of the Japanese train ferry *Toya Maru* in a typhoon in 1954 provided an early indication of the vulnerability of ferries fitted with un-partitioned decks for vehicles or rolling stock to the risk of capsizing. (Arnold Kludas)

on board urgently need enhanced stability potential and hence require strengthened regulatory guidelines.'

The free surface effect is a phenomenon that in certain conditions can cause a craft to become so unstable, through interference to its attitude, that it may, ultimately, cause it to capsize. The tendency of a vessel to roll due to the motion of the waves, the force of the wind or in making a rapid turn is normally countered by the natural righting moment designed into its stability characteristics. However, the momentum of a free mass moving laterally within the hull in the direction of the roll can impede the righting effect by moving the ship's centre of gravity beyond a safe limit towards the lowered side. In extreme cases, sometimes as a consequence of the accumulated energy of several severe rolls, it can result in a vessel turning over. Typically, this condition is associated with unrestricted fluid movement but it can also be induced by aggregates of solids such as seeds or fine gravel. Similarly, stability can be adversely affected by a body of people if they make a sudden and uncontrolled shift of their weight to one side, as happened on the *Dona Paz*.

Subsequent to the *Estonia* disaster of 1994, more purposeful efforts were initiated to determine a 'New Damage Stability Standard', in effect to provide sufficient residual stability on Ro-Ro vessels to allow enough time for the orderly evacuation of passengers and crew in an emergency. The outcome was the Stockholm Agreement, an enhancement of the SOLAS 90 rules on ship stability and hull-subdivision then in force. But for one ship in particular, it came too late.

More recent, serious ferry incidents have involved the *Estonia*, which sank in the Baltic Sea on 28 September 1994 … (Frank Heine)

… and the *Princess of the Stars*, which foundered off the Philippines on 22 June 2008. These incidents suggest that the fundamental design weakness of ships of the Ro-Ro ferry type has not yet been satisfactorily resolved. (Private source)

LE JOOLA (11/1990)

Government of Senegal

The roll-on roll-off ferry *Le Joola*, built in Germany in 1990, was owned by the Senegalese government and operated on a regular domestic service between Dakar, the capital, and the southern city of Ziguinchor in the Casamance enclave.

Though only twelve years old by 2002, the year of her loss, the *Le Joola* had suffered from persistent technical and certification problems. Georg Höckels, the Managing Director of her builders, Germersheim Schiffswerft, stated that the ship had not been seen again since it had been delivered because the Senegalese owners had elected to perform all maintenance and repair work themselves. However, there had been issues with the execution and standard of work that had been deemed necessary, which, in turn, impacted on the *Le Joola*'s classification.

Bureau Veritas (BV) had originally issued a permanent certificate for the ship, valid from 12 November 1990 through to 11 November 1995, subject to periodic inspections. However, in 1994, the classification certificate was suspended partly through the owners' failure to implement corrective actions identified on annual surveys, but also because the government of Senegal had defaulted on its fees. Lacking any certification whatsoever for six years, a reclassification request made in November 2000 necessitated a comprehensive dockyard refit, which lasted until June 2001. Even then, the BV inspector was only prepared to issue a provisional class certificate to run from 25 July to 31 December 2001. This, too, carried endorsements, stipulating the completion of remedial work:

- to repair the closure mechanisms of the rear and lateral doors
- to change the tight seal on the rear door
- to restore to a fit state the electrical power generation supplying the fire detection system

As the owners of the *Le Joola* failed to meet these requirements, the provisional certificate also lapsed.

Against this background, the *Le Joola* sailed from Ziguinchor at 13.30 hours local time on 26 September 2002. En route for Dakar, she called at the island of Carabane near the entrance to the Gambia River where there were no formal exit or entry arrangements for passengers. During the call, 185 unmanifested people boarded *Le Joola* to join the more than 1,046 ticketed travellers who had embarked at Ziguinchor. Among the latter were many schoolchildren returning to the capital for the beginning of the new term at the end of their school holidays. By these figures alone, it was evident that the *Le Joola* was excessively overloaded. Her design specification, the basis of her classification, had provided for a maximum of 536 passengers and sixty-four crew, and thirty-five cars on the vehicle deck.

At 22.00 hours, the ship transmitted a routine message to the maritime security centre at Dakar advising that conditions were clear and she was making good

The Senegalese ferry *Le Joola* loading via her stern doors at Zuiginchor. (Private source)

progress. Within an hour, however, she had sailed into a storm, though it is not known whether she was warned of worsening weather. Caught in rough seas and powerful winds, the *Le Joola* was soon overwhelmed and she capsized within minutes.

Only one lifeboat was deployed, which provided refuge for just twenty-five people. There had been quite literally insufficient time in the circumstances to launch more. Another twenty-two people managed to clamber onto the ferry's upturned hull, which remained on the surface until 15.00 hours the following day before it disappeared into the depths. Everyone else was lost, but the question was, as in so many other disasters, how many had in fact been aboard *Le Joola* and how many had died?

Declarations were immediately made by the authorities in Senegal that the *Le Joola* had not been overloaded, but the manifest of ticketed passengers alone clearly indicated otherwise. As many as 676 remained trapped within the overturned ship, doomed to a slow death, whereas others perished in the sea while waiting for rescue. Rescue boats reported hearing screams and shouts from within the upturned hull before it slipped beneath the surface, unable to do anything to free them. Local fishermen, who had been the first on the scene, rescued some survivors, but the government rescue team was slow to respond and did not reach the capsized ferry until the following morning. Only sixty-four people in total were rescued and just 551 bodies were recovered, all taken to Banjul.

Lloyd's List sheds light on the progressive revelation of the extent of the *Le Joola*'s complement. By 3 October 2002, it was reporting that it had been admitted that at least 1,034 people had been aboard the ferry, 'but it had been conceded that the true toll might be even higher'. As had happened on the *Dona Paz*, many passengers had not been issued with a ticket: those who had boarded at Carabane, children under the age of 5, and stowaways. Ultimately, it transpired that between 1,863 and 1,935 had been killed, making it Africa's worst ever shipping disaster.

Having presided over a failed transport regulatory system, senior members of the Senegalese government were quick to express their outrage at the horror of the sinking and contrition for the official ineptitude. The Senegalese president, Abdoulaye Wade, said it had been established that the ship was overloaded and the State would compensate the victims' families. 'The responsibility of the State is clear,' he said. The prime minister, Ms Mame Madior Boye, referring to the questionable seaworthiness of the *Le Joola* and pre-empting criticism of the ferry's condition, declared, 'For the moment the state of the vessel has not been called into question.' Angry relatives denounced the authorities, claiming that the ship had, in fact, been listing to starboard when she sailed and should never have been allowed to leave port.

A period of three days of national mourning was declared from midday on 27 September 2002. No doubt in a bid to deflect critical attention away from himself, the president promptly sacked the prime minister. The reason given was 'mishandling of the rescue'. A number of senior coastguard and army officials also became casualties of what may be reasonably regarded as a tokenistic cull, but no one was ever prosecuted.

An inquiry into the disaster was set up, which closed a year later with an official report. It was inconclusive and short on recommendations, giving as justification for this that the captain's death had inhibited the inquiry's ability to reach more definite conclusions. No one was held to account for allowing the *Le Joola* to be overloaded, or for her run-down and unseaworthy state.

Technical specialists elsewhere were, however, able to reach a reasonably satisfactory explanation for why the *Le Joola* foundered so dramatically. Survivors' testimonies revealed that when the storm had struck the ship, passengers on her exposed outer decks, by far the majority, had sought shelter on the leeward side. Given that the weight of 536 people, her permitted load, would have been around 40 tons, this weight would have been exceeded by almost another 100 tons through the massive overloading. The sudden shifting of this much excess weight to one side critically destabilised the already tender *Le Joola*. The rough seas and strong winds would have contributed to the ship heeling over to a degree of inclination from which it would have been impossible to recover.

The families of each victim were offered US$22,000 compensation, but it was declined by families in France who continue to pursue indicted Senegalese officials and the authorities in general through the French courts.

--==◉==--

The *Le Joola* disaster demonstrated that the actions taken in the wake of the *Estonia* disaster had not proliferated sufficiently. The Stockholm Agreement, implemented in 2003 as a supplement to SOLAS 90, had the effect of worsening the situation in the

View of the memorial to the *Le Joola* disaster erected at Zuiginchor, Senegal. (Ji-Elle)

emerging world by instigating the transfer of problematic vessels that could not conform to the new rules from countries in the developed world to poorer countries working ferry routes in the Red Sea and in Indonesia and the Philippines.

The International Maritime Organisation (IMO) would insist that it is being and has been proactive in its efforts to improve the safety of ferries and of passenger ships in general. The work of the Maritime Safety Committee (MSC) in conjunction with the Worldwide Ferry Safety Association and Interferry, along with the enhancements to the SOLAS agreements, certainly deserve recognition as do, notably, the endeavours to lift exemption from compliance with the SOLAS rules of ferries that operate either inland or on solely domestic routes, the so-called 'non-convention vessels'. Given the wringing of hands and the uttering of profound but hollow words of concern by Third World officials with each new tragedy, rarely accompanied by any meaningful action, this had been long overdue.

In the final analysis, enduring and coherent remedies to the epidemic of ferry accidents will not be found until certain essential questions, such as those posed by Catherine Lawson and Roberta Weisbrod in their paper 'Ferry Transport: The Realm of Responsibility for Ferry Disasters in Developing Nations', have been answered, among them:

- Are vessels designed properly for their purpose?
- Are the regulations adequate to the conditions of operation?
- Are the regulations enforced and, if so, how?
- Is there a relationship between the record of training and ferry fatalities?
- Is there a formal system in place for search and rescue in the region?

In the quest for prevention the debate continues but, in the meantime, as borne out by the relatively recent losses of the *Al Salam Bocaccio 98* and *Princess of the Stars*, fatal accidents continue to occur.

14

A CLOSE CALL

The concerns associated with increased size and capacity and their potential implications in an emergency are not confined to giant ferries but are equally applicable to the modern generation of super-cruise ships, aboard which the mandated evacuation time, as stipulated by international regulations, would be nigh on impossible to achieve. Here too, design considerations that have maximised the provision of outside cabins with balconies have been realised to some extent at the expense of safety features.

Likewise, there may also be a hint of over-reliance on technology to provide the necessary protection of ships and their occupants from danger, and insufficient attention to the basic principles, practices and skills that are fundamental to good maritime safety measures. As one shipping correspondent has put it, 'The suspicion is that intense competition and the drive to reduce operating costs, prompting moves to greater deregulation, have compromised much in the way of the latter.' Evidence of this can be seen in the widespread reduction of deck department manning. With a greater emphasis on the hotel and entertainment aspects of sea travel, there is now increasing dependence in emergencies, in a shift of key responsibilities, on inexperienced hotel and catering personnel whose routine function has little to do with on-board safety equipment, systems or procedures.

Voices of concern have been raised because it is considered professionally that many of these developments have had a retrograde effect on safety and may be increasing the risk of a future tragedy. Thus, under the auspices of the International Maritime Organisation (IMO), conferences have been held to consider all aspects of passenger ship safety, but so far little substantive has emerged that could make a real difference. Central to this lack of progress has been the dichotomy between the interests and views of professional mariners on the one side and ship operators on the other, the latter fearing that fundamental design changes could cost them business or impact on profitable performance.

Perhaps more worrying is the implication that pressure has been put on the regulatory authorities to resist stricter mandatory safety requirements. In his article 'Safety of Large Passenger Vessels', Allan Graveson, Senior National Secretary of Nautilus UK, says:

The passenger shipping industry, represented internationally by the International Council of Cruise Lines and the International Chamber of Shipping, robustly defends the status quo in seeking to prevent the introduction of new safety measures or changes in construction and design of these vessels. All measures likely to incur additional costs and reduce revenue are vigorously opposed.

Clearly, passenger vessel operating conditions must provide for competitive performance and be such that investors will be sufficiently content their money will generate an appropriate return, but nothing would undermine both public and business confidence more than another major shipping disaster, especially to a giant cruise ship. Nothing could blight the cruise industry more than another human tragedy on a massive scale.

In making these observations, it is recognised that this book is first and foremost devoted to relating the accounts of those most serious shipping disasters of the past which have been overshadowed by the *Titanic*. However, to demonstrate that such extreme events are not consigned to the past, but could recur in the future, should a combination of factors be allowed to emerge, it is also fitting here to look forward as well as backwards in time. It should be emphasised that the reflections expressed here draw extensively from the opinions articulated in professional journals by officer-grade mercantile personnel, who fear that the simple extrapolation of the rules relating to ship design and construction and the proposed amendments to evacuation procedures are raising the spectre of further major disasters at sea, once more needlessly putting lives in peril.

It has to be said without exaggerating that, beset by potential hazards and unheeded concerns, there is about our present circumstances something of an echo of the past in the run up to the tragic loss of the *Titanic* a hundred years ago, when there was an apparently similar indifference to the warning signs.

COSTA CONCORDIA (6/2006)

Costa Crociere, Genoa, Italy

Built by Fincantieri, Genoa-Sestri (yard number 6122)
114,147 gross tons; 955ft (290.2m) length overall; 117ft (35.5m) beam
diesel-electric engines; twin Azipod propulsion.

The preceding comments regarding the safety of large passenger vessels, essentially the cruise ships of the latest generation, were written late in 2011 as the intended postscript to this book. Little did we know that an incident would occur within weeks that would raise the spectre of a tragedy of major proportions occurring, reinforcing the concerns that had been expressed by professional mariners.

On the face of it, the stranding of the *Costa Concordia* on rocks off the Isola del Giglio on 14 January 2012 was the result of an avoidable navigational error. Carrying 4,229 people (split approximately as 3,200 passengers and 1,000 crew), all of whom, apart from thirty-five – either confirmed dead or missing presumed dead –

survived the incident, the outcome, with relatively few casualties, appeared to endorse the currently prescribed design standards and evacuation arrangements. The latest SOLAS safety provisions mandated for passenger-carrying vessels would appear to have been adequate.

Thus, there is a possibility that the inquiry into this stranding, still due to take place (at the time of writing), will dwell on what has been alleged to be the reckless endangering of the ship and the abandonment of its occupants by her master, Captain Francesco Schettino, rather than give due attention to the evident inability of the emergency systems to adequately cope with the damage sustained. In the final analysis, whatever the cause of a potentially fatal threat to a ship, be it human error, fire, collision or environmental hazard, it should be possible for it to be evacuated in a reasonably safe and timely fashion and for essential on-board systems to continue to function at least until full abandonment has been satisfactorily achieved.

There has been much press speculation about what happened to cause the *Costa Concordia* accident, as well as the subsequent behaviour of those responsible for the ship and the well-being of its passengers. The facts will only become clear when the inquiry finally delivers its report. What is known for certain is that the *Costa Concordia* was ripped open by the reef onto which she had been too closely steered but, it should be kept in mind, equally serious damage could have been caused in a collision. Luckily, land was close by and it has to be said that, despite anything that her master may or may not have been guilty of in causing the ship to be damaged in the first place, he appears to have manoeuvred his stricken vessel with considerable skill, given that she had lost power; ensuring that she stranded rather than foundered in

The cruise ship *Costa Concordia* on 31 July 2009. (Ray Woodmore)

deep water. Had the ship not made it to Isola del Giglio, then, with a 160ft-long gash in her underwater hull, she would almost certainly have capsized completely and sunk rapidly. Realistically, many fewer people would have escaped from her. It had been a dangerously close call and the consequences could have been far more serious. Potentially dwarfing the number of victims of the *Titanic*, it could have become one of the worst ever peacetime shipping disasters.

As it was, it took hours for the *Costa Concordia* to be fully abandoned, far longer than the thirty minutes stipulated by IMO regulations, and with extreme difficulty. The reason for that was what would appear to be a fundamental Achilles heel of the design of the *Costa Concordia* and other ships of her class – and equally true of the majority of other large modern cruise ships.

The rules stipulate that lifeboats should not be stowed higher than 50ft (15m) above sea level. Having increased the superstructure height in these giants to provide more stateroom balconies, designers have therefore been obliged to place the lifeboats low down, virtually within the side structure. In the case of the *Costa Concordia*, a twelve-deck vessel, they are on deck three, with much of the ship's side towering above. This necessitates the organisation of emergency disembarkation from within the interior spaces rather than from an open boat deck as in the past, which may in itself be viewed as a matter of some concern. It also means that many passengers are required to enter and go down into the ship to reach their lifeboat muster points, a direction that conflicts with instinctive human behaviour to head for open spaces.

Of greater concern is the location of the lifeboat stations. As outlined in the previous chapter, when the integrity of a ship's hull has been compromised and is flooding, the free surface effect can cause it to list to one side. As the flooding continues, the list would gradually worsen to a point where the ship may not be able to right itself. Ultimately, if the ship's centre of gravity has been shifted beyond the point of recovery it will turn over onto its beam ends and may sink altogether. The top hamper of high-sided ships like the *Costa Concordia* can, given the worst set of circumstances possibly accentuated by making a sharp turn, increase the risk of this happening.

From a practical, life-saving point of view, a severe list on ships like the *Costa Concordia* whose lifeboats are stowed low down on her sides can result in their use being potentially and rapidly lost on both sides (see the diagrams overleaf). Those on the side of the list, threatened beneath the lofty hull wall, will, if they have not been loaded and launched in good time, be submerged on their davits as the list increases. Any people who remain in the ship on that side as this happens would be trapped and risk being drowned. On the opposite side, as the ship rotates around its length, the lifeboat stations will be taken upwards to a position where the boats will foul the ship's side as they are launched, with the risk of spilling their occupants. On a ship the size of the *Costa Concordia*, the drop to the sea will also increase alarmingly as the list worsens. Eventually, it will be impossible to launch boats on that side at all. As already stated, the facts of this particular case are awaited, but this scenario appears to have been what was experienced with the *Costa Concordia*.

The *Titanic*, which sank by the head because of the nature of her damage and the way that she flooded, carried insufficient lifeboats to save all of her passengers. The

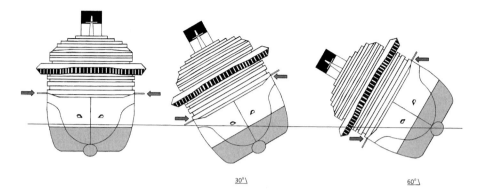

Arguably, in the most unfavourable conditions, cruise ships of the *Costa Concordia* type have effectively fewer lifeboats than the *Titanic*. These bow elevations of a cruise ship of the *Costa Concordia*-class show the locations of the lifeboat stations and how, as the ship lists, deployment of boats stowed low down becomes, at 30 degrees, dangerous or, at 60 degrees, impossible. (David L. Williams)

The *Titanic* carried twenty lifeboats, a greater number than were stipulated by the Board of Trade. Realistically, though, to provide for her maximum complement in an emergency, she needed three times as many. (Harland & Wolff)

SOLAS rules that were introduced in the wake of her loss were intended to ensure that, in future, passenger ships would carry more than enough lifeboats for all and, in terms of numbers, that is definitely now the case. But if, as in an incident such as that which afflicted the *Costa Concordia*, the use of the majority can be lost because they cannot be deployed, this may be of little benefit. It could be argued that in situations of severe list leading to a vessel capsizing completely, some modern cruise ships have greater vulnerability in this respect than the *Titanic*, having in effect a worse lifeboat provision.

As mentioned, voices of professional dissent have long drawn attention to such discrepancies and the pressing need to address them before it is too late. As seen in an earlier quotation, it has been intimated that some ship owners are resisting changes that they see as imposing unnecessary costs on their operations, even though the consequences of a lost ship and multiple deaths would be far more damaging to their businesses. Some commentators have gone much further in their criticisms of what is seen as an absence of meaningful regulatory intervention. Kendall Carver, chairman and founder of the US-based cruise industry watchdog group, Cruise Victims Association, certainly expressed such a view in the most outspoken terms. He said of the *Costa Concordia* disaster that it was linked to a 'cosy relationship between regulators and the industry'.

One trusts that all parties with a stake in the cruise industry, indeed the passenger shipping industry as a whole – owners, designers, builders, professional mariners and the regulatory authorities – will together seek and implement the safety solutions that are essential and, no doubt, attainable in the twenty-first century to prevent another *Titanic* disaster from occurring. The modern world demands and is entitled to something better, but it could be argued, quite reasonably, that the ship passenger of today is being shortchanged.

As this book was approaching completion, I entered into a discussion with a close friend and retired marine engineer as to whether the *Titanic* could be considered to have been a safe ship. 'Certainly!' was his emphatic response, because in his view she had been built to and in accordance with the standards laid down at that time by the Board of Trade, the body then charged with the responsibility for the rules governing British ship construction and operation. In addition, the threat of extreme circumstances such as those encountered on 14 April 1912 was so remote that they could not reasonably have been perceived in advance.

In my view, however, the *Titanic* *was* an unsafe ship, if only because, subsequent to the disaster and the publication of the inquiry proceedings, her sister ship *Olympic* received extensive modifications to make her a 'safer' ship, most notably increased lifeboat provision and improvements to her system of watertight compartmentation. It is worthy of note that there had been a call for the *Titanic* to have forty-eight lifeboats instead of the twenty she actually carried, implying that her life-saving equipment was inadequate and, therefore, potentially unsafe – this never happened, partly because it was deemed unnecessary but also because of the delusion that she was 'unsinkable'.

Today, it would be argued that the *Costa Concordia*, also designed and built to the latest rules and regulations, was a 'safe' ship, yet she too came to grief in an unanticipated accident that so easily could have resulted in calamity. As Simon Calder, travel correspondent of the *Independent*, said: 'It is unbelievable this this should happen to a 21st Century ship.'

The question of how, today, safe practice is determined for the establishment of the rules for construction and operation of passenger ships is an interesting one, if only because such a vital dimension of maritime regulation appears to have a less rigorous basis than it should. The improvements that followed the *Titanic* and, if there are any, those that will be adopted after the *Costa Concordia* inquiry has reached its conclusions are of a reactive nature. The emphasis in the shipping world remains one of 'cure' rather than 'prevention'.

My personal working experience was in the aviation industry where the processes and procedures for determining the safety of new aircraft types are incredibly strict, justifiably. The aircraft industry safety record is steadily improving, with casualties at an all time low given the number of aircraft now in operation. The reverse seems to be the case with passenger shipping, which has been seeing an increase in numbers of lost lives.

As with ships, aircraft undergo model tests and type approval (flight) trials but their designs are also subjected to a form of risk analysis known as a Failure Modes, Effects and Criticality Analysis (FMECA), carried out on the entire airframe, each main assembly and sub-assembly and every system and individual piece part. Under an FMECA, all potential hazards, no matter how extreme or unlikely, are identified and assessed for their likelihood of occurrence and gravity of outcome in the event of a failure. If the analysis concludes that any potential failure could be catastrophic, that is it would cause the total loss of the aircraft and/or heavy loss of life, the requirement for redesign is mandatory. Without it, type approval would not be granted. As far as is known, such a critical design tool, aided by computer analysis of empirical disaster data, is not applied to the safety aspects of ship design and construction.

As a final thought, is it not perhaps time that it was?

SHIPS LIST

Name	Year	Former Names	Builders	YN	E/S	GRT	LOA/LPP		Beam		Loss			CAS	SURV
							ft	m	ft	m	Date	Cause	Position		
AKITSU MARU	1942		Harima, Aioi	333	ST1	9,186	473	143.8	64	19.5	15/11/1944	Torpedo (USS Queenfish)	33.17N, 128.11E	2,046	?
ARISAN MARU	1944		Mitsui, Tamano	376	ST1	6,886	450	137.3	60	18.2	24/10/1944	Torpedo (USS Snook)	20.46N, 118.18E	c.1,820	8+
ARMENIA	1928		Baltic S.B. & E.Works, Leningrad	?	M2	4,727	354	107.6	51	15.5	7/11/1941	Bombs	44.15N, 34.17E	c.7,000	8
AWA MARU	1943		Mitsubishi, Nagasaki	770	M2	11,249	536	163.0	66	20.0	1/4/1945	Torpedo (USS Queenfish)	24.41N, 119.29E	2,070	1?
CAP ARCONA	1927		Blohm & Voss, Hamburg	476	ST2	27,561	676	205.9	84	25.7	3/5/1945	Bombs	54.04N, 10.51E	c.4,200	316
DONA PAZ	1963	ex-Don Sulpicio, ex-Himeyuri Maru	Onomichi Zosen	118	M1	2,324	305	93.1	45	13.6	20/12/1987	Collision (oil tanker Victor)	approx. 13.10N, 121.40E	4,386	27
DONIZETTI	1928		Cantieri Navale Triestino, Monfalcone	195	M1	2,428	294	89.4	41	12.3	23/9/1943	Gunfire (HMS Eclipse)	approx. 35.45N, 27.30E	1,835	0
EDOGAWA MARU	1944		Mitsubishi, Kobe	679	ST1	6,968	450	137.3	60	18.2	18/11/1944	Torpedo (USS Sunfish)	33.35N, 124.35E	2,114	175+
GOYA	1942		Akers M.V., Oslo	479	M2	5,230	430	130.7	57	17.3	16/4/1945	Torpedo (L-3)	55.13N, 18.20E	c.6,200	183
GRUZIA	1928		Krupp Deutsch Werft, Kiel	493	M2	5,008	380	110.6	51	15.5	13/6/1942	Torpedo?	44.60N, 33.40E	c.4,000	?

Name	Year	Ex-names	Builder	No.	Type	Tonnage					Date	Cause	Position		
HAI CHU	1923	ex-Kaishu Maru, ex-Hang Cheong	Taikoo, Hong Kong	203	T2	1,086	179	54.3	36	10.8	8/11/1945	Mine explosion	22.50N, 113.36E	c.1,907	c.283
HISAGAWA MARU	1944		Kawasaki, Kobe	?	M1	6,886	509	154.6	62	18.9	9/1/1945	Bombs	23.40N, 119.57E	2,283+	?
HSUAN HUAI	1945	ex-Teng 1402, ex-Northern Master, ex-Samuel R. Curwen	Avondale Marine Ways, Westwego	51	T1	1,926	260	78.9	42	12.8	2/11/1948	Fire & explosion	approx. 40.30N, 121.30E	c.3,000	c.3,000
JUNYO MARU	1913	ex-Sureway, ex-Hartmore, ex-Harland Point, ex-Ardmore	R. Duncan, Port Glasgow	324	T1	5,131	406	123.4	53	16.2	18/9/1944	Torpedo (HMS Tradewind)	02.53S, 101.12E	5,620	c.900
KAMAKURA MARU	1930	ex-Titibu Maru, ex-Chichibu Maru	Yokohama Dock Co.	170	M2	17,526	584	178.0	74	22.6	28/4/1943	Torpedo (USS Gudgeon)	10.25N, 121.50E	2,211	465
KIANG YA	1939	ex-Hsing Ya Maru, re Dong Hang Fong 8	Harima, Aioi	274	T2	3,731	323	98.2	50	15.2	3/12/1948	Mine explosion	30.37N, 122.25E	2,353	c.1,091
KOSHU MARU	1937	ex-Teishu Maru	Uraga Dockyard	421	C1	2,612	296	89.9	45	13.7	4/8/1944	Torpedo (USS Ray)	03.59S, 117.54E	1,540	c.525
LACONIA	1922		Swan Hunter & Wigham Richardson, Newcastle	1125	ST2	19,695	625	190.0	74	22.3	12/9/1942	Torpedo (U-156)	05.05S, 11.38W	c.1,690	976
LANCASTRIA	1922	ex-Tyrrhenia	William Beardmore, Glasgow	557	ST2	16,243	579	176.3	70	21.4	17/6/1940	Bombs	47.09N, 02.20E	c.3,500	2,477
LE JOOLA	1990		Germersheim Schiffwerft	847	M2	2,087	262	79.5	41	12.5	26/9/2002	Capsized – storm	approx. 13.25N, 17.50W	1,863	64

Name	Year	ex-names	Builder		Type	Tonnage					Date	Cause	Position		
LENIN	1909	ex-Simbirsk	F.Schichau, Danzig	832	T1	2,713	312	94.8	42	12.7	11/8/1941	Mine explosion	44.20N, 33.44E	c.4,500	643
LIMA MARU	1920		Mitsubishi, Nagasaki	334	T2	7,250	444	135.6	58	17.7	8/2/1944	Torpedo (USS Snook)	32.18N, 129.20E (Lloyds) 31.05N, 127.37E (Japanese)	2,765+	c.135
MAYASAN MARU	1942		Mitsui, Tamano	300	M1	9,433	461	140.0	63	19.0	18/11/1944	Torpedo (USS Picuda)	33.21N, 124.42E	3,536	c.880
NIKKIN MARU	1920	ex-Hokusei Maru, ex-Canadian, ex-Golden West, ex-West Ivan	J.F.Duthrie, Seattle	30	T1	5,587	412	125.1	54	16.5	30/6/1944	Torpedo (USS Tang)	35.05N, 125.08E	3,219	?
ORIA	1920	ex-Norda IV, ex-Sainte Julienne, ex-Oria	Osbourne Graham, North Hylton	222	T1	2,127	286	86.9	44	13.3	12/2/1944	Wrecked – storm	approx. 37.35N, 24.05E	c.4,150	
PETRELLA	1923	ex-Capo Pino, ex-Aveyron, ex-Pasteur	Gironde, Harfleur	p1	T1	4,785	364	110.6	49	15.0	8/2/1944	Torpedo (HMS Sportsman)	35.35N, 24.18E	c.3,700	975
PRINCIPE UMBERTO	1909		Riuniti, Palermo	13	Q2	7,929	476	145.1	54	16.3	9/6/1916	Torpedo (KuK U-5)	40.19N, 19.10E	1,826+	779
RIGEL	1924		Burmeister & Wain, Copenhagen	326	M2	3,828	368	112.0	52	15.7	27/11/1944	Bombs (aircraft from HMS Implacable)	65.49N, 12.21E	2,571	267
RYUSEI MARU (1)	1911	ex-Mabuhay II, ex-Havo, ex-Bra-Kar	Tyne Iron S.B. Co, Willington Quay	177	T1	4,787	386	117.3	44	13.5	25/2/1944	Torpedo (USS Rasher)	07.55S, 115.15E	4,998	1,700+
SAKITO MARU	1939		Mitsubishi, Nagasaki	723	M2	7,158	509	154.7	62	19.0	29/2/1944	Torpedo (USS Trout)	22.40N, 131.50E	2,280+	1,720

Name	Year	Builder	Former names		Class	Tonnage		Length		Speed	Fate date	Cause	Position		
SINFRA	1929	Akers MV	ex-*Sandhamn*, ex-*Fernglen*	434	M2	4,470	386	117.4	55	16.7	9/10/1943	Bombs	approx. 37.50N, 24.30E	2,098	566
STEUBEN	1923	Vulcan Werke, Stettin	ex-*General von Steuben*, ex-*Munchen*	669	T2	14,690	552	167.8	65	19.8	10/2/1945	Torpedo (*S-13*)	54.41N, 16.51E	3,608	659
TAI PING	1921	Newburgh Shipyard, New York	ex-*Choluteca*	18	T2	2,499	302	91.8	42	12.9	27/1/1949	Collision (*Kien Yuan*)	30.37N, 122.25E	c.1,550	35
TAMATSU MARU	1944	Mitsui, Tamano		314	M1	9,589	461	140.0	63	19.0	19/8/1944	Torpedo (USS *Spadefish*)	18.49N, 119.47E	4,755	0
TANGO MARU (1)	1926	Vulcan Werke, Hamburg	ex-*Toendjoek*, ex-*Rendsburg*	639	M1	6,200	451	137.2	58	17.7	25/2/1944	Torpedo (USS *Rasher*)	07.46S, 115.09E	c.3,000	500
TEIA MARU	1932	Méditerranée, La Seyne	ex-*Aramis*	1206	M2	17,537	567	172.5	70	21.2	18/8/1944	Torpedo (USS *Rasher*)	18.18N, 120.13E	2,665+	c.2,685
TEIYO MARU	1924	Blohm & Voss, Steinwerder	ex-*Saarland*	460	ST1	6,863	450	136.7	59	17.8	3/3/1943	Bombs	06.56S, 148.16E	1,914	9+
THIELBEK	1940	Lubecker Werft	ex-*Goldbek*, re *Reinbek*, re *Magdalena*, re *Old Warrior*	382	C1	2,815	345	105.0	48	14.7	3/5/1945	Bombs	54.04N, 10.51E	c.2,700	c.125
TOYAMA MARU	1915	Mitsubishi, Nagasaki		243	ST2	7,089	462	140.4	58	17.7	29/6/1944	Torpedo (USS *Sturgeon*)	27.47N, 129.05E	3,730+	600+
TSUSHIMA MARU	1914	Russell, Port Glasgow		666	T2	6,754	445	135.4	58	17.7	22/8/1944	Torpedo (USS *Boufin*)	29.33N, 129.30E	1,529	83
UKISHIMA MARU	1937	Mitsui, Tamano		225	M1	4,730	357	108.4	52	15.7	24/8/1945	Deliberate/mine?	35.30N, 135.22E	c.3,670	c.310
URAL MARU	1929	Mitsubishi, Nagasaki		452	ST2	6,374	406	123.5	55	16.8	27/9/1944	Torpedo (USS *Flasher*)	15.45N, 117.19E	c.2,400	c.350
WILHELM GUSTLOFF	1937	Blohm & Voss, Hamburg		511	M2	25,484	684	207.9	78	23.6	30/1/1945	Torpedo (*S-13*)	55.07N, 17.42E	c.9,350	1,239
YOSHIDA MARU NO.1	1919	Asano Dockyard		8	T1	5,425	401	121.9	53	16.2	26/4/1944	Torpedo (USS *Jack*)	18.06N, 119.40E	3,000+	0

				YN	E/S	GRT	LOA	LPP						CAS	SURV
YOSHINO MARU	1907	ex-*Kleist*	Schichau, Danzig	775	Q2	8,990	465	141.3	58	17.5	31/7/1944	Torpedo (USS *Parche* and *Steelhead*)	19.10N, 120.58E	2,495	?
SULTANA	1863		John Litherbury, Cincinnati	?	CP	1,719	260	79.0	?	?	23/4/1865	Explosion	Near Memphis, Mississippi River	1,653	741
TITANIC	1912		Harland & Wolff, Belfast	401	T3 +LP	46,329	883	268.3	93	28.2	14/4/1912	Collision (iceberg)	41.16N, 50.14W	1,503	703

Notes:

(1) Japanese source states combined casualties of *Ryusei Maru* and *Tango Maru* were 11,007.

Abbreviations:

C	Compound steam reciprocating	1	single screw propeller	YN	yard number
M	Motorship (diesel)	2	twin screw propellers	E/S	engines/screws
Q	Quadruple expansion steam reciprocating	3	triple screw propellers	GRT	gross registered tonnage
ST	Steam turbines	4	quadruple screw propellers	LOA	length overall
T	Triple expansion steam reciprocating	P	paddle wheels	LPP	length between perpendiculars
				CAS	casualties
				SURV	survivors

BIBLIOGRAPHY & RESEARCH SOURCES

Books

Bekker, Cajus, *Hitler's Naval War* (Corgi, London, 1976)

Benegal, Ramesh S., *Burma to Japan with Azad Hind – A War Memoir 1941–1945* (Lancer, New Delhi, 2009)

Braynard, Frank O., *Lives of the Liners* (Cornell Maritime Press, New York, 1947)

Brustat-Naval, Fritz, *Unter-Nehmen Rettung* [*Under-Taking Rescue*] (Koehlers, Hamburg, 1970)

Dobson, Christopher, *The Cruellest Night* (Hodder & Stoughton, London, 1979)

Hooton, Edward R., *Luftwaffe at War*, 4 volumes (Chevron/Ian Allen, Hersham, 2007)

Jones, Allan, 'Hellships – Scourge of the Japanese', in *The Suez Maru Atrocity – Justice Denied!* (privately published, Hornchurch, 2002)

Kimura, Rei, *Awa Maru – The Titanic of Japan* (Global Book Publishers, Beverly Hills, California, 2008)

Koburger, Charles W., *Steel Ships, Iron Crosses & Refugees: The German Navy in the Baltic 1939–1945* (Greenwood Press, Westport, Connecticut, 1989)

Komamiya, Shinshichiro, *Senji Yuso Sendan Shi* [*Wartime Transportation Convoys History*] translated by William G. Somerville (Shuppan Kyodosha, Tokyo, 1987)

Martin, Roy V., *Ebb and Flow* (Brook House, Southampton, 2010)

Michno, Gregory, *Death on the Hellships* (United States Naval Institute Press, Annapolis, 2001)

Miller, David, *Mercy Ships* (Continuum UK, London, 2008)

Miller, J., Payne, R. & Fenby, J., *The Sinking of the Lancastria* (Simon & Schuster, London, 2005)

Nepomniaschy, Nicholas, *Military Disaster at Sea* (Veche, Moscow, 2001)

Schön, Heinz, *Die Cap Arkona Katastrophe* (Motorbuch Verlag, Stuttgart, 1989)

—, *Die Gustloff Katastrophe* (Motorbuch Verlag, Stuttgart, 1984)

—, *Die KdF-Schiffe und ihr Schicksal* [*The Strength Through Joy Ships*] (Motorbuch Verlag, Stuttgart, 1987)

—, *Ostsee '45 – Menschen, Schiffe, Schicksale* [*Baltic 1945 – People, Ships, Shipwrecks*] (Motorbuch Verlag, Stuttgart, 1984)

Sellwood, A.V., *The Damned Don't Drown* (Tandem, London, 1974)

Smith, Peter C. & Walker, Edwin R., *War in the Aegean: The Campaign for the Eastern Mediterranean in World War II* (Stackpole Military History, Mechanicsburg, Pennsylvania, 2008)

Thorwald, Jürgen, *Flight in the Winter* (Hutchinson, London, 1953)

Wilson, Edward A., *Soviet Passenger Ships 1917–1977* (World Ship Society, Kendal, 1978)

Winser, John de S., *BEF Ships – Before, During & After Dunkirk* (World Ship Society, Gravesend, 1999)

Articles & Reports

'7,000 People Killed in Biggest Shipwreck of WWII', *Pravda* (5 May 2005)

'Chinese Shipping Disasters', *The Times* (6 December 1948)

'Commission d'Enquete Technique sur les Causes du Naufrage du "Joola" – Rapport d'Enquete' ['Commision of Inquiry into the Causes of the Sinking of the Le Joola'], *Republique de Senegal*, Dakar (4 November 2002)

'Ferry Tragedy Prompts Safety Moves', Lloyd's List (19 April 1988)

'HMT Lancastria – 70 Years Since Britain's Worst Ever Maritime Disaster', *Merchant Navy Association commemorative brochure* (Merchant Navy Day, 2010)

'Hospital Ship Armenia: The Most Horrifying Incident during the World War', *Marine Insight* (27 December 2011), http://www.marineinsight.com/marine/life-at-sea/maritime-history/

'How They Sank the Gustlow', *Soviet Weekly* (10 May 1986)

'Jiangya Shipwreck in 1948 – A Tragedy More Serious Than Titanic', *China Peoples Daily*, http://english.peopledaily.com.cn

'La Nave della Vergogna' ['Ships of Shame'], *Storie di Guerra e di Relitti* [*Stories of War Shipwrecks*] (unknown source)

'Lest We Forget – The Story of the Lancastria', *This England* (Summer 1985)

'Naufrage du Transbordeur Senegalais Le Joola – Rapport d'Expertise de Messieurs Jean Raymond Thomas, Pierre Lefebvre & Michel Tricot' ['Specialists Report into the Sinking of the Senegalese Ferry Le Joola'], *Tribunal de Grande Instance d'Evry*, No. de Parquet 0309100098; no. Instruction 9/03/35 (24 November 2005)

'Ships with the name Lenin', *Sudostroine* (unknown date, *c.*1960)

'Soviet Merchant Marine Losses in WW2', *Ships Nostalgia*, http://www.shipsnostalgia.com/guides/Main_Page

'The Military Disaster at Sea', *Veche*, Moscow (2001)

'The Sinking and the Salvage of the Awa Maru' (unknown source, May 1981)

Arthur, Max, 'RAF Pilots Tricked into Killing 10,000 Camp Survivors at End of War', *Independent* (16 October 2000)

Chi-hao, Hsu, 'The Tai Ping Accident', *Ta Kung Pao*, Shanghai (27 February 1949)

Donahue, James 'Over 3,000 Die in Kiang Ya Disaster', http://perdurabo10.tripod.com/ships/id312.html

Gagelonia, Ding Guzman, 'Sinking Ships & Stolen Lives: Another Sulpicio Lines Tragedy' (23 June 2008)

Graveson, Allan, 'Safety of Large Passenger Vessels', Senior National Secretary, Nautilus UK (c.2008)

Helgason, Gudmundur, 'The Laconia Incident', http://uboat.net/ops/laconia.htm

Jamkowski, Marcin, 'Ghost Ship Found (*Steuben*: A Wreck Revealed)', *National Geographic* (February 2005)

Kainic, Pascal, 'The Dramatic Collision of the Tai Ping', http://www.oceantreasures. org/pages/content/shipwrecks-stories/the-oriental-titanic-a-chinese-disaster-37-years-later.html

Koichi, Enoki, 'Army Soldiers Fate Aboard Merchant Ships', http://sky.geocities.jp/ enokiec/enokiepisode/E-Soldier.htm

Lawson, Catherine T. & Weisbrod, Roberta E., 'Ferry Transport: The Realm of Responsibility for Ferry Disasters in Developing Nations', *Journal of Public Transportation*, Volume 8, Issue 4, Special Edition (2005)

Maydon DSO RN, Lt Cdr Stephen L.C. (ed.), 'Extract from HMS Tradewind Report of Patrol, 8 September to 4 October 1944'

McCutcheon, Campbell, 'A Very British Tragedy', *Ships Monthly* (December 2010)

Moratti, Alfio, and Amos, Conti, 'The Sinking of the Ship Principe Umberto', *Ricerche Storiche, ISTORECO*, No.106 (October 2008)

Nijland, Yfke, 'De Ondergang van de Junyo Maru' ['The Sinking of the Junyo Maru'], *Stichting Icodo*, Utrecht: http://www.geschiedenis24.nl/andere-tijden/afleverin-gen/2002-2003/De-ondergang-van-de-Junyo-Maru.html

Pike, Dag, 'Ferries in Peril', *New Scientist* (8 August 1985)

Venning, Annabel, 'The Nazi with a Heart', *Daily Mail* (2010)

Vollrath, Captain Paul, 'Tragedy of the Wilhelm Gustloff', *Sea Breezes* (April 1981)

Williams, David L., 'The Kraft durch Freude Cruise Ships', *Sea Breezes* (September & October 1980)

Letters from Heinz Schön, Herford, Germany, to the author (22 July 1996 and 7 September 1996)

The National Archives Documents

AIR 27/1138, 1157, 1169, 1170 & 1548 RAF Squadron Operations Record Books

HW 23 'Government Code & Cypher School, Bletchley Park – Naval Section: Reports of Japanese Naval Decrypts'

WO 309/1592 *Neustadt Bay, Germany: Death of allied Nationals on board Ship* including 'Report on Investigations by Major Noel O. Till, Investigating Officer, No.2 War Crimes Investigation Team Headquarters, British Army of the Rhine – Part (b): Disaster at Neustadt Bay' (September 1945)

WO 325/101 *Loss of Lives in Sinking of Junyo Maru* including 'Summary of Examination of Matsushita Yoshiaki, ex Chief Officer of *Junyo Maru*, 9 May 1947'

Other Internet Sources

http://www.combinedfleet.com/ (Nihon Kaigun)
http://www.jsu.or.jp/siryo/sunk/tairyou.html (All Japan Seamen's Union – JSU)
http://www.militaryhistoryonline.com/wwii/articles/wilhelmgustloff.aspx
http://www.naval-history.net
http://www.subsim.com
http://www.uboat.net/wwi/ships_hit/
http://www.ubootwaffe.net/ops/shipindex.cgi
http://www1.uni-hamburg.de/rz3a035//arcona.html
http://www.warsailors.com/freefleet/shipindex.html
http://www.west-point.org/family/japanese-pow/

General Shipping Information Sources (Disasters & Technical)

Hocking, Charles, 'Dictionary of Disasters at Sea in the Age of Steam', Lloyd's Register of Shipping (London, 1969)
Hooke, Norman, *Modern Shipping Disasters* (Lloyd's of London Press, London, 1989)
Watson, Milton H., *Disasters at Sea* (Patrick Stephens, Sparkford, 1987 and 1995)
Williams, David L., *Dictionary of Passenger Ship Disasters* (Ian Allan, Hersham, 2009)
——, *Wartime Disasters at Sea* (Patrick Stephens, Sparkford, 1997)
Williams, David L. & de Kerbrech, Richard P., *Damned by Destiny* (Teredo Books, Brighton, 1982)

Lloyd's List – various
Lloyd's Register of Shipping - various
Lloyd's War Loss Cards – various
Lloyd's Weekly Casualty Reports – various
Marine News, World Ship Society (Nos 1 & 2, 1989), (No.12, 2002), (No.4, 2007) and (No.3, 2012)
Miramar Ship Database
Safety at Sea (various issues, including Annual Reviews 1987 & 1988)

INDEX

[Numbers in italics refer to pictures]